American
Nation-Building

American Nation-Building

Case Studies from Reconstruction to Afghanistan

KEVIN DOUGHERTY *and*
ROBERT J. PAULY, JR.

McFarland & Company, Inc., Publishers
Jefferson, North Carolina

Library of Congress Cataloguing-in-Publication Data

Names: Dougherty, Kevin, author. | Pauly, Robert J., 1967– author.
Title: American nation-building : case studies from Reconstruction
    to Afghanistan / Kevin Dougherty and Robert J. Pauly, Jr.
Description: Jefferson, North Carolina : McFarland & Company, Inc.,
    Publishers, 2017 | Includes bibliographical references and index.
Identifiers: LCCN 2017024474 | ISBN 9780786497966 (softcover :
    acid free paper) ♾
Subjects: LCSH: Nation-building—Cross-cultural studies. | Nation-
    building—United States.
Classification: LCC JZ6300 .D68 2017 | DDC 327.1—dc23
LC record available at https://lccn.loc.gov/2017024474

British Library cataloguing data are available

ISBN (print) 978-0-7864-9796-6
ISBN (ebook) 978-1-4766-2821-9

Front cover: Iraqi commandos training under the supervision
of soldiers from the U.S. 82nd Airborne in December 2010
(United States Army photograph)

Printed in the United States of America

McFarland & Company, Inc., Publishers
    Box 611, Jefferson, North Carolina 28640
        www.mcfarlandpub.com

This book is dedicated to all of
America's past and present participants
in nation- and state-building projects

Table of Contents

Preface

Over the past quarter-century, few foreign and national security policy tools have been employed by the United States and broader international community more often, or generated as many challenges for policymakers and practitioners situated across the developing world, as nation- and state-building projects. Those challenges cut across a range of issue areas, analytical frameworks and academic disciplines, and they affect the ways in which policymakers and practitioners of both the civilian and military varieties carry out their duties across on a daily basis. This book assesses the evolution of the field of nation- and state-building from multiple academic perspectives, but with emphases on the disciplines of history and political science, with the former specifying what occurred in each of the cases considered and the latter providing the requisite frameworks to explain why.

The analytical perspectives employed reflect the backgrounds of the two authors, both of whom have academic backgrounds and doctoral degrees that are interdisciplinary in nature, Dr. Kevin Dougherty in history, international development and international security, and Dr. Robert J. Pauly, Jr. in international studies, which blends history and political science. With their respective backgrounds providing a complementary point of departure, the authors traced the history of nation- and state-building chronologically and thematically, with cases varying geographically and culturally and each blending disciplines to provide informed, incisive analysis that provides a comprehensive examination of the field of study overall.

Evolution of Nation and State Building: Pre–World War II

American participation in nation- and state-building projects dates deep back in U.S. history, to the Civil War and Reconstruction periods of 1861–77 in particular. The American federal government engaged in nation- and state-building efforts both during the war against the Confederacy and the attempted (but ultimately unsuccessful) political reconstruction of the South that followed. During the Civil War, efforts to build and maintain a "state" for escaped slaves in Mitchelville, South Carolina, illustrate the challenges associated with developing enduring institutions amidst an ongoing intra-state conflict. Following the conclusion of that war, the North learned what most victors do: imposing political and social reforms on a defeated state (in this case the Confederacy) presents daunting challenges that often prove insurmountable, particularly where cultural differences are involved. There are also significant costs involved, whether of the economic or political variety. The Reconstruction programs of the post–Civil War period, for instance, failed in large part because, ultimately, the costs involved were more than the American federal government was willing to bear.

The domestic challenges the United States faced during Reconstruction proved a preview of those it has had to manage in its nation- and state-building operations abroad since then. The most significant such examples came as a direct result of the U.S. victory in the Spanish-American War of 1898. The conflict itself lasted less than eight months. The nation- and state-building projects that followed in the territories the United States claimed from the Spanish—Cuba just across the Florida Straits, and the Philippines in the South Pacific—were of a considerably long-term nature. The former signaled a re-emphasis of the Monroe Doctrine, with the United States using its victory over the Spanish to reassert American economic and military power and political influence in the Western Hemisphere under Presidents William McKinley and Theodore Roosevelt. It also helped set Cuba on a path that ultimately rejected American leadership and values through the 1959 revolution, by which that country adopted the autocratic communist political system it has maintained since then. Considerably further afield, the case of the Philippines, in the context of which American forces successfully countered an insurgent movement from 1899 to 1902, proved a preview of comparable challenges the United States has faced since the end of World War II, most notably during the Cold War and post–Cold War eras.

Germany and Japan: Models and Lessons for the Future

The two most often cited examples of effective nation- and state-building projects are the cases of Germany and Japan in the aftermath of World War II. In the former case, U.S.-led nation- and state-building operations provided the foundation for the development of cohesive liberal democratic transatlantic and Western European communities, including West Germany, in opposition to the autocratic communist political systems the Soviet Union imposed on the states of Central and Eastern Europe it occupied at the end of the war. In the latter, comparable efforts by the United States produced a democratic Japan that has been a staunch American ally in the Pacific ever since.

Notwithstanding the positive outcomes of nation- and state-building operations in Germany and Japan alike, it is extraordinarily important to recognize the distinctive characteristics of those countries and the circumstances on the ground therein, as well as their broader economic and geopolitical importance regionally and globally in the aftermath of World War II, all of which contributed markedly to those outcomes. In particular, the ethnic and cultural homogeneity prevalent in West Germany and Japan, their past exposure to—if not acceptance of—Western economic and political norms, and American control over the territory of both countries, as well as their centrality to U.S. interests, rendered them far more promising candidates for nation- and state-building projects than has proven the case for any other country since.

Post–Cold War Nation- and State-Building Projects: Opportunities and Challenges

Among the most daunting challenges the United States has faced in the contexts of nation- and state-building operations in which it has participated to date are those continuing to unfold in Afghanistan and Iraq. The George W. Bush administration launched both projects, the former through the prosecution of Operation Enduring Freedom in Taliban-controlled Afghanistan in response to al Qaeda's terrorist attacks against America on 11 September 2001, and the latter via the conduct of Operation Iraqi Freedom against the regime of President Saddam Hussein in the spring of 2003. In neither case has the objective of developing enduring liberal democratic institutions in the context of stable and secure environments been achieved.

The cases of Afghanistan and Iraq are addressed in depth in this volume, as are those that preceded them during the 1990s, with emphases on the examples of Somalia and Bosnia-Herzegovina. The book also touches on the transitory incorporation of nation- and state-building efforts into American strategy in the Vietnam War. Ironically, the ill-fated U.S. intervention in Vietnam drove subsequent presidential administrations to limit engagement in such endeavors under even broadly comparable circumstances, an approach that lasted through the end of the Cold War. From there, however, three successive administrations, those headed by William J. Clinton, George W. Bush and Barack H. Obama, either initiated or maintained American-led nation- and state-building operations entailing economic and military costs greater than any other such efforts since Vietnam. Those costs will almost certainly ensure a significant temporal pause before the United States considers launching any similar initiatives again.

Closing Observations

Above all, the volume that follows is designed to afford readers an opportunity to ground their understanding of American-led post–Cold War nation- and state-building projects in the Balkans and Greater Middle East in the historical and conceptual analyses of such initiatives. By tracing the history of U.S. participation in such projects at home and abroad and the challenges and implications that had to be managed along the way, the book serves as a useful guide to academics and policymakers and practitioners alike on how best to manage nation- and state-building initiatives under myriad circumstances. Most significantly, the myriad cases explored demonstrate that no one example is identical to another, whether in terms of U.S. and broader allied interests or evolving characteristics and circumstances on the ground at a given temporal juncture. The more informed scholars, policymakers and practitioners are with respect to the conceptual approaches to the planning and implementation of nation- and state-building projects under perpetually changing conditions on the ground in culturally distinct environments across the world, the more fruitful such efforts are likely to be moving forward.

Introduction

What this book and most other contemporary literature calls "nation-building" has otherwise gone by such names as "nation assistance," "modernization," "peaceful revolution," "middle class revolution," and "state-building."[1] This litany of names suggests an evolving understanding of the concept, and different observers certainly emphasize different aspects when discussing this broad idea.

Francis Fukuyama writes that nation-building is part of the effort to "promote governance in weak states, improve their democratic legitimacy, and strengthen self-sustaining institutions."[2] James Dobbins adds a military component to this understanding, arguing that nation-building "involves the use of armed force as part of a broader effort to promote political and economic reforms with the objective of transforming a society emerging from conflict into one at peace with itself and its neighbors."[3] Indeed, the U.S. military has played a significant role in nation-building efforts, especially with the end of the Cold War, and the 1993 edition of the Army's capstone field manual FM 100-5, *Operations*, included a detailed discussion of "nation assistance," which it defined as "diplomatic, economic, informational, and military cooperation between the U.S. and the government of another nation, with the objective of promoting internal development and the growth of sustainable institutions within that nation."[4] The manual cited the goals of nation assistance are "to promote long-term stability, to develop sound and responsive democratic institutions, to develop supportive infrastructure, to promote strong free-market economics, and to provide an environment that allows for orderly political change and economic progress."[5] This process, the manual continued, "corrects conditions that cause human suffering and improves the quality of life of the nation's people."[6] Interestingly, FM 100-5 was largely silent on the military component of all this, save for the casual allusion contained in the statement "in United Nations terms, nation assistance equates to peace-building operations."[7]

Following FM 100-5's invitation to explore "peace-building" reveals that the United Nations has gone through its own evolutionary understanding of this concept. In the 1992 report "An Agenda for Peace," Secretary-General Boutros Boutros-Ghali defined peacebuilding as "action to identify and support structures which will tend to strengthen and solidify peace in order to avoid a relapse into conflict." By 2000, the Report of the Panel on United Nations Peace Operations (perhaps better known as the Brahimi Report) defined peacebuilding as "activities undertaken on the far side of conflict to reassemble the foundations of peace and provide the tools for building on those foundations something that is more than just the absence of war." In 2007, the UN Secretary-General's Policy Committee agreed on a conceptual basis that peacebuilding "involves a range of measures targeted to reduce the risk of lapsing or relapsing into conflict by strengthening national capacities at all levels for conflict management, and to lay the foundations for sustainable peace and development."[8]

This last iteration of the United Nations definition introduces the notion of "development," another complicated and slippery term. Among its numerous definitions and connotations, one common theme is that development encompasses "change" in a variety of aspects of the human condition.[9] Robert Chambers notes that the preference is for "good change," but because "any development agenda is value-laden," interpretations of what "good change" is are also problematic.[10] As Ravi Kanbur observes, "Since [development] depend[s] on values and on alternative conceptions of the good life, there is no uniform or unique answer."[11] Lynnell Simonson and Virginia Bushaw point out that even a seemingly innocuous needs assessment is "by definition, a value judgment comparing the current state of affairs with some more desirable conditions."[12] In part because of these difficulties, development and nation-building are subjective processes that, whatever their good intentions, may not be perceived as such by the recipient.

Nonetheless, development is a critical component of nation-building, especially as it relates to security. David Tucker posits that nation-building assumes that "underdevelopment causes conflict and this cause must be treated or the counterinsurgency effort will not succeed."[13] Tucker's depiction is useful in understanding why nation-building requires a military component to end conflict and a developmental component to sustain the peace. Purely military action involves merely defeating an enemy. Purely developmental activity requires a certain level of security as a foundation. Nation-building combines these two spheres in a complex, ambiguous, and changing environment that presents enormous challenges.

Recognizing this condition, the essays contained in this volume are designed to present multiple, different, and at times conflicting views and analyses of a selection of nation-building themes. Chapter 1 places nation-building in the broad strategic context, and Chapter 2 lays out the cases for and against nation-building. Chapters 3 and 4 highlight different motivations for nation-building. Chapter 3 offers Somalia as an example of an altruistic effort, and Chapter 4 looks at the U.S. operations in Central America as a result of Roosevelt's Corollary to the Monroe Doctrine as the self-interested variety. Security is essential to any nation-building operation, and Chapter 5 discusses the different sequencing options used in the Philippines and Germany. Chapter 6 continues this discussion by analyzing the challenges to security presented during Reconstruction in the U.S. South. While acknowledging the reality of resource limitations, nation-building experts argue that "working at all levels produces the best results."[14] To this end, a set of three essays discusses Vietnam as an example of nation-building at the local level (Chapter 7), Iraq as an example of nation-building at the national level (Chapter 8), and Mitchelville, South Carolina (Chapter 9), as an example of nation-building and civil society. The last pair presents the roles of different actors in nation-building. Chapter 10 looks at the United States Agency for International Development in Afghanistan as an example of the government as nation-builder, and Chapter 11 examines the role of nongovernmental organizations (NGOs) and international governmental organizations (IGOs) in Bosnia.

In addition to providing analysis of nation-building from a variety of perspectives, the selection of the case studies is designed to represent the chronological breadth of America's nation-building experience. Two examples are from the Reconstruction era, two from America's imperialistic period, two from the Cold War, two from the post–Cold War era, and two from the Global War on Terrorism. The volume concludes with some thoughts on the future of nation-building in Chapter 12.

CHAPTER 1

Nation-Building in Context

The "state" as an institution dates back some 6,000 years to the first agricultural societies that sprang up in Mesopotamia. States use their centralized power to provide order, security, law, and property rights.[1] One of the most popular definitions of a state is the one offered by Max Weber in 1946 which describes the state as "a human community that (successfully) claims the monopoly of the legitimate use of physical force within a given territory." Francis Fukuyama interprets this definition as saying "the essence of stateness is … enforcement: the ultimate ability to send someone with a uniform and a gun to force people to comply with the state's laws."[2]

Failed States

States that do not meet this requirement are often referred to as "failed states."[3] Precisely defining these states is problematic because of the continuum upon which they reside, so most definitions describe them by what they are not. An example would be Stephen Lamy and his co-authors, who write that failed states are those that "do not have a monopoly of force at home and lack complete control over their own territory." Additionally, such states are "incapable of executing meaningful agreements with other countries." Because of their "unstable and ineffective" key governing institutions, they "do not have the capacity to provide even basic services for their citizens."[4]

While Fukuyama routinely uses the expression "failed state" in his *State-Building: Governance and World Order in the 21st Century*, he offers no definition. He does describe weak state strength as "meaning a lack of institutional capability to implement and enforce policies, often driven by an underlying lack of legitimacy of the political system as a whole." He says "weak governance undermines the principle of sovereignty."[5] In Fukuyama's context, weakness is a function of the state's strength, which he describes as "the ability of states to plan and execute policies and to enforce laws cleanly and transparently," rather than scope, which he says "refers to the different functions and goals taken on by governments."[6]

Fukuyama associates strength with capacity.[7] Stewart Patrick goes one step further, arguing that "state weakness is not just a question of capacity but also of will." He uses this distinction to describe four categories of weak states: relatively good performers that have strong will and high capacity (e.g., Senegal and Honduras); weak but willing states with low capacity and strong will (e.g., Mozambique and East Timor); unresponsive/corrupt/repressive states with low will and high capacity (e.g., Burma and Zimbabwe); and weak and not willing states with low capacity and low will (e.g., Sudan and Haiti).[8]

Determining when a state is failing or failed is as much art as it is science. No standard set of criteria for assessment exists, though examples are numerous. In her "CRS Report for Congress; Weak and Failing States: Evolving Security Threats and U.S. Policy," Liana Wyler lists peace and stability, effective governance, territorial control and porous borders, and economic sustainability as the determinants of state weakness. This list is commonly used within the U.S. government.[9]

Another list is offered by the Fund for Peace (FfP), which, in compiling its "Failed States Index," considers a state to be failing if it has the following attributes:

—the loss of physical control of its territory or a monopoly on the legitimate use of force

—the erosion of legitimate authority to make collective decisions

—an inability to provide reasonable public services

—the inability to interact with other states as a full member of the international community.

The FfP explains its methodology in greater detail than does Wyler, noting that it uses twelve indicators—Demographic Pressures, Refugees/IDPs, Group Grievance, Human Flight, Uneven Development, Economic Decline, Delegitimization of the State, Public Services, Human Rights, Security Apparatus, Factionalized Elites, and External Intervention—to assess state vulnerability. These indicators cover a wide range of elements of the risk of state failure, such as extensive corruption and criminal behavior, inability to collect taxes or otherwise draw on citizen support, large-scale involuntary dislocation of the population, sharp economic decline, group-based inequality, institutionalized persecution or discrimination, severe demographic pressures, brain drain, and environmental decay.[10]

World Views

Traditional realists and liberalists view the phenomenon of these under-performing states and the efficacy of nation-building as a response from their own unique perspectives. During the Cold War, realism was the dominant theoretical tradition of international relations and national security was the clear priority. According to the realist viewpoint, nation-building should be considered as it relates to security interests. In the post–Cold War era's absence of the threat of a superpower collision, realism's clearly stated and preferentially ranked goals became increasingly elusive. The self-help and completive approach to security gave way to liberalism's emphasis on internationalism and cooperation. According to the liberalist viewpoint, nation-building is at least in part a function of values. The post–September 11 era generated another opportunity to reconsider the utility of different international relations paradigms to inform efforts to combat terrorism. Interestingly, in this era, nation-building has been simultaneously discussed in realist and liberalist terms.

Realism

Realists can trace their roots to Thucydides, who in "The Melian Dialogue" championed the Athenian view of security that "the strong do what they can and the weak suffer what they must."[11] More recently, Hans Morganthau articulated six principles that have come to define classical realism:

—Politics is governed by objective laws that have their roots in human nature.

—Interest is defined in terms of power.

—Interest defined as power is an objective category which is universally valid, but whose meaning can change.

—Universal moral principles cannot be applied to the actions of states in the abstract; the circumstances of time and place must be considered.

—The moral laws that govern the universe are distinct from the morals of any one nation.

—Politics is an autonomous sphere that needs to be analyzed as an entity, without being subordinated to outside values.[12]

Realists like Morganthau view security largely in terms of the accumulation of the traditional elements of power, namely military and economic power.

The realist world view stems from the assumption of anarchy—there is no authority that exists that can enforce agreements between states. Therefore it is possible for any state to attack another at any time, and in the name of prudence, each state must arm itself to protect against this danger. The result, according to arch-realist Edward Carr, is "the supreme importance of the military instrument ... [based on] the fact that the *ultima ratio* of power in international relations is war." Carr calls military power "an essential element in the life of the state" and "not only an instrument, but an end unto itself." Because "of its association with the military instrument," Carr also views economic power as critical to the survival of a state. He argues that military and economic powers are "indivisible."[13] Thus for a realist, state security is based primarily on military and economic power, and any potential nation-building effort would be weighed based on its impact in these areas.

Liberalism

Liberalism, the other dominant international relations paradigm, emphasizes international law, reciprocity, international organizations, nonstate actors, international norms, free trade, and the connectedness of the international arena. Liberalism's popularity is generally associated with peaceful interludes in world history, which is why it enjoyed a resurgence in the post–Cold War era. Like realism, liberalism has various branches; but at its core, liberal theory, according to Andrew Moracsvik, is grounded in three key components:

—The key actors in the international scene are societal—individuals and private groups.

—States are not the central actors. They are mere representatives of the individuals and private groups. However, states are the transmission belt that delivers the preferences of these societal actors to the international scene.

—Interdependent preferences constrain state behavior and establish the basis for international cooperation.[14]

Modern liberalist thought draws on a strong historical foundation that includes Adam Smith's arguments for free trade, Hugo Grotius's arguments for international law, and Immanuel Kant's thoughts on collective security.

In *Perpetual Peace*, Kant advocated that "standing armies shall be gradually abolished," and instead, "for the sake of its own security," individual nations should join a "federation of nations" that would create a "league of peace."[15] Kant's philosophy is part of the idealism that emerged from Enlightenment concepts that stressed scientific rationality, freedom, and the inevitability of human progress. Although some modern scholars continue to use the label "idealism," most descendants of the paradigm's founders are better described as liberals or constructivists.[16] For the Kantian idealist, security is grounded in governments that emphasize individual rights, constitutionalism, democracy, limitations on the powers of the state, and economic policies that promote market capitalism as the organization that best promotes the welfare of all because it efficiently allocates scarce resources within the society. By a cooperative effort to safeguard individual freedom and economic well-being, idealists believe security is enhanced because competition is reduced.

Perhaps the best-known modern-day idealist is Woodrow Wilson, who followed idealist theory when he proposed his "Fourteen Points" as a basis for the World War I armistice. Rather than the realist-based proposals of the British and French that would prevent war by weakening Germany's power, Wilson's proposal was based on the idea of creating a new world order built on a respect for law, the acceptance of shared universal values, and the development of international organizations. Wilson proposed the types of guarantees that Kant envisioned would be necessary to establish peace, including "a general association of nations" to supervise it all. According to David Baldwin, Wilson "joined the idea that free trade promotes peace with the idea of a universal international organization to promote the same goal."[17] The end of the Cold War offered a new opportunity to consider security in the context of liberalism. Francis Fukuyama argued in 1992 that the demise of the Soviet Union proved that liberal democracy had no serious competitor and that projection of its principles to the international realm provides the best prospects for a peaceful world order because "a world made up of liberal democracies ... should have much less incentive for war, since all nations would reciprocally recognize one another's legitimacy."[18] Thus theorists like Fukuyama argue that security is best enhanced by promoting liberal democracy both at home and abroad.

Fukuyama's argument is consistent with Michael Doyle's articulation of the democratic peace theory that contends

President Woodrow Wilson is inexorably associated with the international relations paradigm of idealism based on his Fourteen Points proposal, which included provisions to end all economic barriers between countries, to provide for self-determination, and to establish a League of Nations "to guarantee the political and territorial independence of all states." (Library of Congress Prints and Photographs Division LC-USZ62-20570.)

democratic states are less likely to go to war with other democratic states than other types of states. Doyle's theory contends there is a natural tendency for ruling elites to wage war because it increases their power by allowing them to expand their bureaucratic apparatus and increase their control over their citizens. The people end up bearing the burden of war by increased taxes, casualties, compulsory military service, and war-associated hardships. However, in liberal democracies, individual liberties such as free speech, universal suffrage, and rule of law allow the citizens to express their innate peace-loving nature and curb the ruling elites' appetite for war. According to Doyle, "When the citizens who bear the burdens of war elect their governments, wars become impossible."[19] Thus Doyle's theory suggests that expanding democracy worldwide increases security by reducing war.

Liberals also see security benefits in free trade and commerce, which they argue help overcome the artificial barriers between individuals and unite them everywhere into one community. Among the early champions of this understanding was David Ricardo, who in 1817 wrote that free trade "binds together, by one common tie of interest and intercourse, the universal society of nations throughout the civilized world."[20] This dynamic reduces international tension and increases contacts and understanding. Unfettered commercial exchanges encourage links across borders and shifts loyalties away from the nation-state. The resulting interdependence replaces national competition and defuses unilateral acts of aggression and reciprocal retaliation.

Commercial liberalism in particular links free trade with peace. Thomas Friedman offers a popular explanation of this connection in his "Dell Theory of Conflict Prevention." "No two countries," Freidman argues, "that are part of a major global supply chain, like Dell's, will ever fight a war against each other as long as they are both a part of the same global supply chain."[21] Thus security for a commercial liberalist is enhanced by economic interdependence.

Because liberalism stresses cooperation rather than competition among states, its adherents view nation-building as an opportunity to improve relations throughout the international community. Likewise, liberalism's emphasis on individual rights is consistent with the humanitarian potential of nation-building. Liberalism also sees nation-building as a means of promoting peace by spreading democratic values.

Similarities

In spite of the strong contradictory rhetoric, realism and liberalism are not without their points of agreement. Inis Claude has challenged the "notion of the essential opposition of realism and idealism" and suggests that they "are more properly regarded as complementary rather than competitive approaches to international affairs." John Herz concurs with Claude and has described his own position as "realist liberalism." Joseph Nye has echoed the sentiment that the two paradigms are complementary and expressed hope that "the 1990s will be able to synthesize rather than repeat the dialectic 1970s and 1980s."[22] David Baldwin describes his *Neorealism and Neoliberalism* as "a step toward such a synthesis."[23]

Indeed, in the post–September 11 era, realism and liberalism seemed to merge in the neoconservative movement that was highly influential in the George W. Bush administration. Bush began his presidency intending to roll back President Bill Clinton's internationalism, stating as a candidate, "I don't think our troops ought to be used for what's called nation-building."[24] Nonetheless, as early as 1999, while acknowledging America's military preponderance, President Bush noted that "military power is not the final measure of might. Our realism must make a place for the human spirit."[25]

After the attacks of September 11, 2001, President Bush became increasingly influenced by key advisors such as Vice-President Dick Cheney and Deputy Secretary of Defense Paul Wolfowitz, who championed the neoconservative belief that America should practice an assertive and robust foreign policy that involved such concepts as regime change, benevolent hegemony, unipolarity, preemption, and American exceptionalism.[26] As a result, after September 11, the Bush Administration "did not do a *volte-face* in its policy, but it did change from classical realism to what we would describe as 'defensive realism' that incorporated a distinct form of idealism."[27] President Bush came to accept that the "internal characteristics of regimes matter,"[28] and he declared in November 2003 that "the global expansion of democracy" should be a key pillar of American security.[29] In pursuing what Walter Russell Mead called "Revival Wilsonianism," President Bush believed in the spread of democracy and the goodness of American intentions and actions, without Wilson's embrace of international laws and institutions.[30] Hence, the United States' invasion of Iraq became an exercise in nation-building.

The result is that realism, liberalism, and neoconservativism all view nation-building both differently and similarly. Rather than diverging rays on a single linear continuum, the paradigms occasionally intersect as they pursue similar goals by different means. One of these means is nation-building.

CHAPTER 2

The Cases for and Against Nation-Building

It is interesting that two observers may agree on the need for a nation-building operation for entirely different reasons. A liberalist may have supported the U.S. intervention in Haiti in 1994 on the humanitarian grounds of protecting Haitian citizens from the human rights abuses of the Cedras regime. A realist may have supported it based on the national security interest of stemming the tide of Haitian boat people fleeing to America. Likewise, realists and liberalists might oppose a nation-building operation for different reasons. The realist may have seen no national security interest at stake in Somalia in 1993. A liberalist may have seen a greater humanitarian crisis in Sudan and instead favored an intervention there. Even more fundamental than differences of opinion about specific situations is the argument about the validity of nation-building as a concept.

The Case for Nation-Building

Ambassador Richard Williamson argues that "there are both moral motives and pragmatic reasons of self-interest to nation-build."[1] As part of a broader discussion, Paul D'Anieri employs similar logic in identifying motivations to battle global poverty. These arguments can be used to defend nation-building from both liberalist and realist perspectives.

Morality

D'Anieri's first reason that can be used to support nation-building is the normative notion that "it seems immoral or unethical not to try to do something" to alleviate the less fortunate.[2] There is an obvious moral appeal to such a concept of nation-building: an altruistic ideal of helping people and

16

The moral justification for nation-building includes assisting unfortunate victims of hardship, chaos, and disorder, such as these Somali children. (Department of Defense photograph DD-SD-00-00762 by Perry Heimer.)

governments better themselves. When Americans witness conditions abroad that they consider to be deplorable, their natural inclination is to help. As an illustration of this sentiment, Gerald Parshall describes the nation-building effort in Vietnam as merely the end result of a series of attempts to help others that began with GIs handing out candy bars in World War II.[3]

The moral argument has been codified in the "responsibility to protect" mandate that emerged from the 2005 World Summit in the aftermath of the international community's failure to intervene in the genocide that swept Rwanda in 1994. Still reeling from the disaster in Somalia, the United States was unwilling to enter another risky venture, and the United Nations was paralyzed and passive in the void left by the American position. In 1998, both President Bill Clinton and United Nations Secretary-General Kofi Annan apologized for the inaction. President Clinton lamented, "We did not act quickly enough after the killing began. We should not have allowed the refugee camps to become safe havens for the killers. We did not immediately call these crimes by their rightful name: genocide. We cannot change the past. But we can and must do everything in our power to help you build a future without fear, and full of hope." Annan, who was the United Nations Under-Secretary-General for Peacekeeping at the time of the crisis, echoed, "The world must deeply repent this failure. Rwanda's tragedy was the world's tragedy.... We will not deny that, in their greatest hour of need, the world failed the people of Rwanda."

While the legacy of Somalia was the principal reason for the international paralysis, issues of sovereignty also hamstrung decision-makers regarding Rwanda. Roméo Dallaire, commander of the United Nations Assistance Mission for Rwanda, lamented that he was denied permission to shut down RTLM, the national radio station that was rhetorically fueling the genocide, because to do so "would violate international convention on sovereignty."[4]

The "responsibility to protect" doctrine addresses the issue of sovereignty: "The duty to prevent and halt genocide and mass atrocities lies first and foremost with the State, but the international community has a role that cannot be blocked by the invocation of sovereignty. Sovereignty no longer exclusively protects States from foreign interference; it is a charge of responsibility where States are accountable for the welfare of their people.... If a State is manifestly failing to protect its populations, the international community must be prepared to take collective action to protect populations, in accordance with the Charter of the United Nations."[5]

The "responsibility to protect" mandate and revised interpretation of state sovereignty fall within a broader concept of "human security." This understanding of society emphasizes the importance of the basic necessities, quality of life, and individual dignity humans need to feel secure. War and large displacements of populations threaten this sense of human security, especially in areas already operating on the margins.[6] The implications for nation-building are that "security policy requires a holistic approach that views human security as critical to building state capacity and legitimacy."[7]

Self-Interest

Like Williamson, D'Anieri also points out that there is a certain self-interest associated with nation-building.[8] These motivations include reducing the spillover problems associated with failed states, promoting peace through democracy, and creating economic benefits by expanding global markets. In this sense, nation-building is consistent with the liberalism theory of international relations and its belief that such ideals as cooperation, democracy, and free trade are essential to peaceful and mutually beneficial relations among nations.[9] By making more stable and capable individual nations, nation-builders create better conditions for all.

By the same token, nation-building can appeal to realism's focus on self-interest because the problems typically associated with failed states are not contained at the state's borders. As they spread, they threaten security in other countries. Therefore, mitigating the spillover effects of terrorism, immi-

Piracy is an example of the spillover problems created by failed states. Here members of a visit, board, search and seizure team from the USS *Gettysburg* and U.S. Coast Guard Tactical Law Enforcement Team South Detachment 409 approach a suspected pirate mothership in the Gulf of Aden. (U.S. Navy photo 090513-N-0743B-057 by Eric L. Beauregard.)

gration, crime, and health threats can motivate nation-building from a realist perspective.[10]

Perhaps the most oft-cited threat to other countries' self-interest posed by failed states is that they are prone to becoming safe havens for transnational terrorist groups. Al Qaeda's presence in Afghanistan is the most common example of this situation. In 1996, Michael Ignatieff noted the humanitarian concern posed by the "violence, misery, and hunger" spreading across the southern frontiers of the former Soviet empire. On the other hand, however, he wondered, "If Afghanistan bleeds to death, will American strategic interests be the worse?"[11] Only when Afghanistan's lack of domestic control made it a safe haven for Osama bin Laden and al Qaeda did the answer become clear.

Even though several scholars argue Afghanistan represents the exception rather than the rule, the magnitude of the September 11, 2001, attack indicates that this threat is ignored only at great risk. The inability of failed states to control their borders also poses threats to their neighbors in the form of illegal immigrants fleeing poverty, and refugees seeking shelter from the ravages of war and ethnic violence. Black-marketeers, pirates, and drug lords also take advantage of the lack of control in failed states to export criminal activity. Finally, the epidemic diseases such as HIV/AIDS present in many failed states pose international health threats. Because of spillover factors such as these, the 2002 United States National Security Strategy asserted, "America is now threatened less by conquering states than we are by failing ones."[12]

In addressing this threat, several theorists argue that shoring up failed states is in the self-interest of potential nation-builders because creating democratic institutions promotes peace. The origins of this idea can be traced to Immanuel Kant, who believed that the natural state of the world was war, not peace. Therefore, one had to work for peace. In a phrase that captures the same connotation as "building" a nation, Kant wrote that a state of peace "must be established."

Kant argued that this peace was dependent on the internal character of governments. He reasoned that republics, with a legislative branch that can hold the monarch in check, will be more peaceful than autocracies. Drawing on Kant, Michael Doyle's democratic peace theory argues that democracies are unlikely to go to war with other democracies because of three factors. First of all, the nature of democratic society—elections, freedom of speech and political opposition—gives citizens a voice in the state's decision to go to war, and because the citizens pay a heavy price in terms of taxes and casualties, they are reluctant to go to war. The result is that "liberal wars are only fought for popular, liberal purposes" and a strong domestic check replaces "monarchical caprice."[13] The second explanation of the democratic peace theory is that democracies have shared norms such as an assumption of each other's pacific nature, reasonableness and regard for respect of sovereignty. The result is a predisposition toward compromise. As Doyle explains, "Domestically just republics, which rest on consent, presume foreign republics to be also consensual, just, and therefore deserving of accommodation."[14] The final reason is that "cosmopolitan law" produces market, economic, and trade incentives that rest on cooperation and accommodation. Furthermore, the interdependence of modern commercial relations helps "create crosscutting trans-national ties that serve as lobbies for mutual accommodation."[15] Doyle concludes, "No one of these constitutional, international or cosmopolitan sources is alone sufficient, but together (and only where together) they plausibly connect the characteristics of liberal polities and economies with sustained liberal peace."[16]

The post–Cold War era ushered in what many saw as an unprecedented opportunity to capitalize on the potential of the democratic peace theory. In his 1992 book *The End of History and the Last Man*, Fukuyama hypothesized, "What we may be witnessing is not just the end of the Cold War, or the passing of a particular period of post-war history, but the end of history as such: that is, the end point of mankind's ideological evolution and the universalization of Western liberal democracy as the final form of human government."[17] Although Fukuyama's optimism was subsequently revealed as being misplaced, it did represent the faith in the American way that was embraced by the "neoconservative" movement represented by several key advisors in President George W. Bush's administration. By tying America's well-being to the expansion of freedom and liberty around the world, President Bush represents the argument that nation-building serves America's self-interest. He explained in a 2003 speech in London that "lasting peace is gained as justice and democracy advance."[18] Nation-building is seen by many to be one way of facilitating this advance.

Another argument in favor of nation-building is an economic one. The post–World War II Bretton Woods international economic system is designed to foster international trade in order to increase prosperity.[19] A major component of this model is the free trade ideology that eliminates or minimizes barriers to the exchange of goods, services, and investments among states. Such a system is premised on the assumption that free trade delivers mutual gains to all players because of the condition of comparative advantage.[20]

Williamson notes that in an integrated, cooperative market such as the one envisioned by Bretton Woods, failed states "curtail American economic opportunities and growth." Failed states possess "hundreds of millions of workers and consumers." In their dysfunctional state, these populations "buy fewer goods, produce less for the world economy, create no businesses, and invent no products."[21] Furthermore, failed states often possess vast natural resources that are critical to the global economy. Nation-building turns the unrealized economic potential of failed states into development that benefits not just the state, but through free trade, the world.[22]

Proponents of nation-building acknowledge its difficulties but argue that these real threats and potential gains justify its practice. They consider it both a "necessary response" to present danger and a "strategic investment" in the future.[23] They point to America's history of nation-building and its important successes in Germany and Japan.[24] While they counsel such imperatives as the need to consider lessons learned, flexibility, better organization, and humility, they insist nation-building is in the national interest and therefore should be pursued affirmatively.

Others are less enthusiastic about nation-building's inherent goodness, but instead point to its inevitability. Francis Fukuyama is typical of this philosophically pragmatic approach. He acknowledges that avoiding nation-building altogether is simply an untenable position "given the kinds of security and foreign policy needs the United States faces and will face."[25] As an example, he notes that in spite of the Bush Administration's initial resistance to nation-building, the United States has "willy-nilly gotten dragged into it in Afghanistan and Iraq."[26] For pragmatists like Fukuyama, nation-building is largely a foregone conclusion, and the discussion thus focuses on how to best undertake the inevitable.

The Case Against Nation-Building

In contrast to Fukuyama's cautious pragmatism, some critics of nation-building are absolute and definitive. Representative of this set is David Tucker, who declares in his "Facing the Facts: The Failure of Nation Assistance" that the very idea of nation assistance "is a bad one, and should be expunged from policy, doctrine, and practice."[27] Certainly nation-building is not for the faint of heart and should not be undertaken without a full awareness of its challenges. These include the rationale and results, the resources required and their costs, cultural factors as they apply to both the nation-builders and the recipient of the effort, and the difficulty in overcoming recipient unwillingness.

Rationale and Results

Critics of nation-building find fault with both its altruistic and self-interested purposes. Well-intentioned efforts to bolster state strength, promote democracy, enhance human rights, reduce violence, and any of the other justifications for altruistic nation-building all reside on a continuum that makes it difficult to objectively articulate a standard that justifies both the affront to state sovereignty and the costs associated with nation-building. It is a question similar to the one posed by Robert Tomes in his analysis of Kosovo: "Is there some threshold at which human rights violations become unacceptable and a state's sovereignty no longer precludes intervention? Is it the 500th slain ethnic citizen or the next refugee after 10,000 have been forced to leave home that triggers intervention or makes it legitimate?"[28]

Critics of nation-building also argue that much of the logic of "self-interest" used to justify some nation-building is faulty. Specifically they point to what they consider an exaggerated fear of failed states supporting terrorists. In fact, Anna Simons and David Tucker contend that international terrorists "do not appear to come predominantly or even significantly from failed states."[29] In fact, they argue that "entire states never fail." Instead, "*all* states consistently fail some portions of their population." They allow that from these "disenfranchised populations can come foot soldiers, [and] from alienated populations can come terrorists." Yet Simons and Tucker contend this same phenomenon can occur anywhere, "including our own backyard."[30]

Thus instead of nation-building, they argue the United States should focus its efforts on helping governments "secure the goodwill of local populations."[31]

Setting aside the difficulties in determining a rationale to justify a particular nation-building effort, critics argue "nation building has an extremely poor track record."[32] James Dobbins assesses West Germany and Japan as "very successful" nation-building exercises but notes that the standards they set for "postconflict transformation ... have not since been equaled."[33] Francis Fukuyama does not even consider these commonly cited successes to be representative of true nation-building because of the strong bureaucracies that existed in both states before the United States became involved. Instead, all he credits the United States with doing was "to change the basis of legitimization in both cases from authoritarianism to democracy and to purge members of the old regime that had started the war."[34] Of the cases he considers true American nation-building efforts, Fukuyama counts only South Korea as a success, and he gives South Korea more credit for that than he does the United States.[35] A small handful of observers such as Jeremi Suri optimistically include post–Civil War Reconstruction as a success, but the standard interpretation is more along the lines of the South lost the war but won the peace.[36] Certainly nation-building has a mixed record of success, and its high costs lead many to deem it a poor investment.

High Costs and Paucity of Proper Tools

James Dobbins notes that most historical nation-building operations can be categorized as either peacekeeping or peace enforcement missions. He estimates that a hypothetical light peacekeeping mission (one with a permissive entry, an acquiescent population, and some level of local capacity for governance and security) requires 9,000 international soldiers and police and costs $1.5 billion a year. He calculates a heavy peace enforcement mission (one with a forced entry, a more hostile or divided population, and little or no immediately available indigenous capacity for governance and security) as requiring 80,000 personnel and costing $15 billion a year. Both types of operations are expensive, but Dobbins notes that full-scale peace enforcement actions are so costly that they "are feasible only when the intervening authorities care a great deal about the outcome and, even then, only in relatively small societies."[37] Generating sufficient interest, and sustaining it in the face of casualties and over time, is a serious challenge to nation-building.

Former United Nations Secretary-General Dag Hammarskjöld famously quipped, "Peacekeeping is not a job for soldiers, but only soldiers can do it," and nation-building indeed has often suffered from an over-reliance on the military. Detractors argue that this reality both diminishes military combat readiness and is ill-suited for the variety of skills required by a nation-building

The post–World War II nation-building effort in Germany served American geopolitical strategic interests. Here American and Soviet tanks square off at Checkpoint Charlie in Berlin in October 1961. (Photograph courtesy the United States Army Military Heritage Institute.)

operation. At a minimum, the frequency and duration of post–Cold War nation-building has stressed and stretched the American military.

Charles Dunlap argues that nation-building may have "the perverse effect of diverting focus and resources from the military's central mission of combat training and warfighting."[38] While today's military has become remarkably flexible and versatile, it seems intuitive that energy spent training and resourcing the "soft skills" required of nation-builders must come in part at the expense of other activities. As Dunlap notes, "Each moment spent performing a nontraditional mission is one unavailable for orthodox military exercises,"[39] and David Tucker declares nation-building is a "distraction" to the military.[40] There is certainly logical concern that an Army devoted to nation-building may well become an Army short of traditional warfighting skills.

Others argue that an overuse of the military in nation-building not only is a disservice to the military, but also is detrimental to the nation-building effort itself. Instead, Kenneth Allard argues that "while military power may well set the stage for such action, the real responsibility for nation-building must be carried out by the civilian agencies of the government better able to specialize in such long-term humanitarian efforts."[41] He warns that "an institution built around can-do attitudes and the expectation of success" may be tempted to try to do too much, and instead needs to focus on tasks derived from mission analysis and clearly defined objectives.[42]

> Such a phenomenon existed in the late 1960s when Douglas Blaufarb observed that "military intellectuals were advancing the notion that the U.S. Army was the arm of the government best equipped to carry out in the field the entire range of activities associated with 'nation-building.'"[43] Hindsight reveals the fundamental flaws in this philosophy as it manifested itself in the United States' nation-building efforts in Vietnam. In 1976, Chief of Staff General Fred Weyand, a former MACV commander, concluded that in Vietnam.... The major military error was a failure to communicate to the civilian decisionmakers the capabilities and limitations of American military power. There are certain tasks the American military can accomplish on behalf of another nation. They can defeat enemy forces on the battlefield. They can blockade the enemy's coast. They can cut lines of supply and communication. They can carry the war to the enemy on land, sea, and air. These tasks require political decisions before they can be implemented, but they are within the military's capabilities. But there are also fundamental limitations on American military power ... the Congress and American people will not permit their military to take total control of another nation's political, economic, and social institutions in order to completely orchestrate the war.... The failure to communicate these capabilities and limitations resulted in the military being called upon to perform political, economic, and social tasks beyond its capability while at the same time it was limited in its authority to accomplish those military tasks of which it was capable.[44]

Rather than this overreliance on the military instrument of power that also epitomized the nation-building effort in Somalia, Allard recommends a more balanced application of military, diplomatic, and humanitarian efforts.[45] To date, however, the military retains its dominant role in the process.

Cultural Factors

From a cultural perspective, Francis Fukuyama argues that the very word "nation" building conjures up unrealistic expectations. Although sometimes used interchangeably, especially in the United States, states and nations are not the same thing. While a state exercises sovereign authority over a defined territory, a nation is "a community bound together by shared history and culture." Thus, Fukuyama asserts that "nation-building in the sense of the creation of a community bound together by shared history and culture is well beyond the ability of any outside power to achieve.... Only states can be deliberately constructed. If a nation arises from this, it is more a matter of luck than design."[46]

Fukuyama's argument is more than an academic mincing of words. It plagued United States efforts in Somalia, where Major General S.L. Arnold recognized from the beginning that when it came to making a nation out of the chaotic situation his 10th Mountain Division encountered, "history was not on our side." "For centuries," Arnold explains, "the Somali warrior had been fiercely independent, uniting with extended family and other subclans only when challenged from external forces; showing some limited loyalties to the clan and demonstrating little, if any, sense of national unity. Even with a common language and religion, homogeneity in Somalia was a myth."[47]

Another difficulty with nation-building from a cultural perspective involves the insensitivity of nation-builders to situations other than their own, as well as the inherent obstacles to democratization critics argue are present in some societies. The American version of nation-building has long assumed a superiority of American culture and technology that it offers as a model to the developing world. The Manifest Destiny of the 1840s, for example, was designed "to bring the blessings of liberty and democracy, Christianity and commercialism, to backward peoples."[48] The free-labor ideology of the Reconstruction era assumed the superiority of Northern business practices and saw them as a model for Southern economic development.[49] In 1899, Rudyard Kipling called upon America to "take up the White Man's burden" and bestow the blessings of higher culture and civilization to a Filipino people "half-devil and half child."[50]

In the late 1950s and 1960s, modernization theory offered an even more encompassing vision of the values and institutions, in addition to capital and technology, necessary to transform traditional societies.[51] According to Arthur Schlesinger, a "middle-class revolution" was needed. Unless land reform, industrialization, tax reform, and public health and sanitation were initiated in the Third World, he argued, "new Castros will infallibly arise." Among the most influential modernization theorists was Walter Rostow, who served as head of the policy planning staff under President John Kennedy and as national security advisor under President Lyndon Johnson. Considered by some to be "the chief architect of the Vietnam War,"[52] Rostow declared "modern societies must be built and we are prepared to help build them."[53]

Thomas Paterson argues that Rostow's version of nation-building failed in Vietnam in part because it "simply did not pay proper attention to the world's diversity and complexity" or "the varied traditions of other cultures." Instead, Rostow and others "chose to project the American experience onto aliens" in a way Paterson decries as "blindly ignorant." Whatever its intentions, the "pro-capitalist, private enterprise bias" of American nation-building in Vietnam was "traditionally identified with exploitation" in the Third

World.[54] David Tucker agrees: "Our ideal of a 'wealthy, equitable, democratic, stable, and autonomous' society, like the notion of development itself, is not indigenous to most of the world, which may conceive of the good society as one that is 'simple, austere, hierarchical, authoritarian, disciplined, and martial.'"[55]

Some argue that not just cultural expectations, but also cultural characteristics can affect nation-building efforts. David Landes, for example, concludes, "If we learn anything from the history of economic development, it is that culture makes almost all the difference."[56] The status and role of women, what Landes argues is "the best clue to a nation's growth and development," is one example of such a cultural characteristic. After admitting that "even the so-called advanced societies of the West can do better in this regard," Landes writes that "if we view gender relations as a continuum running from nothing to full equality, the Muslim countries, especially the Arab Muslim countries, would bottom out the scale."[57] While Landes appears to be supportive of nation-building, asserting that "rich countries" must "help the poor to become healthier and wealthier,"[58] his linkage of culture and economic development certainly serves as caution regarding what nation-building can reasonably be expected to do.

Recipient Willingness

Landes's argument about inherent cultural characteristics segues to another problem associated with nation-building—a certain degree of cooperation from the recipient of the effort is critical to success. Whether for the cultural reasons Landes argues, or for other motivations such as a self-interested desire to preserve the status quo, or a simple preference for local autonomy, the recipient of a nation-building effort gets a vote in the process. As a result, the United States has met resistance in a large number of its nation-building efforts.

One reason for resistance is that nation-building often threatens those in power. As nation-building expert James Dobbins explains, "The very act of intervention alters, often radically, the power balance and social dynamic in the subject nation and its region. By virtue of an intervention, losers suddenly become winners, and winners become losers."[59] Benjamin Schwarz, for example, found the U.S. efforts in El Salvador were spurned because "to reform radically threatens to alter fundamentally the position and prerogatives of those in power. The United States, with its 'revolutionary' means of combatting insurgency, is threatening the very things its ally is fighting to defend. Those reforms that we have deemed absolutely essential—respect for human rights, a judicial system that applies to all members of Salvadoran society, radical land redistribution—are measures no government in El Salvador has been able to achieve because they require fundamental changes in the country's authoritarian culture, economic structure, and political practices."[60] Major General Thomas Montgomery reported a similar situation in Somalia, where he found building a nation "was not in the best interest of the warlords, who wanted, each of them, to control."[61]

Another obstacle occurs when would-be indigenous reformers realize that American pursuit of its own self-interest gives the recipient a large amount of leverage, even in an environment of blatant intransigence. Nepotism, repression of the Buddhists, favoritism of the Catholics, failure to implement land reforms, black marketeering, and election fraud plagued South Vietnam, but President Ngo Dinh Diem was emboldened to "resist American pressures for reform because the United States needed his regime as an anti–Communist bastion. Thus he became, as one American official then in Saigon put it, 'a puppet who pulled his own strings—and ours as well.'"[62] Schwarz found the same situation in El Salvador, where "the Salvadorans had America trapped. They realized that the United States was involved in their war for its own national security interests.... So while the ruling Salvadorans gestured appropriately in response to U.S. conditions, whenever the U.S.-imposed reforms threatened to alter fundamentally the status quo—their very object—they were emasculated."[63]

Motives

If the United States forcefully overcomes such recipient unwillingness, it subjects itself to charges of imperialism. Then-Governor Bush tried to allay such perceptions in a carefully worded 1999 speech. "America cherishes that freedom, but we do not own it," he explained. "We value the elegant structures of our own democracy—but realize that, in other societies, the architecture will vary. We propose our principles, we must not impose our culture." "Precisely because we have no territorial objectives," he continued, "our gains are not measured in the losses of others. They are counted in the conflicts we avert, the prosperity we share and the peace we extend."[64] Whatever were the President's intentions, he was soon plagued by vehement accusations of hubris and oil-lust as the real motivations for the U.S. intervention in Iraq.[65]

In the final analysis, these myriad challenges ensure that, if nothing else, nation-building is not for the faint of heart. Fukuyama reminds us that nation-building has "an extremely troubled record of success,"[66] and warns that "most nation-builders soon find their ability to shape the local society is very limited."[67] He is joined by a chorus of observers bent on inserting some reality into characteristically over-optimistic expectations. Edward Mansfield and Jack Snyder call for "humility about the ability of any outsider to re-engineer a country's political institutions,"[68] Thomas Carothers contends that outsiders can rarely have a huge effect on a society's choice of political trajectory,[69] and Rory Stewart cautions that the international community "knows much less and can do much less than we pretend."[70] All this returns the discussion to Fukuyama's pragmatic conclusion that while nation-building may be difficult, it is also necessary. With that in mind, it is prudent to examine historical cases of nation-building efforts in hopes of improving understanding, at least, and perhaps performance as well.

Chapter 3

Altruistic Nation-Building: Somalia

U.S. involvement in Somalia came as a response to the anarchy, drought, civil war, and banditry that had reduced Somalia, a country encompassing approximately 637,540 square kilometers on the Horn of Africa, to a virtual wasteland. Some 300,000 Somalis had died between November 1991 and March 1993, and another 1.5 million lives were at immediate risk because of famine. Nearly 4.5 million of Somalia's 6 million people were threatened by severe malnutrition and related diseases. Another 700,000 had sought refuge in neighboring countries.

To help relieve the mass starvation, the United Nations Security Council approved Resolution 751, which established a humanitarian aid mission known as United Nations Operation in Somalia (UNOSOM I) in April 1992. UNOSOM I's success was severely limited because Somali warlords, most notably Mohamed Farah Aideed of the Habr Gidr subclan, and Ali Mahdi Mohamed of the Abgal subclan, refused full cooperation, and the limited mandate was not strong enough to compel compliance. The warlords, whom Kimberly Martin noted "maintain their authority only by preventing the emergence of a functioning state,"[1] kept the UNOSOM I troops from leaving Mogadishu Airport, and only 500 of the authorized 3,500 troops deployed.[2]

The failure of UNOSOM I quickly became apparent, and the United States found itself under increasing pressure to act. Because there was little national interest at stake in Somalia, any decision regarding intervention would be based on humanitarian considerations. As such, Somalia represents a host of the issues associated with altruistic nation-building. These include a decision-making process shaped by values instead of interests, the complications that arise when even non-biased humanitarian intervention inevitably alters the country's existing balance of power, pressures to expand the mission, and the difficulty in maintaining domestic interest in the face of such problems.

The Decision-Making Process

As policy-makers considered options, they did so without the familiar Cold War decision-making process that had served them well in the past. Then, after the 1983 disaster in Beirut, Secretary of Defense Caspar Weinberger had developed what became known as the "Weinberger Doctrine"—strategic criteria to help guide "the painful decision that the use of military force is necessary to protect our interests or to carry out our national policy."[3] The overarching concern of the criteria was that the objective, commitment, and other conditions would be strong enough to ensure perseverance. The Weinberger criteria required the following:

—The United States should not commit forces to combat unless the vital national interests of the United States or its allies are involved.

—United States troops should only be committed wholeheartedly and with the clear intention of winning. Otherwise, troops should not be committed.

—United States combat troops should be committed only with clearly defined political and military objectives and with the capacity to accomplish those objectives.

—The relationship between the objectives and the size and composition of the forces committed should be continually reassessed and adjusted if necessary.

—United States troops should not be committed to battle without a "reasonable assurance" of the support of US public opinion and Congress.

—The commitment of US troops should be considered only as a last resort.[4]

The Weinberger Doctrine had emerged as the definitive yardstick for measuring the application of military force, but by the time of the Somalia crisis, the success of Operation Desert Storm and the collapse of the Soviet empire were changing both America's perception of its military and the nature of the threat. To many, Weinberger's strict criteria for the use of force seemed to require revision.[5] They sought new roles and missions for the U.S. military in the globalized era and a foreign policy that supported not just U.S. interests, but also U.S. values.[6]

There had been other postwar periods in which an emphasis on values in American foreign policy rose to the fore. After World War I, President Woodrow Wilson championed what became known as "Wilsonian idealism," which held:

—Moral principle should be the guide to U.S. actions abroad.

—The Anglo-American values of liberty and liberal democratic institutions are worthy of emulation and promotion worldwide. Indeed, they are necessary if world peace is to be realized.

—The old order, based on balance-of-power and interest politics, must be replaced by an order based on moral principles and cooperation by all states against international aggression.

—The United States must continue to take an active role in bringing about these global reforms.[7]

According to Wilson's vision of foreign policy, the interests of humankind and global reform would take precedence over any narrowly defined national interest.[8]

Similarly, the nation-building effort in Somalia reflected what President Clinton's National Security Advisor Anthony Lake described as "pragmatic neo–Wilsonianism." No American vital interests were at stake in Somalia, but in their place were the peripheral interests of promoting American values and a favorable world order. While such interests did not meet Weinberger's high bar, it appeared that the application of military power was likely the only option that had a reasonable prospect of producing favorable results in Somalia at an acceptable cost.[9] As one contemporary observer described it, Somalia was without American precedent as "a major military action in the name of morality."[10] Another described the "startling new way" of using American forces "for humanitarian purposes, with no national interest at stake."[11] At the same time, however, there was a consensus that "the rules for compassionate intervention have not been spelled out with enough clarity."[12]

Thus, rather than being the result of deliberate and methodical exposure to criteria such as Weinberger's that sought to pursue national interests, the decision to intervene in Somalia was based on a series of domestic influences that related to values. This phenomenon marked another deviation from the Cold War's emphasis on realism as a foreign relations paradigm. Rather than realism's assertion that international relations and domestic politics are two separate spheres, President Clinton found himself in an environment where he noted "the dividing line between foreign and domestic policy is increasingly blurred."[13]

The shift in foreign policy focus away from interests and toward values was compatible with a media elite value "to use government power to 'do good.'"[14] Indeed, an onslaught of media coverage soon portrayed starvation conditions in Somalia and created the impression that only U.S. intervention could save the country. The ability of the media to project such compelling imagery was a fairly recent phenomenon.

In 1980, the Cable News Network, or CNN, became the first television channel to provide twenty-four-hour-a-day news coverage. With the deployment of communications satellites, CNN and other modern news outlets could now broadcast "real-time" reports from anywhere on earth. Collectively, this expanded news coverage creates what many observers call the "the CNN curve" or "CNN effect," which "has come to represent the influence that this new kind of 'real-time' reporting can have—that dramatic images of starving masses, shelled populations, or dead American soldiers can induce public demands for action from elected officials."[15]

The CNN effect manifests itself in several ways concerning foreign policy decision-making, but the one most present in the case of Somalia was as an "agenda setting agent." Agenda-setting involves using emotional and compelling coverage of events to reorder foreign policy priorities.[16] It is in this way that the media defines the "problem" as a "problem" and "decides what is decided."[17]

The media is capable of an agenda-setting role by both "framing" and "priming." Framing holds that how the media casts an issue affects substantive judgments people make about the issue. Priming argues that the priority the media gives to an issue affects the priority people give to the issue. The result is noted by Bruce Jentleson, who says, "The mass media may not be successful in telling people what to think, but the media are stunningly successful in telling their audience what to think about." Jentleson then asks, "If a tree falls in the woods and CNN doesn't cover it, did it really fall?"[18]

Numerous high-level decision-makers and observers recognize the impact of the media as an agenda setter. Former Secretary of State James Baker argues, "All too often, television is what determines what is a crisis."[19] Similarly, former Secretary of Defense James Schlesinger believes, "National policy is determined by the plight of the Kurds or starvation in Somalia, as it appears on the screen," and Jessica Matthews, former Deputy Under Secretary of State for Global Affairs, states, "The process by which a particular human tragedy becomes a crisis demanding a response is less the result of a rational weighing of need or of what is remediable than it is of what gets on the nightly news."[20] In the case of Somalia, Michael Mandelbaum concludes that "televised pictures of starving people created a political clamor to feed them, which propelled the U.S. military into action."[21]

Proponents of the media's impact on Somalia focus on the statements of those in the decision-making process. White House Press Secretary Marlin Fitzwater acknowledges this impact of the press coverage, saying, "After the election [of November 1992], the media had free time and that was when the pressure started building up.... We heard it from every corner, that something had to be done. Finally the pressure was too great.... TV tipped us over the top.... I could not stand to eat my dinner watching TV at night. It made me sick."[22] Perhaps the most telling testimony is Craig Hines's report of the media coverage's impact on President George H.W. Bush. Hines writes:

> Bush said that as he and his wife, Barbara, watched television at the White House and saw "those starving kids ... in quest of a little pitiful cup of rice," he phoned Defense Secretary Dick Cheney and Gen. Colin Powell, Chairman of the JCoS [Joint Chiefs of Staff]: "Please come over to the White House." Bush recalled telling the military leaders: "I—we—can't watch this anymore. You've got to do something."[23]

Although the true situation was pockets of hunger rather than widespread starvation, the media created a popular perception of universal life-

Marines and Somalian civilians load bags of food onto trucks for transport and delivery in Somalia in support of Operation Restore Hope. (Department of Defense photograph DD-SD-00–00668.)

threatening conditions that demanded action.[24] Anthony Lake explained, "We know that when the all-seeing eye of CNN finds real suffering abroad, Americans want their government to act—as they should and we should."[25] However, these public demands for action based on media coverage can negatively affect policy decision-making, especially in the context of traditional national interests and the rational actor model. Former Secretary of State Lawrence Eagleburger lamented, "The public hears of an event now in real time, before the State Department has had time to think about it. Consequently, we find ourselves reacting before we've had time to think. This is now the way we determine foreign policy—it's driven more by the daily events reported on TV than it used to be."[26] Donald Snow adds that such intense media coverage of "atrocious violence can create the public perception of a vital interest (one worth fighting over) on humanitarian grounds in situations where a more dispassionate, abstract analysis would not suggest that intensity of interest. Given the pressures that seem to emerge, one can call this temptation the 'do something syndrome.'"[27]

In addition to the domestic media coverage, there were other influences impacting American decision-making concerning Somalia. In the aftermath of the end of the Cold War and the victory in Operation Desert Storm, there was tremendous domestic and international pressure on the U.S. to use its status as the world's only superpower to create a favorable new world order. Indeed, in 1990, President Bush had declared:

> We stand today at a unique and extraordinary moment. The crisis in the Persian Gulf, as grave as it is, also offers a rare opportunity to move toward an historic period of cooperation. Out of these troubled times, our fifth objective—a new world order—can emerge: a new era—freer from the threat of terror, stronger in the pursuit of justice, and more secure in the quest for peace. An era in which the nations of the world, East and West, North and South, can prosper and live in harmony.... A hundred generations have searched for this elusive path to peace, while a thousand wars raged across the span of human endeavor. Today that new world is struggling to be born, a world quite different from the one we've known. A world where the rule of law supplants the rule of the jungle. A world in which nations recognize the shared responsibility for freedom and justice. A world where the strong respect the rights of the weak.[28]

Somalia was just one of many crises demanding U.S. attention as Bush and others sought to forge this new world order. Bosnia was another, but the seemingly open-ended nature of an intervention there served to fracture American will and popular interest in becoming involved. Somalia, on the other hand, seemed a much less complicated way of dealing with the pressure for U.S. action and a way of buying time for America to come to grips with what its role in Bosnia should be.[29]

The end result was that the American decision to intervene in Somalia was not based on the traditional rational actor model. Indeed, one contemporary observer described it as "more generous impulse than thought-out policy."[30] It certainly gave the appearance of being a "largely tactical decision reached to solve a current, concrete problem with little apparent concern for the longer term strategic implications."[31] Such misgivings notwithstanding, the United States won United Nations Security Council approval in December 1992 of Resolution 794, which established Unified Task Force (UNITAF), a large, U.S.-led peace enforcement operation known as Operation Restore Hope. UNITAF made great progress, and humanitarian agencies soon declared an end to the food emergency. By January 1993, food was getting to all areas of the country, leading 10th Mountain Division commander Major General S.L. Arnold to soon declare, "We have come very close to establishing the right environment to enable the Somalis to arrive at a *'Somali solution.'*"[32] In light of these improvements, U.S. forces began withdrawing in mid–February, and on May 4, UNOSOM II took over operations from UNITAF.

The Unintended Consequences of Intervention

In the wake of this success, subsequent experience in Somalia revealed that even as seemingly innocent an operation as providing humanitarian assistance can threaten legitimacy because of its inescapable political and military consequences. This risk is especially prevalent in an environment like Somalia where no government existed.[33] As James Dobbins explains, "The very act of intervention alters, often radically, the power balance and social dynamic in the subject nation and its region. By virtue of an intervention, losers suddenly become winners, and winners become losers."[34] In Somalia's clan-ridden society, aid was not seen as neutral or impartial if it was provided to a rival group. Indeed, strengthening any of the warring factions altered the balance of power and created a perception of peacekeeper bias.[35] Walter Clarke and Jeffrey Herbst explain, "When U.S. troops intervened in December 1992 to stop the theft of food, they disrupted the political economy and stepped deep into the muck of Somali politics. By reestablishing some order, the U.S. operations inevitably affected the direction of Somali politics and became nation-building because the most basic component of nation-building is to end anarchy."[36]

Norman Cooling argues that UNOSOM II continued this error. He claims, "Disregarding the long-established Somali cultural order, the UN felt that, in the interest of creating a representative, democratic Somali government, they would be better served by excluding the clan leadership."[37] The

A Marine patrol surrounding a weapons cantonment site of Mohamed Farah Aideed in northern Mogadishu. (Department of Defense photo DD-SD-00–00730 by Terry Mitchell.)

problem was that since 1988, more than fourteen Somali clans and factions had fought a civil war for control of their own territory.[38] In its expanded mission, UNOSOM II directly threatened these warlords' hold on power. UNOSOM II deputy commander Major General Thomas Montgomery observes, "That [to build a nation] was not in the best interest of the warlords, who wanted, each of them, to control, and of course Aideed was the strongest of the warlords."[39] Nonetheless, 10th Mountain Division commander Major General Arnold argued equally correctly that in his view, "The center of gravity of the operation in Somalia is the erosion of the independent power of the warlords.... It must take place if Somalia is ever to return to normalcy and attempt to rule itself."[40] But by concentrating on Aideed and Ali Mahdi, Somalia's two main warlords, William Wunderle argues that the UN created the unintended consequence of actually increasing "the warlords' degree of power and authority, which was desirable to the warlords but led to the marginalization of other clans, thereby upsetting the traditional balance of the Somali kinship system."[41] Moreover, the action that Arnold noted as critical to mission accomplishment was the same one that Montgomery explained would render the effort illegitimate in the eyes of the Somali base of power.

Mission Creep

The differences in scope between UNOSOM II and UNITAF were striking. While UNITAF focused on the southern parts of Somalia, UNOSOM II covered the entire country. While UNITAF strictly limited its activities to securing humanitarian assistance, UNOSOM II took on the much more dangerous task of disarmament. While UNITAF had no role in nation-building, UNOSOM II was mandated to assist Somalia in rehabilitating its political institutions, rebuilding its economy, and promoting national reconciliation and political settlement.[42]

The logic behind this expanded role was the inexorable connection between Somalia's humanitarian crisis and its underlying cause. Somalis were not starving exclusively from a devastating act of nature. Instead, as Clarke and Herbst explain, "The famine that gripped Somalia in 1992 resulted from the degeneration of the country's political system and economy."[43] President Bush had dispatched troops for the limited purpose of distributing food in hopes of curtailing the crisis and departing quickly. He had no intention, as President Clinton's Ambassador to the United Nations Madeleine Albright put it, of embarking on a plan "for the restoration of a country."[44] Yet observers at the time of Bush's modestly intended commitment noted, "It may not be enough just to police the Somalis and feed them. If the American-led multinational force does not also begin to rebuild the nation—pacifying the factions, creating at least a bare-bones local government and repairing the infrastructure—chaos could resume the minute it leaves."[45]

The expanding UNOSOM II mission drew political criticism in some circles, but few immediate protests. One of the earliest opponents was Senator Robert Byrd, who called for a withdrawal of U.S. forces, stating that while he supported the initial short-term humanitarian assistance, he did not have "nation-building in mind."[46] Nonetheless, the operation muddled along with little real effort to transform Somalia into a state, but with increasing confrontation and problems.[47] The most serious tensions arose from the fact that UNOSOM II's expanded mandate posed a threat to the delicate clan-based balance of power in Somalia. As a result, by June, UNOSOM II was at war with various Somali parties and was suffering high casualties, including twenty-five Pakistanis killed in an ambush on June 5. United Nations Security Council Resolution 837 was passed the next day and called for the immediate apprehension of those responsible. The result was that U.S. soldiers became involved in a highly personalized manhunt for Mohamed Ali Farrah Aideed, the most powerful of the warlords.

This effort climaxed on October 3 with Operation Gothic Serpent. The operation began favorably with a force of Army Rangers and Delta commandos conducting a daylight raid on a suspected location of Aideed and his lieutenants at the Olympic Hotel. The Americans captured twenty of Aideed's men, but the mission quickly unraveled when Somalis shot down three U.S. helicopters. The Americans soon became surrounded by thousands of Somalis, and the relief column was ambushed on its way to rescue the beleaguered soldiers. It was more than nine hours before help arrived. By the time it did and the evacuation was complete, eighteen Americans had been killed.

The Problem of Perseverance

Although it is estimated that the Americans inflicted up to two thousand casualties on the Somalis during the Battle of Mogadishu, the American losses and the chaotic nature of the operation created a domestic outcry in the United States.[48] As a peripheral interest, Somalia had never evoked a deep U.S. commitment, and the October fiasco led to the Clinton administration's decision to withdraw U.S. troops by March 1994. "It is not our job," President Bill Clinton explained, "to rebuild Somalia's society."[49] The U.S. withdrawal compelled the UN to terminate UNOSOM II and withdraw all peacekeepers by March 1995.

David Rieff attributes the American decision not simply to the casualties, but to the nature of the American mission in Somalia:

The American public came to think of the hunt for Aideed, even though they knew it was being carried out by U.S. Army Rangers, not as war but as police work. Casualties in war are understood to be inevitable. Soldiers are not only supposed to be ready to kill, they are supposed to be able to die. But casualties in police work are a different matter entirely. There, it is only criminals who are supposed to get hurt or, if necessary, killed, not the cops. Again, the fundamental problem has not been some peculiar American aversion to military casualties. Rather, there has been an essential mistake in the way such operations are presented to the public, and, perhaps, even in the way they are conceived of by policymakers. Under the circumstances, it should hardly be surprising that public pressure on Congress and the president to withdraw U.S. troops predictably arises at the first moment an operation cannot be presented in simple moral terms, or when casualties or even the costs start to mount.[50]

Because the objective of nation-building in Somalia was not broadly accepted by the American people or important to U.S. national interests, perseverance could not be sustained in the wake of growing numbers of casualties. The U.S. experience in Somalia shows a clear connection between the domestic legitimacy of the objective and the public's willingness to exhibit perseverance when the operation undergoes difficulty. It is a phenomenon that makes all altruistic nation-building efforts subject to a rapid loss of interest.

Conclusion

The lure of altruistic nation-building is easy to understand because humanitarian crises indeed tug on the heartstrings. Unfortunately, the reality requires more than just emotion. As Anthony Lake noted, "When I wake up every morning and look at the headlines and the stories and the images on television of these conflicts, I want to work to end every conflict, I want to save every child out there." While the needs may be near infinite, however, capabilities are not. Lake understands this limitation, adding, "But neither we nor the international community have the resources nor the mandate to do so."[51]

Yet even critics of altruism see its moral and practical application. While Michael Mandelbaum decries President Clinton's expansion of the mission in Somalia as "a branch of social work" and "the foreign policy of Mother Teresa," he acknowledges that by some estimates the U.S. intervention saved as many as half a million lives.[52] The problem then becomes to determine how to balance American interests and values, and then how to leverage U.S. power in a way that preserves the humanitarian good of Somalia while mitigating its unintended negative consequences.

From its very inception, observers recognized Somalia as a "test case" for the use of military intervention for humanitarian purposes in the post–Cold War "new world order."[53] There was an emerging consensus that "human suffering is a reason to act" and that, whether it liked it or not, "America is the world's chief of police." At the same time, however, even before Somalia's disastrous conclusion, it was understood that "Americans can't take charge of policing every beat" and they should "only attempt what's feasible."[54]

As Americans reflected on the failure in Somalia and gained more experience with humanitarian military interventions such as in Haiti and Kosovo, more refined lessons emerged. Among the most common was the need for perseverance. Carl Hodge warns, "National governments have become … inclined to regard military force in the name of human rights as an addition to their toolkit for short-term political and diplomatic contingencies that offer little of lasting value to international peace."[55] Clarke and Herbst echo this theme, noting, "There is no such thing as a humanitarian surgical strike." Instead they depict President Bush's original vision of a short-duration mission in Somalia as indicative of a lack of "will to see a solution through." Somalia showed that "time estimates for interventions must be adjusted."[56] Likewise, the military-civilian partnership must be adjusted as "a humanitarian intervention shifts to nation building" to reflect "increased civilian resources and adequate time to fully complete such a bold undertaking."[57]

The problem associated with mustering the perseverance that humanitarian interventions require is that the initial unbridled altruistic motivation wanes as costs mount. At the beginning of the intervention in Somalia, the U.S. public perceived the "victims" as the starving Somali people. By the end, the American soldiers were the new victims. This changed sentiment manifested itself when a disorderly mob challenged the arrival of the USS *Harlan County* at Port-au-Prince, Haiti, just days after the disastrous Battle of Mogadishu. Senator Robert Dole captured the view of many when he asserted, "The return of [exiled President Jean-Bertrand] Aristide to Haiti is not worth even one American life." Dole then proposed a resolution to cut off funds for U.S. military forces sent to Haiti unless Congress voted to authorize the action, an emergency evacuation of Americans was required, or the "national interest" was at stake and there was not time to obtain congressional approval.[58]

Leslie Gelb and Justine Rosenthal applaud the new era in which "ideals and self-interests are both generally considered necessary ingredients of the national interest."[59] Nonetheless, as the post–Somalia response to Haiti indicates, Hodge warns that a humanitarian intervention "is likely to be effective and perceived as legitimate *only* when it is married to credible self-interest."[60] The challenge Hodge identifies is "establishing a clarity of purpose that is both humanitarian and credibly self-interested."[61] Michael Ignatieff argues that when this reconciliation of "moral idealism with national interest" is accomplished, "American policy has been a triumphant success." He cites the strategic and humanitarian goals of the U.S. efforts to rebuild Europe and Japan after World War II as examples.[62]

This combination eluded the U.S. in Somalia, and indeed the Clinton Administration's overall foreign policy. What is required, according to Ignatieff, is the ability "to match the moralism inherited from the tradition of Woodrow Wilson with muscular action in the style of Harry Truman." Instead, Ignatieff accuses the administration of a "failure to articulate the connection between ethical goals and national interest."[63] Somalia is a good example.

Clarke and Herbst also note that "a clear procedure for handling a failed state and determining that state's relationship to the international community is essential if the mistakes of the Somalia intervention are not to be repeated."[64] As "the first [United Nations] intervention without even pro forma permission in an independent country," Somalia challenged traditional notions of sovereignty.[65] Indeed, Leslie Gelb and Justine Rosenthal note, "Humanitarian intervention ... is the most dramatic example of the new power of morality in international affairs. The notion that states could invade the sovereign territory of other states to stop massive bloodshed (call it genocide or ethnic cleansing or whatever) was inconceivable until the 1990s.... Just think of it: states endorsing the principle that morality trumps sovereignty."[66]

With no working economy, no police force, and no government, Strobe Talbott described Somalia as a place where "Mad Max characters have been conducting an experiment in anarchy." In such an environment, "the logical and necessary next step is for the U.N. to step in and run Somalia until there is once again a functioning government." Talbott notes that such an administration is the traditional trusteeship, but that, "especially in Africa [the idea] smacks of the white man's burden." Nonetheless, he argues, trusteeship, albeit under some other name, is what such situations require.[67]

Clarke and Herbst agree that "a new term is needed to express the idea that a state's fundamental institutions have so deteriorated that it needs long-term external help, not to institutionalize foreign control but to create stronger domestic institutions capable of self-government." They call for "the development of an international political equivalent to American bankruptcy law."[68] James Fearon and David Laitin call this new construct "neotrusteeship" and compare and contrast it with classical imperialism:

Similar to classical imperialism, these efforts involve a remarkable degree of control over domestic political authority and basic economic functions by foreign countries. In contrast to classical imperialism, in these new forms of rule subjects are governed by a complex hodgepodge of foreign powers, international and nongovernmental organizations (NGOs), and domestic institutions, rather than by a single imperial or trust power asserting monopoly rights within its domain. In contrast to classical imperialism but in line with concepts of trusteeship, the parties to these complex interventions typically seek an international legal mandate for their rule. Finally, whereas classical imperialists conceived of their empires as indefinite in time, the agents of neotrusteeship want to exit as quickly as possible, after intervening to reconstruct or reconfigure states so as to reduce threats arising from either state collapse or rogue regimes empowered by weapons of mass destruction (WMD).[69]

They call for "the current, ad hoc and underrationalized arrangements ... to be reformed in the direction of neotrusteeship."[70] David Rieff goes one step further in championing a revisitation of the mandatory system that was instituted after the Treaty of Versailles. While he admits the system was flawed in its execution, he sees promise in President Wilson's original idea to take temporary control over certain territories in order "to build up in as short a time as possible ... a political unit that can take charge of its own affairs."[71] If the situation "boils down to imperialism or barbarism," he argues "half-measures ... represent the worst of both worlds. Better to grasp the nettle and accept that liberal imperialism may be the best we are going to do in these callous and sentimental times."[72] Such an all-in or all-out approach is a common theme. Stephen Walt characterizes the United States in the era of Somalia as "the half-hearted hegemon,"[73] and Donald Snow points to the dangers of "ad hocracy."[74]

In order for such recommendations to be heeded, Clarke and Herbst note that another lesson from Somalia is that "the proper intervention forces must be developed." They contend that such a force must be capable of "executing complex political-military operations" that require the mix of civil affairs, psychological operations, and intelligence units "necessary to interact with the local population and promote reconciliation."[75] At the same time, however, they remind that it was the absence of heavy forces that hamstrung the relief of the lightly armed Rangers during the Battle of Mogadishu.[76] Indeed, Fearon and Laitin conclude that "in a country with a fractured state and an environment conducive to guerrilla war, a successful PKO [peace-keeping operation] requires a dominant military force that can act decisively, establish a clear chain of command, and take responsibility." For that reason they argue there must be "a lead state or regional organization with advanced technical and organizational capabilities to be the principal contractor with the UN for PKOs sent to collapsed states."[77] Even altruistic nation-building cannot ignore the requirement for security and force protection.

The U.S. experience in Somalia points to the chief danger associated with altruistic nation-building. While genuine humanitarian concern may be sufficient to initiate an intervention, sustaining that motivation for the lengthy period of time required to solve the underlying cause of the problem is difficult. Charities of all sorts battle the phenomenon of donor fatigue, and altruistic nation-building faces this same challenge. The difficulty in sustaining commitment worsens as monetary and human costs increase. More broadly, the lack of self-interest affects not just perseverance, but also decision-making because of the tendency to make decisions based on emotion rather than analytical process. This less rational approach can blind decision-makers to some of the practical obstacles to achieving their humanitarian vision. The lesson learned from Somalia then is that even altruistic nation-building interventions should be subjected to a deliberate and detailed decision-making and planning process, and unless an acceptable degree of self-interest is articulated in conjunction with the altruism, perseverance in the face of nation-building's inevitable difficulties will be hard to sustain.

CHAPTER 4

Self-Interested Nation-Building: Roosevelt's Corollary

In 1890, naval theorist Alfred Thayer Mahan wrote *The Influence of Sea Power upon History, 1660–1783*, and created an intellectual justification for a maritime power construct that was a tightly knit system of institutions, facilities, commercial carriers, and naval fleets that worked as an integrated whole to promote national interest.[1] The United States, Mahan argued, should regard the oceans as "a great highway" across which America would carry on world trade.[2] Mahan's vision became a practical reality with the Caribbean and Pacific interests the United States obtained after the Spanish-American War. A canal across the Central American isthmus would be necessary to conveniently connect these markets, and in 1901 the United States lent covert assistance to the Panamanian movement for independence from Columbia and soon gained a perpetually renewable lease on a canal zone. Mahan cautioned that an isthmian canal "may bring our interests and those of foreign nations in collision," and therefore "we must without any delay begin to build a navy which will at least equal that of England ... and must begin to build as soon as the first spadeful of earth is turned at Panama."[3] A dedicated naval expansion program followed, and by 1904, the U.S. Navy ranked fifth in the world. By 1907, it was third.[4]

With the Panama Canal in hand, it was necessary to make sure the Caribbean basin was secure. Secretary of State Elihu Root explained that the countries there had been placed "in the front yard of the United States" by the Canal, and President Theodore Roosevelt added that they now must "behave themselves."[5] As Root explained, "The inevitable effect of our building the Canal must be to require us to police the surrounding premises. In the nature of things, trade and control, and the obligation to keep order which go with them, must come our way."[6]

Believing that regional instability would invite European intervention, President Roosevelt announced what became known as the Roosevelt Corollary to the Monroe Doctrine in 1904: "Chronic wrongdoing, or an impotence which results in a general loosening of the ties of civilized society, may in America, as elsewhere, ultimately require intervention by some civilized nation, and in the Western Hemisphere the adherence of the United States to the Monroe Doctrine may force the United States, however reluctantly, in flagrant cases of such wrongdoing or impotence, to the exercise of an international police power."[7] This "unilateral declaration sanctioned only by American power and national interest" was used by the United States to take over the customs of debt management of the Dominican Republic in 1905, of Nicaragua in 1911, and of Haiti in 1916, and to restore domestic stability in Cuba in 1906 and Nicaragua in 1909.[8] This particular study focuses on the Dominican Republic.

The Roots of the Crisis
in the Dominican Republic

Ulises Heureaux had first been elected president in 1882, and governed the Dominican Republic in a mock-constitutional fashion until his assassination in 1899. Under his rule, the Dominican government greatly expanded its external debt. While some of the money was used to generate infrastructure improvements, a significant amount also went to support Heureaux's personal extravagances and the financial requirements of his police state. This misuse of funds exacerbated both domestic budget deficits and shortfalls in the external balance of payments. Hoping to head off complete bankruptcy, the government turned to the familiar expedient of printing paper money. A huge issuance in 1897 debased the currency so much that even Dominicans refused to accept it. The economic crisis compounded popular discontent with Heureaux's increasingly oppressive rule, and in May 1899 he was assassinated.[9]

Following a brief provisional government, Juan Isidro Jiménez Pereyra was elected president in November 1899. He quickly was confronted by a fiscal crisis when European creditors, led by the French, began to call in loans that had been contracted by Heureaux. Customs fees represented the only significant source of government revenue at that time, and the Jiménez government pledged forty percent of its customs revenue to repay its foreign debt. This move agitated the San Domingo Improvement Company, a United States–based firm that had lent large sums to the Heureaux regime. As a result, the Improvement Company had not only received a considerable percentage of customs revenue, but also had been granted the right to administer Dominican customs in order to ensure regular repayment. The directors of the Improvement Company protested the Jiménez government's resumption of control over its customs receipts to the United States Department of State, and the review of the case prompted a renewed interest in Washington in Dominican affairs.[10]

Jiménez's handling of the economic crisis brought him in conflict with several Dominican nationalists who accused him of bargaining away the country's sovereignty in return for financial settlements. Horacio Vásquez Lajara, who had earlier established the anti–Heureaux Young Revolutionary Junta, led the government forces that quelled some early uprisings, but personal and political competition soon brought Jiménez and Vásquez into serious conflict. Vásquez's forces proclaimed a revolution on April 26, 1902, and Jiménez, with no real base of support, fled his office and his country a few days later. However, once in control, Vásquez lacked the strong leadership skills necessary to bring order to the chaotic situation, and general unrest culminated in the seizure of power by ex-president Woss y Gil in April 1903.[11]

At this point Dominican politics was polarized into two largely nonideological camps: the *jimenistas*, who supported Jiménez, and the *horacistas*, who supported Vásquez and fellow Young Revolutionary Junta member Ramon Cáceres Vasquez. Woss y Gil, a *jimenista*, made the mistake of seeking supporters among the *horacista* camp and was overthrown by the *jimenista* general, Carlos F. Morales Languasco, in December 1903. Morales set up a provisional government and announced his candidacy for the presidency with the *horacista* Cáceres as his running mate. While this cooperation with the *horacistas* incited another *jimenista* rebellion, Morales and Cáceres were inaugurated on June 19, 1904.[12]

With its Panama Canal interests at stake, the United States closely monitored the Dominican Republic's economic and political saga. The Roosevelt Administration negotiated an agreement in June 1904 whereby the Dominican government bought out the holdings of the San Domingo Improvement Company. Nonetheless, regional unrest continued to the point that Roosevelt felt compelled in his December 1904 annual message to Congress to caution that the United States would intervene in the affairs of a Caribbean country whose "inability or unwillingness to do justice at home and abroad had violated the rights of the United States or had invited foreign aggression to the detriment of the entire body of American nations."[13]

In a further effort to reverse the Dominican Republic's financial straits, the United States and the Dominican Republic signed a financial accord on February 7, 1905, by which the United States government assumed responsibility for all Dominican debt and for the collection of customs duties and the allocation of those revenues to the Dominican government and to the repayment of its domestic and foreign debt. Although the United States Senate rejected parts of the agreement, it was still the basis for the establishment in April 1905 of the General Customs Receivership. It was through this office that the United States government would administer the finances of the Dominican Republic.[14]

While these economic arrangements were developing, the Morales-Cáceres administration was plagued by a partisanship that hamstrung the government. By late 1905, Morales had so lost effective control to Cáceres and the cabinet that Morales resolved to lead a coup against his own government. Before he could act, however, his plan was discovered by the *horacistas*, and Morales was captured and sent into exile. Cáceres assumed the presidency on December 29, 1905.[15]

With the General Customs Receivership freeing him from the burden of dealing with creditors, Cáceres attempted to reform the political system. Local *ayuntamientos* (town councils) were placed under the power of the central government, the presidential term was extended to six years, and the office of vice-president was eliminated. Cáceres also nationalized public utilities and established a bureau of public works to administer them.[16]

President Roosevelt was initially enthusiastic about the developments in the Dominican Republic, reporting to Congress in December 1905, "Under the course taken, stability and order and all the benefits of peace are at last coming to Santo Domingo, danger of foreign intervention has been suspended, and there is at last a prospect that all creditors will get justice, no more and no less."[17] Many Dominican nationalists, however, were less sanguine about what they saw as challenges to local authority and encroachments on sovereignty. Cáceres soon found himself plagued by opposition fomented in exile by Morales, Jiménez, and others. These intrigues culminated on the evening of November 19, 1911, when a small group headed by Luis Tejera assassinated Cáceres as he drove through the streets of Santo Domingo.[18]

Cáceres was succeeded by Eladio Victoria y Victoria, who squandered most of the fiscal benefits that had resulted from the 1905 receivership on military campaigns against rebellious partisans. In the wake of the continued violence and instability, President William H. Taft dispatched Brigadier General Frank McIntyre, the chief of the War Department's Bureau of Insular Affairs, and William T.S. Doyle, the chief of the Latin American division in the State Department, to Santo Domingo on September 24, 1912, to mediate among the warring factions. The commissioners were accompanied by a force of 750 United States Marines, which no doubt helped convince the Dominicans of the seriousness of Washington's threats to intervene directly. As a result, Victoria agreed to step down in favor of a neutral figure, Roman Catholic archbishop Adolfo Alejandro Nouel Bobadilla, who assumed office as provisional president on November 30.[19]

With the installation of Nouel, the commissioners returned to Washington. Two months later the Marines also withdrew, leaving Nouel to his own devices to deal with the various factional leaders in control of different sections of the country. While ostensibly recognizing the provisional government's authority, Nouel's rivals insisted on offices and money for themselves in exchange for their support. Efforts to placate the factions only emboldened them, and Nouel was reluctant to compel cooperation with force. Within days of his inauguration, Nouel was ill from overwork and discouragement. He sent his resignation to Congress on December 15, but Ambassador William Russell persuaded him to withdraw it. Nonetheless, little changed, and on March 31, 1913, Nouel finally stepped down. The Congress selected José Bordas Valdés as the provisional president with the stipulation that elections for a constitutional president would be held within a year.[20]

Like his predecessors, Bordas was unable to restrain the factional fighting, and once again, Washington intervened to mediate a resolution. This time, the rebellious *horacistas* agreed to a cease-fire based on an American pledge to oversee elections for members of local *ayuntamientos* and a constituent assembly that would draft the procedures for presidential balloting. The process, however, was flagrantly manipulated and resulted in Bordas's reelection on June 15, 1914. Both *horacistas* and *jimenistas* objected and rebelled against Bordas.[21]

Woodrow Wilson had succeeded Taft as president in 1913, and he followed his predecessor's firm approach toward the Dominicans. In spite of Wilson's historical legacy as an idealist, the self-interest expressed in Roosevelt's Corollary to the Monroe Doctrine continued to guide American policy in the Caribbean. President Wilson expressed full agreement with Secretary of State Robert Lansing, who explained in November 1915, "The possession of the Panama Canal and its defense have in a measure given to the territories in and about the Caribbean Sea a new importance from the standpoint of our national safety. It is vital to the interests of this country that European political domination should in no way be extended to these regions…. Because of this state of affairs, our national safety, in my opinion, requires that the United States should intervene and aid in the establishment and maintenance of a stable and honest government, if no other way seems possible to attain that end."[22] The potential of German intrigue in Central America as part of an effort to deter American entry in World War I presented another concern.[23]

With these security interests in mind, President Wilson had a plan presented whereby the contending factions would lay down their arms and select a provisional president. If they could not agree upon one, the United States would name one. The new government would then hold an election under close United States observation. If the election was conducted satisfactorily, the United States would support the new constitutional government. If the election was not free and fair, a new election would be held, "at which the mistakes observed will be corrected."[24]

President Wilson dispatched former New Jersey Governor John Franklin Fort, New Hampshire attorney Charles Cogswell Smith, and Envoy Extraordinary and Minister Plenipotentiary James Sullivan to the Dominican Republic to deliver the plan with instructions to "see that it is complied with." The commissioners were further advised that "no opportunity for argument should be given to any person or faction." To back up these demands, the United States sent a detachment of Marines to Cuba to be on hand if American interests were threatened in the Dominican Republic or Haiti. An additional contingent of Marines accompanied the commissioners to the Dominican Republic but remained on board their transport vessels during the negotiations. A combination of this strong show of force and a general weariness from the continuous fighting led all the principal faction leaders except Desiderio Arias to accept the plan. Dr. Ramón Báez Machado, a physician who had previously been relatively inactive politically, was made provisional president on August 27, 1914.[25]

Comparatively fair presidential elections began on October 25, and Jiménez was elected president with 40,000 votes compared to 35,000 for Vasquez. He was inaugurated on December 5. In an effort to build cooperation, Jiménez appointed leaders and prominent members of the various political factions to positions in his government, including making Arias his secretary of war. Jiménez's well-intended move only resulted in more internecine conflicts, which weakened the government and the president. With encouragement from the Federico Velasquez faction, Jiménez broke with Arias and imprisoned the commander of the fortress at Santo Domingo City and the chief of the Republican Guard, two of Arias's

Charges of inappropriate financial dealings made James Sullivan's posting in the Dominican Republic short and controversial. Appointed on August 12, 1913, he resigned on July 23, 1915, after an investigation determined him to be "unfit." (Library of Congress Prints and Photographs Division LC-DIG-hec-17549.)

principal lieutenants. The troops of the fortress, however, remained loyal to Arias, and the leaders of the opposition parties offered him their support. Armed with this backing, Arias seized control of both the armed forces and the Congress, which he compelled to impeach Jiménez for violation of the constitution and the laws.[26]

In the midst of the turmoil, the State Department authorized Ambassador Russell to give Jiménez "all support," and two American warships arrived at Santo Domingo City and off-loaded a contingent of 150 Marines commanded by Major Frederick Wise. After an aborted effort using his own men, Jiménez asked the American forces to take the city for him, but then reconsidered and opted to step down on May 7, 1916. Washington authorized Russell and Admiral William Caperton, the military administrator in neighboring Haiti after that country had been occupied by the United States in 1915, to take whatever action they deemed necessary to remove Arias. On May 13, they advised Arias they would attack Santo Domingo unless he surrendered. Major Wise recounted the conversation:

> I told him that this damned business of having revolutions in San Domingo had to cease; that he must get out and let the President come back into the capital without a row; that the United States meant business and if he didn't do it we were going to put him out.
> "I do not intend to leave," he said.
> "Oh, yes, you will," I told him.[27]

Faced with this firm stand, Arias quietly withdrew to the interior, and the Marines, with the addition of 400 reinforcements commanded by Major Newt Hall, occupied the capital without bloodshed on May 15.[28]

By this point, "The United States government had apparently tired of its recurring role as mediator and had decided to take more direct action."[29] Three days after the showdown with Arias, the first Marines landed and established effective control of the country within two months. On July 25, apparently without any consultation with American officials, the Dominican Congress appointed Dr. Francisco Henriquez y Carbajal as provisional president for a term of five months. When it appeared that Arias, whom the United States had determined to be the principal reason for the failure of previous peace efforts, appeared likely to become constitutional president, President Wilson "with the deepest reluctance" agreed to a military occupation, having become "convinced that it is the least of the evils in sight in this very perplexing situation." On November 29, Rear Admiral Harry Knapp, Caperton's replacement as commander of the Special Service Squadron, proclaimed the establishment of a military occupation with himself as military governor.[30]

Knapp's proclamation explained that the intervention was "designed to assist the country to return to a condition of internal order which would

On May 23, 1916, Colonel Theodore Kane came ashore with additional forces and assumed command of all Marines in the Dominican Republic. He deployed his companies to secure Santo Domingo, including these camped at Fort Ozama. (Official Marine Corps Photo # QHCR67PZMRY4-276-70.)

enable it to observe the terms of the treaty concluded with the United States in 1907 [the American-Dominican Fiscal Convention of 1907], and the obligations which must rest upon it as one of the family of nations."[31] Indeed, the existence of the receivership created a U.S. interest in Santo Domingo that made it impossible to remain indifferent when civil war occurred. Customs receiver William Pulliam argued that even the Dominicans understood that "the increased or unauthorized public debt was of an internal nature and caused by internecine warfare when the Government became demoralized and unpaid bills and salary accounts were neglected and accumulated."[32] Under these circumstances, Knapp quickly issued orders censoring the press, telegraph, and mail, and forbidding the possession of firearms and explosives by individuals. At the same time, it was announced that budgetary payments would resume immediately.[33]

Hoping initially to establish a situation similar to that in Haiti, where the president and congress continued to function under the protection of the American forces, Knapp instead experienced an "unexpected evolution" when the members of the cabinet simply deserted the posts. As a result, American naval authorities assumed direct control of all branches of the central government. The military governor simply took the place of the Dominican government and acted "for and in behalf of that government—in a sense as a trustee."

Knapp "suspended" the Dominican Congress and issued those laws that he considered warranted. On the other hand, Dominican officials at the provincial and municipal levels largely remained in office and continued their customary functions under American supervision.[34]

The Marines were an active and highly visible part of the military government, "personif[ying] the American regime for the individual Dominican." The Marines exercised their civil affairs duties through the military districts into which the country was divided. The Marine commander of each district acted as the civil governor of his area of responsibility. He supervised a Marine provost marshal who extended the occupational authority to the town and village level through the power of arrest and through the provost courts. Indeed, the Marines had no nationwide program for improving the economic and social conditions in the Dominican Republic, but efforts at the district level and below represent the local approach to nation-building that will be discussed in greater detail, using Vietnam as an example, in Chapter 7. The Marines also performed the arduous task of disarming the civilian population, collecting some 53,000 firearms throughout the course of the occupation.[35]

While most Dominicans received the proclamation without enthusiasm, it was accompanied by much less violence than was anticipated, and most Dominicans seemed content to passively comply with the decrees of the military government. Indeed, the surface effects of the occupation were largely positive. The country's budget was balanced, its debt was diminished, and economic growth resumed. Significant reforms were made to an obsolete and abusive prison system, the postal service was reorganized, and the telephone and telegraph systems were rebuilt. Infrastructure projects produced new roads that linked all the country's regions for the first time in its history, moving one observer to report these "new arteries of the national life brought about the unity of the Dominican family." As is common in most developmental efforts, educational improvements were very popular. New buildings were constructed, teacher salaries were raised, and student attendance jumped from 12,000 to over 100,000.[36]

The Marines restored order throughout most of the republic, with the exception of continual problems with banditry in the sparsely settled eastern end of the island in the provinces of El Seibo and San Pedro de Macorís. There several groups had operated independently during the governmental chaos and did not wish to lay down their weapons. A guerrilla movement known as the *gavilleros* developed and enjoyed the benefits of considerable support among the population and a superior knowledge of the terrain. The movement was resilient enough to survive the capture and the execution of its leader, Vicente Evangelista, and some initially fierce encounters with the Marines. However, the Marines' superior firepower, air power, and aggressive counterinsurgent methods eventually overwhelmed the *gavilleros*.[37] By May 31, 1922, organized banditry was determined to have ceased in the eastern district, and the country could be considered fully pacified.[38]

The Constabulary

This imposition of order was greatly facilitated by the creation of the *Guardia Nacional Dominicana* (Dominican Constabulary Guard), a professional military organization that replaced the partisan army, navy, *Guardia Republicana*, and frontier guard forces that had fueled the republic's historic struggles for power. Knapp had made the creation of a constabulary recruited and trained by the Marines one of his first objectives, but it was not formally established until April 7, 1917, by Executive Order 47. The initial strength was set at 88 officers and 1,200 enlisted men, and $500,000 was provided for its support. Its purpose was to perform police functions, guard the border with Haiti, and aid the Marines in counterinsurgency operations.[39]

The *Guardia Nacional Dominicana* (GND) was commanded by a Marine officer who reported to the commanding general of the 2nd Brigade. Soon, the GND developed its own central staff and adopted a territorial district organization that paralleled that of the Marine brigade. A company of GND was stationed in each province. Nonetheless, the development of the GND suffered from frequent changes in the top command, a lack of systematic training, inadequate budget and equipment, and limited expertise among the Marine trainers on the specifics of constabulary work. Additionally, there was some tendency among GND members to continue the corrupt and arbitrary methods of earlier Dominican constabularies. In spite of these handicaps, the GND provided a valuable contribution to the Marines' anti-banditry efforts. The official Marine history of the Dominican intervention concludes, "There can be no question that between 1917 and 1924 the Marines had created a disciplined, modern police force out of the rag-tag remnants of the former regime's motley constabulary."[40]

There was, however, a sinister component of this transformation of the GND into a powerful organization. Its new-found efficiency and discipline gave its officers a potential political power that surpassed even that of the old-style Dominican *caudillos*.[41] In what Richard Millett calls the "unintended foundation of tyranny," the first class of officers graduating from the new training center at Haina included Rafael Leonidas Trujillo.[42] Trujillo rose rapidly through the ranks, and in 1925 he was promoted to Colonel Commandant of the *Policia Nacional Dominica* (PND), a new name given to the GND to emphasize the organization's character as a police agency and to eliminate residual mental associations with the corrupt forces of the pre-occupation era. Realizing that the military represented the best route to power, Trujillo began an ambitious drive that catapulted him to the position of one of the Caribbean's most enduring and repressive dictators.[43]

Trujillo's early rise in the PND coincided with a declining American interest in the Dominican Republic. With the end of World War I, the public was ready to "return to normalcy" and forego global involvement in favor of a reaffirmation of isolationism.[44] Indeed, Warren Harding, who succeeded Wilson as president in March 1921, had campaigned against the occupations of both Haiti and the Dominican Republic.[45]

Once in office, the new administration presented the "Harding Plan," which called for an American withdrawal accompanied by Dominican ratification of all acts of the military government, approval of a loan of $2.5 million for public works and other expenses, the acceptance of United States officers for the PND, and the holding of elections under American supervision. Some moderate Dominican leaders favored the proposal, but in the face of significant public protests and nationalist opposition that argued the plan continued too much American control, the negotiations came to an impasse. More productive discussion was revived in March 1922 between Dominican negotiator Francisco Peynado and Secretary of State Charles Evans Hughes. By this point, Hughes was more willing to seek compromise after a year of stalled negotiations, and Peynado was also willing to take a pragmatic approach. To address the concerns of the Dominican nationalists, Harding dispatched Sumner Welles to establish a Commission of Representatives to modify the plan set forth in the Peynado-Hughes agreement. Welles's commission announced a final draft of the plan on September 23, 1922. By this time, Dominican public opinion had generally shifted in support of the Peynaldo-Hughes agreement, largely based on the realization that a U.S. withdrawal was inevitable.[46]

Under the supervision of Welles, Juan Bautista Vicini Burgos assumed the provisional presidency on October 21, 1922. With his inauguration, the Marine brigade lowered its profile, serving "for Dominican politicians [as] a final reserve upon which they could call if their experiment in keeping order among their own people broke down."[47] Such a crisis did not arise, and in the presidential election of March 15, 1924, Horacio Vásquez Lajara handily defeated Peynado. When Vásquez was inaugurated on July 13, control of the republic returned to Dominican hands. The last U.S. forces handed over police authority to the PND and left the Dominican Republic on September 18.[48]

Even critics of the intervention had to concede that the United States left the Dominican Republic materially better than it found it. The improvements, however, did not last long, and it soon became apparent that they were dependent on the Marine presence rather than being of a self-sustaining nature.[49] One observer concludes, "After the marines left, the roads decayed, the telephones stopped functioning, and thugs once again took control of the machinery of government."[50] Ironically, the infrastructure improvements the Marines had made to unite the country ultimately served to afford new ways for authoritarianism to be projected to heretofore remote areas.

Indeed, the Vásquez administration has been described as "a star amid a gathering storm" in Dominican history. While Vásquez engineered a brief period of progress, Trujillo was establishing his base of power behind the scenes. Using the army to harass, intimidate, and eliminate opposition, Trujillo declared victory in the May 1930 election with ninety-five percent of the vote. He then proceeded to rule the Dominican Republic as a feudal lord for thirty-one years.[51]

Max Boot correctly notes that the United States certainly did not deliberately install a dictator in the Dominican Republic. Indeed, "the marines had tried hard to plant constitutional government but found it would not take root in the inhospitable soil of Hispaniola." The only thing Boot notes that could have interrupted Trujillo's authoritarian rule was another intervention—"precisely the course that critics of American 'imperialism' had deplored in the first place." Caught in this dilemma, Boot laments that "the only thing more unsavory than U.S. intervention, it turned out, was U.S. nonintervention."[52]

To be sure, there was some element of altruism present even in this age of American imperialism. As President Roosevelt explained in his 1905 annual address to Congress: "This brings me to what should be one of the fundamental objects of the Monroe Doctrine. We must ourselves in good faith try to help upward toward peace and order those of our sister republics which need such help."[53] Likewise, Secretary Root had a genuine like for Latin Americans as individuals and in the finest tradition of liberal internationalism spoke of an effort "to help all friends to a common prosperity and a common growth."[54] Certainly President Wilson's Dominican foreign policy represented a combination of American self-interest and a sincere belief in the moral duty to promote democratic government in the countries within the American sphere of influence.[55] To this extent, the U.S. intervention in the Dominican Republic comes close to Carl Hodge's vision of "establishing a clarity of purpose that is both humanitarian and credibly self-interested" in nation-building.[56]

Likewise, the experience in the Dominican Republic represents some of the characteristics of a revisited "neotrusteeship" advocated by Walter Clarke, Jeffrey Herbst, James Fearon, David Laitin, and others. Even under these conditions, however, the intervention suffered the difficulties in sustaining a long-term commitment to nation-building. Stephen Fuller and Graham Cosmas explain the reversal wrought by Trujillo in the post-occupation era by lamenting, "Probably in the time the Military Government had, with the resources available and with the local conditions it faced, it never could have built a stable Dominican democracy."[57] As such, like Somalia, it remains another cautionary tale of the perseverance and commitment required of any nation-building effort.

CHAPTER 5

Sequencing Security:
The Philippines and Germany

Nation-building experts like James Dobbins agree that "security is an essential precondition" to any development associated with a nation-building operation.[1] Throughout its history with nation-building, the United States has experimented with different means of pursuing this prerequisite. In the Philippines after the Spanish-American War, the United States practiced a form of nation-building in which "persuasion and force went hand in hand."[2] Reflecting a certain degree of cultural awareness, the United States attempted to create security by accommodation, education, and civil society. However, when an insurgency developed, the United States was quick to use decisive force to crush it. This sequencing model can be described as "civic action backed by coercion." In Germany after World War II, the United States established initial security by a "blanket occupation" that "showed the Germans that they were defeated and their country occupied."[3] Once Germany was adequately demilitarized and denazified, the United States progressively shifted its effort to cooperative civil programs such as the Marshall Plan. As part of this transition, security was sustained by a police-type constabulary force backed by a small mobile strike force. This sequencing model can be described as "coercion and then civic action." Both of these approaches had advantages and disadvantages and provide lessons learned about sequencing, hard and soft power, and national will that can benefit current and future nation-building efforts. The most important lesson, however, is that, one way or another, security must be established for nation-building to have a chance.

The Philippines:
Civic Action backed by Coercion

America's long-held interest in ending the presence of European powers in the Western Hemisphere and three years of Cuban revolutionaries fighting to gain independence from Spanish colonial rule served to create palatable political tensions between the United States and Spain. This delicate situation reached its boiling point on February 15, 1898, when the U.S. battleship *Maine* exploded and sank in Havana harbor under mysterious circumstances. President William McKinley and Congress then initiated a series of measures supporting Cuban independence and preparing America to protect its interests there. On April 22, McKinley implemented a naval blockade of Cuba and issued a call for 125,000 military volunteers on April 23. Spain responded by immediately declaring war on the United States, and on April 25, the United States declared war on Spain.

After suffering more deaths from disease and accidents than battle, the U.S. emerged from what future Secretary of State John Hay declared a "splendid little war" with a resounding victory that was codified by the Treaty of Paris on December 10, 1898. The treaty guaranteed the independence of Cuba, forced Spain to cede Guam and Puerto Rico to the U.S., and arranged for Spain to sell the Philippines to the United States for $20 million.

America was unprepared to assume the global role thrust upon it by the aftermath of the Spanish-American War, and there was broad agreement not to embark on European-style imperialism. Nonetheless, the crumbling Spanish authority threatened to create regional violence that compelled the United States to take up what Rudyard Kipling described as the "White Man's Burden." In the process, the U.S. sought to navigate between "empire and chaos" to build a sovereign Philippines that would be cooperative with U.S. interests.[4] The result was an approach to security that was designed to be based on accommodation but was ultimately achieved by force.

Major General Elwell Otis commanded the U.S. Army forces in the Philippines. His task was outlined in what became known as the "Benevolent Assimilation Proclamation," authored by Secretary of War Elihu Root and issued by President McKinley on December 21. McKinley asserted that the "authority of the United States is to be exerted for the securing of the persons and property of the people of the islands and for the confirmation of all their private rights and relations," and that the occupiers "come, not as invaders or conquerors, but as friends, *to protect* the natives in their homes, in their employments, and in their personal and religious rights." "It should be the earnest wish and paramount aim of the military administration," McKinley continued, "to win the confidence, respect, and affection of the inhabitants of the Philippines by assuring them in every possible way that full measure of individual rights and liberties which is the heritage of free peoples, and by proving to them that the mission of the United States is one of benevolent assimilation substituting the mild sway of justice and right for arbitrary rule." Yet, he added, in fulfilling this higher purpose, "there must be sedulously maintained the strong arm of authority, to repress disturbance and to overcome all obstacles to the bestowal of the blessings of good and stable government upon the people of the Philippine Islands under the free flag of the United States."[5]

Regardless of what the Americans considered to be their benevolent intent, Filipino nationalists led by Emilio Aguinaldo objected to what they saw as a mere change in colonial masters from the Spanish to the Americans. As a result, a conventional war erupted on February 4, 1899, at Manila involving Major General Arthur MacArthur's 2nd Division and Aguinaldo's Filipino Army of Liberation. While MacArthur gained a string of victories, he insisted on the "kind and considerate treatment" of the local population, reminding his men on April 22 that to do otherwise would "impede the policy of the United States and to defeat the very purpose which the army is here to accomplish."[6] Such restrained conduct was commensurate with the philosophy of the "Philippine Commission" that McKinley had appointed on January 22. The commission was chaired by Dr. Jacob Schurman, President of Cornell University, and its members were Charles Denby, a former American minister to China; Dean Worcester, a professor of zoology from the University of Michigan; Commodore George Dewey, victor of the Battle of Manila Bay; and Major General Otis. The commission arrived in the Philippines on March 4, armed with a mandate "to facilitate the most humane, pacific, and effective extension of authority throughout these islands, and to secure with the least possible delay, the benefits of a wise and generous protection of life and property to the inhabitants."[7]

Under the auspices of benevolent assimilation, early Army efforts were "motivated by humanitarian instincts and a reform impulse divorced from the necessities of a military campaign." Indeed, rather than as a predominantly combat-related entity, John Gates describes "the army's role as [being] the advance agent of American culture and government."[8] Otis and many other senior Army leaders embraced this philosophy.[9] For example, Major General William Lawton felt that to pacify the Philippines, "we should impress the inhabitants with the idea of our good intentions and destroy the idea that we are barbarians or anything of the sort."[10] Likewise, MacArthur stated in his field orders that it was "one of the most important duties of American soldiers to assist in establishing friendly relations with the natives by kind and considerate treatment in all matters arising from personal contact."[11]

Otis, MacArthur, and other Army leaders were particularly enthusiastic about school development, and the Filipinos shared this interest in education. In many cases, a school was the first project the Army embarked on when occupying a town. Otis maintained an active interest in such efforts and even took a personal interest in such matters as selecting textbooks. The mutual interest in education generated much goodwill between the Americans and the Filipinos.[12]

This is not to say that the Army did not also maintain its ability to gain security by force. Indeed, Gates astutely captures the mix of civic action and coercion employed by the U.S. Army in the Philippines in his aptly titled *Schoolbooks and Krags*.[13] Thus, while Otis was experimenting with benevolent pacification, he was also preparing for a fall campaign to destroy the Army of Liberation. He began with operations in northern Luzon and then turned his attention south. The results came more quickly and easily than expected, and Otis soon felt that organized insurrection had been broken and only brigandage remained. He was so confident that "the war in the Philippines is already over," that he requested to be relieved from command, and on May 5, 1900, he was succeeded by MacArthur.[14] In a June 16 article in Leslie's *Weekly*, Otis opined, "The insurrection ended some months ago, and all we have to do now is protect the Filipinos against themselves and give protection to those natives who are begging for it." Reflecting a confidence in benevolent assimilation, Otis emphasized that to secure victory, he considered the most important task to be "simply to keep scrupulous faith with these people and teach them to trust us."[15]

To assist MacArthur in the anticipated transition from war to nation-building, President McKinley appointed federal circuit court judge William Howard Taft to lead a Philippine Commission that arrived in Manila on June 3, resolving "to cultivate the good will of the people and to convince them of the purposes of the United States to give them a good government."[16] According to Jeremi Suri, Taft's background as a judge had equipped him with the proper temperament for such an undertaking. "Taft," writes Suri, "had made his career through persuasion and compromise with antagonistic groups, not force or moral self-righteousness."[17] Even "his enormous rotund body" suggested Taft represented "judicious political bargaining" rather than military force.[18]

Taft's approach became known as the "policy of attraction." Designed to win over key elites and other Filipinos who did not share Aguinaldo's vision for an independent Philippines, the policy was built around a significant degree of self-government, social reforms, and plans for economic development. According to the Department of State's official history, "Over time, this program gained important Filipino adherents and undermined the revolutionaries' popular appeal, which significantly aided the United States' military effort to win the war."[19]

In the meantime, however, Aguinaldo responded to the superiority of the American forces by adopting a strategy of guerrilla war. In fact, much of what Otis and others saw as lawless brigandage was really the formative stages of Aguinaldo's guerrilla movement.[20] As this threat grew and became more apparent, the U.S. military increasingly relied on traditional coercive security measures rather than those associated with the cooperative security envisioned by the policy of attraction.

Initially, the problem of security in northern Luzon was expected to be resolved by the establishment of local governments with local police forces. When this measure proved to be ineffective in halting the guerrilla movement, Colonel William Duvall, commander of the 48th United States Volunteers in the particularly lawless La Union province, raised a 400- to 500-man vigilante force from the *Guardia de Honor* to identify *insurrectos* and purge towns of their influence. Local vigilantes then occupied the town while American forces swept the countryside for guerrillas. By breaking and isolating the guerrillas from the towns, Duvall successfully pacified most of La Union by the end of May 1900.[21]

The Americans built on this success by applying the forceful approach throughout the First District. In the process, they became increasing coercive. "I want you to take the most aggressive measures against the natives," instructed 34th U.S. Volunteer commander Lieutenant Colonel Robert Howze to his forces at Badoc. "Clear up that situation even if you have to kill off a large part of the malcontents; do some terrorizing yourself."[22] In Ilocos Norte, Howze ordered civic officials to be warned "that the feeding, sheltering and harboring of the *Insurrecto* element must at once cease, or the vicinity will be laid to waste, even to the extent of destroying their crops.... The most drastic measures will be resorted to in order to put an end to disturbances in this province."[23] Brigadier General Samuel Young, commander of the First District, applauded Howze's work, declaring it "unparalleled" and recommending him for promotion to brigadier general.[24]

In fact, Young was skeptical of the American policy of attraction. Instead, he advocated what he called the harsher "methods of European nations in arms in suppressing rebellions among Asiatics." If such an approach had been pursued earlier, he wrote on December 28, 1900, "the insurrection could have been easily put down a month ago."[25] As an example of his philosophy, Young ordered his command to "shoot anyone you believe to be in any way connected with destruction of telegraph."[26]

Young's superior, Major General Loyd Wheaton, commander of the Department of Northern Luzon, agreed that Young's methods would "speedily end resistance," but also noted that the "vagaries of impracticable public sentiment" warred against their adoption.[27] MacArthur refused to implement all of Young's recommendations, but frustration with the slow pace of pacification was mounting. Even Taft, the champion of the policy of attraction, "often suggested harsher measures than MacArthur took."[28]

By December 1900, MacArthur too was ready to take stronger action. The reelection of McKinley ensured American perseverance in the Philippines, and the rotation home of the volunteer infantry regiments scheduled for the spring created a sense of urgency.[29] On December 28, 1900, MacArthur admitted the progress of pacification was "apparent to me, but still very slow."

Thus he initiated "a more rigid policy" aimed to crush resistance.[30] To that end, MacArthur permitted the use of imprisonment, deportation, execution, and the confiscation and/or destruction of property to punish guerrillas and their supporters to a greater degree than had been permitted heretofore.[31] John Gates notes the new program was a departure from "the unqualified benevolence characteristic of the American policy during the first two years of the war." Instead, Gates opines, MacArthur embarked on a new course designed to ensure "Filipinos no longer interpret American benevolence as weakness."[32]

At the same time, MacArthur and Taft complemented this more aggressive military approach by creating the Federalist Party, a Filipino political organization that supported American rule in exchange for the establishment of representative government and increased local autonomy. Through the Federalist Party, the Americans offered a viable option in the competition with Aguinaldo for the allegiance of the Filipino people.[33] Robert Ramsey describes the resulting dynamic as "the policy of attraction ... stiffened by a policy of coercion."[34]

The trend toward coercion intensified on February 28, 1901, when Brigadier General J. Franklin Bell replaced Young as commander of the First District. If anything, Bell was even more aggressive than his predecessor. Under his command, Major William Bowen likened the district to the Shenandoah Valley after Major General Philip Sheridan's raid there during the American Civil War.[35] In the midst of such pressure, Aguinaldo was captured on March 23. On April 12, explaining the need to make the *insurrectos'* supporters to feel "the full hardship of War," Bell ordered the population of the barrios moved into towns "to stop the system of aid and contributions to the insurgents by the non-combatants and thus bring hostilities to a close."[36] Historian Brian Linn describes Bell as "willing and able to escalate the war to a level that the revolutionary leaders found intolerable, and once they surrendered, he was able to reconcile them to American rule."[37] His tactics seemed to deliver results, and in June, MacArthur declared "the armed insurrection is almost entirely suppressed."[38] On July 4, 1901, Taft assumed duties as governor of the Philippines, and Major General Adna Chaffee replaced MacArthur as commander of the Division of the Philippines. On the strength of the reinvigorated pacification effort, the Philippines were deemed ready for civil rather than military government.[39]

When MacArthur had made his optimistic announcement of near success in June, he did confess that "disorders still continue in several provinces" in the Department of Southern Luzon. His hope that the "progressively diminishing" nature of these incidents would lead to all areas' being "pacified at an early date" was dashed on July 17, when violence in the Batangas province and on the islands of Cebu and Bohol caused military control to be reestablished in those locations.[40] MacArthur's optimistic prediction, like Otis's before him, had proved to be somewhat premature.

The military campaign to conquer the Tagalog provinces in southwestern Luzon began on January 4, 1900, and enjoyed surprisingly rapid success. By early February, American units were occupying towns and beginning the transition to local civil government. They were met, however, by an "unfriendly, if not hostile" population, and "it would soon become apparent that occupation and pacification were very different problems."[41] Using guerrilla tactics, the *insurrectos* frustratingly avoided decisive contact and enjoyed shelter and support from the largely anti–American population.[42]

The Americans experienced great difficulty in forming local governments as a result of the *insurrectos'* grip on the population. Although Colonel Cornelius Gardener, commander of the 30th U.S. Volunteer Infantry, reported the Tayabas province ready for civil government in September, few shared his optimistic view of pacification's progress. In December, Major Matthew Steele, commander at Lucban, complained, "I have tried every argument to persuade various citizens to accept the office of [*presidente*] … without success." All, Steele reported, were afraid to take office because of the *insurrecto* threat to "their lives and property."[43] To Captain John Jordan, the problem was simply, "This business of fighting and civilizing and educating at the same time doesn't mix very well. Peace is needed first."[44] Major General John Bates, commander of the Department of Southern Luzon, also was pessimistic about the efficiency of the benevolent approach. In his annual report of August 15, he complained that *insurrectos* who had been treated kindly quickly showed "their lack of appreciation of the policy of magnanimity."[45] Ramsey summarizes the general conclusion of these observers: "Pacification was not working. Lack of security was considered the problem."[46]

Real progress was not made until November 30, 1901, when Chaffee appointed Brigadier General J. Franklin Bell from the First District in Northern Luzon to command the Third Separate Brigade. Bell brought with him his direct approach to security. On December 1, he briefed his officers, "We have one purpose, and that is to force the insurgents and those in active sympathy with them to want peace."[47]

Bell challenged the assumption that the average Filipino was predisposed to respond positively to the policy of attraction. "You can no more influence him by benevolent persuasion," Bell opined, "than you can fly."[48] Yet Bell did not propose abandoning the policy altogether. He merely was reordering the sequence to establish security first. "After all armed insurgents are forced to submit to constituted authority and peaceful conditions are re-established within the Brigade, we can then be benevolent and generous again and convince the people that we are their real friends," he told his assembled officers. He added, however, that "without first whipping them and convincing them

Among the American forces in the Philippines, around 100 were in Company K of the 17th Infantry. (U.S. Army photo by J.D. Givens.)

that we are able to accomplish our purposes by force if necessary, we can never gain their friendship, because otherwise we can never command their respect."[49]

As he had done in Northern Luzon, Bell took decisive measures to separate the population from the *insurrectos*. "Neutrality should not be tolerated," he advised. "Every inhabitant of this Brigade should either be an active friend or be classed as an enemy."[50] In stark contrast to the policy of attraction, Bell's approach was "based upon the assumption that, with very few exceptions, practically the whole population has been hostile to us at heart." "In order to combat such a population," he concluded, "it is necessary to make the state of war insupportable, and there is no more efficacious way of accomplishing this than by keeping the minds of the people in such a state of anxiety and apprehension that living under such conditions will soon become unbearable."[51]

Bell commenced operations in the Loboo Mountains on January 1, 1902. Under these new forceful conditions, he expected to eliminate insurrection within two months. In fact, the operation lasted throughout April, but it was highly successful in destroying the linkage between the guerrillas in the field and their support structure in the towns. On April 16, *insurrecto* leader Miguel Malvar surrendered, citing as his reason "the measures of General Bell ... reconcentration, the complete cleaning up of food supplies outside the towns, and persecution of the insurgent soldier by the people, and the demoralization of my troops." On May 6, Malvar announced, "I proclaim and make known by means of this edict to all concerned that the war carried on against the authority of the United States by the Filipino people, has ended." On July 4, 1902, President Theodore Roosevelt declared the Philippine Insurrection was over.

The United States fought the Spanish-American War as a limited war and was reluctant to embrace the international role that was then thrust upon it. Perhaps as a function of this moderation, the United States emphasized civic action early in its nation-building effort in the Philippines and hoped to gain security through goodwill and cooperation. Instead an insurgency developed, but the United States was able and willing to overcome this threat to security by force. Secretary of War Root acknowledged "a dual process" of military power and civil initiative, noting, "It is evident that the insurrection has been brought to an end both by making a war distressing and hopeless on the one hand and by making peace attractive."[52] Historian Maurice Matloff agrees: "Ultimately, the United States employed a carrot-and-stick policy to both entice and cower the Filipino population into submission. Force broke the back of the resistance; positive measures undermined it and helped reconcile the nationalists to their defeat. Neither would have been as effective without the other, but finding the right mix of benevolence and coercion had been difficult."[53]

Germany: Coercion and then Civic Action

The United States experience in post–World War II Germany differed significantly from its experience in the Philippines. It approached the situation with a decidedly more aggressive approach to international involvement. It had an unashamed objective of totally defeating its enemy. It faced a much greater security problem. As a result of these factors, the United States took a different approach to nation-building in Germany than it did in the Philippines.

In the Philippines, the United States had found itself unavoidably saddled with Kipling's "White Man's Burden." It was an unwanted obligation that Taft described as having been assumed out of necessity in spite of its being "contrary to our traditions and [occurring] at a time when we had quite enough to do at home."[54] In contrast to this grudging international involvement, one of President Franklin Roosevelt's objectives for the post–World War II period was an expanded role for the United States in world affairs.[55] Indeed, the

Atlantic Charter was replete with references to "hopes for a better future for the world," "the right of all peoples," "all States, great or small," "the fullest collaboration between all nations," and "all of the nations of the world."[56] Clearly, Roosevelt envisioned an active role for the United States in the post–World War II era.

Instead of the more limited approach pursued in the Spanish-American War, President Roosevelt announced at the end of the January 14–24, 1943, Casablanca Conference that he would pursue a policy of unconditional surrender in World War II. In an effort to avoid the situation that allowed Adolf Hitler to exploit nationalist sentiment after World War I, Roosevelt sought to ensure "the destruction of the philosophies in those countries which are based on conquest and the subjugation of other people." A poll conducted in the summer of 1944 showed the American public shared this assessment, with eighty-one percent of those surveyed wanting to enforce unconditional surrender terms on Hitler's regime and reduce Germany to the status of a third-rate power.[57]

In contrast to the attempt in the Philippines to establish security in conjunction with accommodation, the American policy in Germany after World War II was clearly built on a more heavy-handed approach. This strategy was articulated in Joint Chiefs of Staff Directive 1067, "Directive to SCAEF Regarding the Military Government of Germany in the Period Immediately Following the Cessation of Organized Resistance," which declared the intention to establish a "stern, all-powerful military administration of a conquered country, based on its unconditional surrender, impressing the Germans with their military defeat and the futility of any further aggression."[58] Only after this condition had been achieved would more cooperative ventures such as the famous Marshall Plan be initiated.

As in the Philippines, the United States' presence in Germany was impacted by domestic considerations. World War II had been a trying experience for the country, and there was significant pressure to "bring the boys home." Such sentiments, however, were subordinated to the very real concerns about the security vacuum created by the defeat of the German military. Before military governments of the occupying powers could fill that void, the German military would have to be disarmed and demobilized, renegade guerrilla groups would have to be prevented from forming, and Nazi war criminals would have to be identified and brought to trial. Thus, in Germany, the United States pursued a decidedly sequential approach to nation-building with "the first order of business" being to establish security.[59]

This objective was facilitated by the fact that on V-E Day (May 8, 1945), General Dwight Eisenhower had sixty-one U.S. divisions consisting of 1,622,000 men in Germany. This massive force became the occupying army "charged with maintaining law and order and establishing the Allied military presence in the defeated nation.... Its object was to control the population and stifle resistance by putting troops into every nook and cranny." As a result of this overwhelming presence, "almost everything of importance—and some not so important—was guarded."[60]

In the wake of this "blanket occupation," the feared resistance movement never materialized. The German Army was quickly demilitarized, and over three million prisoners of war and disarmed troops were taken into custody by U.S. forces.[61] The war crimes trials that followed began in November 1945 and ultimately lasted four years. An International Military Tribunal (commonly called the Nuremberg Tribunal) was created in August, and in early October twenty-four men were indicted on charges of systematically murdering millions of people and planning and carrying out the war in Europe. Eisenhower was particularly keen on bringing concentration camp commandants and guards to justice, noting that the swift punishment of their crimes would have "a salutary effect on public opinion both in Germany and in Allied countries." Operating with this sense of urgency, by January 1946, the War Crimes Group had referred eighty-one cases to trial and had 2,438 war crimes and 131 mass atrocity (concentration camp) cases on the docket.[62]

Practical considerations, however, made the proposed far-reaching scale of denazification problematic. Instead, German-administered and Occupying Powers–supervised sector-level tribunals called *Spruchkammern* were used as a more realistic alternative. While the result was less complete, James Dobbins concludes, "This more practical policy helped lead to a more-thorough repudiation of Nazi policies by the German populace and eliminated remaining support for the return of such an autocratic regime."[63]

With these actions completed or well underway, Eisenhower could respond to the intense domestic pressure to redeploy significant numbers of troops. The original plan was for an "Occupational Troop Basis" of 404,500 troops to remain in Germany and Austria after the redeployment and readjustment were completed. This target number was to be reached a year and a half after the surrender, but in May, the War Department reduced the time to one year. Then in August, it reduced the number of troops to 370,000 and established a shipping schedule that would meet this goal by the end of January 1946. According to this plan, the low point would be reached in the middle of the first postwar winter, when civil unrest, if it occurred at all, was to be expected in Germany and when the Army would probably still have to care for about a half million displaced persons and guard many thousands of war prisoners and internees.[64]

After Eisenhower's staff noted it would take 100,000 troops just to guard and maintain the six million tons of surplus property left in the theater, the War Department in September approved a Liquidation Force of 337,000 troops, which could be used to postpone the reduction to the Occupational

Troop Basis until July 1, 1946. But as Earl Ziemke notes in his official Army history of the occupation, with the war over "everyone wanted to go home faster than any feasible schedule could move them and with an intensity that was not going to be diverted by any amount of persuasion." Under such pressure, at the end of December, the theater strength was down to 614,000 troops and was 93,000 below the combined total of the Occupational Troop Basis and Liquidation Force.[65] In November 1945, Lieutenant General Walter Bedell Smith, Eisenhower's chief of staff, had already reported, "The forces within this theater are today unable to perform any serious offensive operations. The capability to carry on limited defensive operations is slightly better." Nonetheless, Smith concluded the "ability to perform … occupational duties, to control the German population, and to suppress local uprisings is rated as satisfactory."[66]

Indeed, at this point in time, the U.S. troop strength was within modern-day force planning guidelines. Field Manual 3-24 notes, "Most density recommendations fall within a range of 20 to 25 counterinsurgents for every 1000 residents in an [area of operation]."[67] Ziemke's official history estimates a German population of about 15.5 million in the fall of 1945.[68] Based on that figure, an Occupational Troop Basis of 370,000 would provide about 24 soldiers for every 1,000 Germans.[69]

Such a large occupation force, however, "soon began to look like an outright extravagance after Japan surrendered."[70] Faced with this reality, Eisenhower and his staff began planning a police-type occupation, such as was taking shape in Japan. Beginning with the idea of district constabularies, in the fall of 1945 European planners developed a concept for a United States Constabulary as a self-sufficient security force for the whole zone. Assuming the continued reduction of requirements to guard and process surplus property, displaced persons, and prisoners of war, Eisenhower planned his force size on the basis of one constable (plus signals, supply, and air reconnaissance) for every 450 Germans. Thus he informed the War Department that a constabulary of 38,000 men would be enough to establish police-type control by July 1, 1946.[71]

For the next two years, the Constabulary served as the primary police authority and provided the security needed to facilitate the rebuilding of Germany's political and economic infrastructure. Whatever significant anti–American or pro–Nazi outbreaks the postwar planners feared never materialized, and the Constabulary was able to focus its attention on controlling displaced persons, conducting law enforcement, and enforcing the border. It was also agile enough to adapt to a variety of unforeseen short-term missions.[72]

While the Constabulary must be rightfully recognized for its skillful performance and resounding success, the specific conditions that facilitated

Major General Ernest Harmon inspects a constabulary detachment. Harmon directed the organization, training, equipping, and initial operations of the Constabulary until his return to the United States, where he served as Deputy Commanding General, Army Ground Forces until his retirement in 1947. (U.S. Army photograph.)

this outcome must also be noted. As Kendall Gott astutely concludes in his analysis of the Constabulary, critical to the success of this small force was that in World War II, "Germany met devastating defeat resulting in the wholesale destruction of all major cities, millions of casualties, and the specter of Soviet rule. The Germans simply counted on the United States and its Western Allies to help establish law and order until the Germans could reconstruct their country."[73]

The United States fought World War II as a total war and deliberately and willingly embraced the international role that it assumed in the war's aftermath. As a function of this commitment, the United States emphasized coercion early in its nation-building effort in Germany and hoped to gain security through restructuring German society. Although no insurgency developed, the massive size of the initial occupation force—which likely deterred any insurgency, if one was in fact contemplated—would have been able to suppress it. Once the United States had satisfactorily demilitarized and denazified German society and established itself as the custodian of law and order, a more cooperative approach that would ultimately reintegrate Germany in the international community as an important Cold War ally was pursued. As this transition proceeded, a relatively small Constabulary safeguarded Germany from the civil unrest that has plagued some other nation-building efforts.[74] Germany is often cited as one of America's most successful nation-building operations, and although there are many factors that contributed to this positive outcome, the early emphasis on establishing security through coercion must be counted among them.

Lessons Gleaned

All nation-building operations require security, but that security can be arrived at by different means. On one end of the spectrum is security that is built on overwhelming force and coercion. This type of security is *imposed on* the local population. On the other end of the spectrum is the security that is built on the trust and cooperation gained by civic action. This type of security is *given by* the local population.

Given its present military preponderance, it would seem that the United States is capable of imposing the coercive type of security in most cases. It certainly did so in Germany after World War II. However, such a strategy can be costly in terms of domestic and international support, perseverance, lives, and treasure. For this reason, security gained by civic action may be a more attractive option in many cases. This strategy, however, is dependent on the local population's acceptance of the American effort. Under such conditions, the United States has less control of the situation than it does in the coercive approach. Thus the United States must have the will and flexibility to impose security by force if the local population cannot be convinced to bestow it through civic action. The United States showed this ability in the Philippines.

In *The Prince*, Machiavelli wrote that ideally one could be both loved and feared, but if a choice had to be made, "It is far better to be feared than loved." The United States must be willing to practice such pragmatism in its nation-building. Security must be achieved for nation-building to succeed, so before embarking on a nation-building effort, the United States must decide if it is willing to take security even if it is not given.

CHAPTER 6

Armed Resistance to Nation-Building: The U.S. South during Reconstruction

On June 30, 1865, President Andrew Johnson appointed Benjamin Perry as provisional governor of South Carolina. Before the Civil War, Perry had been a unionist, but when secession came, he supported the Confederate war effort. A member of South Carolina's antebellum elite, he was a strong proponent of slavery and an unabashed believer in white rule.

President Johnson provided his provisional governors little specific direction for the implementation of his vision of Reconstruction and the postwar South. Whether he was himself uncertain of the details or whether out of deference to the notion of states' rights, he left a vacuum that allowed men like Perry to exercise considerable initiative. Perry used this leeway to try to retain as much of the prewar status quo as possible.

A South Carolina state constitutional convention was called to meet on September 13, 1865. Reflecting the expectations that emerged after the Federal victory, on September 4, "a large meeting of freedmen, held on St. Helena Island," petitioned "the Convention about to be assembled at Columbia, on the 13th instant, to so alter and amend the present Constitution of this State as to give the right of suffrage to every man of the age of twenty-one years, without other qualifications than that required for the white citizens of this State."[1] The meeting and the resolution were reported without the dignity of elaboration in the *Columbia Daily Phoenix* on September 23, ten days after the opening of the state convention the freedmen had intended to influence. The convention showed similar indifference to such sentiments. Indeed, in his instructions to the convention members, Perry noted:

> The radical Republican party [members of the] North are looking with great interest to the action of the Southern States in reference to negro suffrage, and whilst they admit that a man should be able to read and write and have property qualification in order

to vote, yet they contend that there should be no distinction between voters on account of color. They forget that this is a white man's government, and intended for white men only; and that the Supreme Court of the United States has decided that the negro is not an American citizen under the Federal Constitution. That each and every State of the Union has the unquestioned right of deciding for herself who shall exercise the right of suffrage is beyond all dispute. You will settle this grave question as the interest and Honor of the State demand.[2]

Taking their cues from the limited demands President Johnson imposed, Perry and the state convention continued South Carolina's prewar defiance of federal authority. Ignoring or downplaying requirements such as "unqualified abolition," declaring secession "null and void," and repudiating Confederate debt, the convention set out to solidify white control of the state. A key component in this effort was to draft a code for the "regulation of labor and the protection and government of the colored population of the State."[3] The result was a "black code" that "clearly indicated the future of Carolina society should whites remain in control."[4]

Instead, the code delivered a "chilling object lesson in the restraints" imposed upon any "self-generated change" by white Southerners, and forced federal action. Having no intention of leaving the matter in the hands of the South Carolinians' "deeply ingrained intellectual, ideological, and racial assumptions," when the Thirty-ninth Congress convened in December, it refused to seat the state's and other Southern representatives.[5] Arguing that President Johnson had exceeded his presidential authority, the Republican majority created a Joint Committee on Reconstruction that would determine new, less conciliatory practices by which the ex–Confederate states would be restored to the Union. As a result of this new agenda, on June 13, 1866, Congress passed the Fourteenth Amendment, which declared that "all persons born or naturalized in the United States … are citizens of the United States" and guaranteed such citizens "due process of law." It also contained provisions which presented office-holding disabilities and disenfranchisement for many white Southerners and established incentives for states either to grant black voting rights or proportionally lose representation in Congress.

Posed with this challenge to his interpretation of "the interest and Honor of the State," Governor Perry took his case to several Northern newspapers. To the *New York Tribune* he warned, "If the negro will be invested with all political power, then the antagonism of interests between capital and labor is to work out the final result." To the *New York Herald* he boasted "that the people of South Carolina have honor and sagacity enough to reject with scorn and indignation this constitutional amendment."[6] He lectured the *Tribune*'s readers, "This Government has been the white man's government, both federal and state. It was formed by white men and for white men exclusively."[7] The paper begged to differ, accusing Perry of wanting to "put the clock four years back," which they assured him was "impossible." Instead, "South Carolina must present herself at the doors of the House next December with words quite other than his on her repentant lips, if she looks to see those doors fly open to her delegation."[8]

This struggle between federal and state authority proved to be much more than a rhetorical one. The Reconstruction Act of 1867 placed the South under military occupation, dividing it into five military districts commanded by officers empowered to use the army to "protect all persons in their rights of person and property, to suppress insurrection, disorder, and violence, and to punish, or cause to be punished, all disturbers of the public peace and criminals." The act also stated that the ex–Confederate states would not be "declared entitled to representation in Congress" until they ratified "a constitution of government in conformity with the Constitution of the United States in all respects, framed by a convention of delegates elected by the male citizens of said State, twenty-one years old and upward, of whatever race, color, or previous condition" and ratified the Fourteenth Amendment.

These developments represented a marked shift in the federal government's approach and the fate of South Carolina. Whereas previous efforts had focused "on influencing, conciliating, and cajoling the white population," the Reconstruction Act "placed the focus on the voting population at large, including the black portion of it."[9] Most states with large black populations accepted the evitable and responded by trying to elect conservatives to their upcoming convention. South Carolina took the opposite approach and attempted a "register and reject" strategy. Conservatives hoped to swell the rolls by registering in large numbers and then boycotting or voting "no" at the election in order to sabotage the requirement that for a convention to be held, a majority of those registered had to vote for it. The tactic nearly worked, but by a slim margin a convention was assembled in Charleston on January 14, 1868. Of the 124 delegates, seventy-three were black, thirty-six were Southern whites who were nearly all Republicans, and the remainder were carpetbagger whites from the North. By the middle of March, a new constitution, which included the required provision for impartial male suffrage, was ready, and elections were held in April. Robert Scott, who had succeeded Rufus Saxton as Assistant Commissioner for the States of South Carolina, Georgia and Florida of Freedmen's Bureau, was elected governor. Along with him, nearly the entire Republican ticket was elected, and the new constitution also passed. It was quickly accepted by Congress, and in June, South Carolina was readmitted to the Union.[10]

Across the South, similarly unprecedented opportunities for black political representation and power were created, to the dismay and horror of the former white elite rule. The vast majority of South Carolina whites rejected the idea of black political power and considered the new government and any

The composition of the first South Carolina legislature after the Civil War was anathema to much of the state's white conservative population. (Library of Congress Prints and Photographs Division LC-DIG-ppmsca-30572.)

actions it might attempt to be illegitimate. Nonetheless, in 1870, South Carolina had a population of 289,667 whites and 415,814 blacks, which translated into a majority of over 26,000 black voters.[11] In a political system in which party affiliation was divided almost exclusively along racial lines, these numbers presented a significant challenge for whites to overcome by purely democratic means.

The Ku Klux Klan

In the spring of 1868, immediately after the failure of the white effort to defeat the new state constitution, the Ku Klux Klan began to appear in South Carolina.[12] Although the Klan originated in Tennessee in 1866, Richard Zuczek notes that it was highly consistent with "two longstanding Carolina traditions." The first was "the localized, community-oriented, extralegal response to fears and crimes which were seen as a threat to Carolina society." The second was "the establishment of organizations that were designed to carry out the tasks desired by the fearful citizens." South Carolina's history of slave patrols is an example of this legacy. "In 1868," Zuczek writes, "these elements combined to create an organization that could operate in a systematic way to confront [the] Republican party in the state."[13]

Indeed, Zuczek is adamant in his description of the Klan as "a political organization with political goals."[14] He supports his assertion with contemporary testimony of men like William Tolbert, who participated in the assassination of Benjamin Randolph, one of two black legislators assassinated during the 1868 campaign. Randolph was originally from Ohio. During the Civil War, he served as a chaplain of the 26th U.S. Colored Troops Regiment and was transferred with the regiment to Hilton Head Island. After the war he stayed in South Carolina and worked for the American Missionary Association. He soon became active in politics, elected both to the state Senate by Orangeburg County and Chair of the State Central Committee of the Republican Party by the party's membership. As chairman of this committee, he actively represented the party across the state.[15] Randolph's political profile made him a likely target for the Klan, a body Tolbert told investigators "was a political organization of the Democratic Party," with goals "to regulate the republican party, break it up if they could, and strengthen the democratic party." Specifically, the Klan existed to "kill out the leaders of the republican party and drive them out of the state."[16]

Randolph's murder was an example of the increase in Klan violence that preceded the November election. Trying to stem the dangerous situation, Governor Scott met first with Colonel L.D. Childs, a close friend of Wade Hampton and a member of the Democratic state central committee, and later with Hampton personally. Hampton was a wealthy antebellum planter and Confederate cavalry hero who enjoyed great respect and loyalty among the white population. Amid strong pressure to arm the blacks, Scott reported he was doing everything possible to prevent black retaliation against the white atrocities, but unless Hampton used his standing to openly speak against white violence, Scott would have no choice but to eliminate his restraints.[17]

Scott's gambit worked. On October 23, newspapers across South Carolina reported Hampton's call for "earnest efforts in the cause of peace and disorder." A palatable decline in violence immediately accompanied Hampton's address, but it was at best a tactical and temporary victory for Scott. More importantly, the outcome indicated the power of Hampton and the white population's willingness to act strategically to achieve their ends. A substantial outbreak of violence, regardless of circumstances, would likely result in federal intervention, a development counter to the white goal of local rule. As Zuczek concludes, "White Carolinians controlled the tempo, and it was their decision to ease up. They were not suppressed, cowed, or intimidated, but merely took a step back, in order to take two steps forward in the future. The terrorist tactic—going underground when the risk becomes too great—was to come into play several more times before Reconstruction was over."[18]

Wade Hampton was one of not just South Carolina's but also the entire South's wealthiest planters and bastions of the Southern aristocracy. He became one of only three Confederates to reach the rank of lieutenant general without formal military training.

For the time being, however, the Republican party in South Carolina weathered its first major storm and the state voted 62,916 for Ulysses Grant in the 1868 presidential election, to 45,237 for Horatio Seymour, the Democratic challenger. Yet, Zuczek notes, there were signs that the Democratic strategy of intimidation "was not a complete failure." In the upstate counties where the Klan violence had been greatest, South Carolinians gave a 14,186 to 10,379 advantage to

Seymour, even though blacks comprised a slight majority of the region's voters. Several counties had notably low turnouts of black voters. In Abbeville, only 800 blacks voted of 2,400 registered. In Laurens County, just 1,174 of almost 2,500 blacks turned out. In Anderson, between 700 and 800 of a potential 1,400 blacks voted. Moreover, Democrats captured two Congressional seats, compared to a Republican sweep in the elections of the previous April.[19]

Such gains, however, were small comfort to white South Carolinians who agreed with James Pike that their home had become "the prostrate state." Indeed, the legislature dominated by blacks, carpetbaggers, and scalawags was corrupt and inefficient. White South Carolinians regarded the state's leaders "as illegitimate usurpers who were dragging the state's proud name through the filth of degradation and disgrace."[20] Between June 1868 and December 1872, the state debt mushroomed from $5.4 million to nearly $15.8 million. Some of these expenditures were due to legitimate educational initiatives and internal improvements, but much of the increase was the result of unscrupulous officials lining their own pockets. The result was the establishment of "a firm link in white Americans' minds, North and South, between 'negro rule' and corruption."[21] Such a dynamic fueled the growth of the Ku Klux Klan in South Carolina, leading one citizen to complain to Governor Scott in July 1869 that there is "a Second Rebellion upon us." Indeed, Klan activity expanded throughout the year.[22]

Scott had to do something to stop the bloodshed, and, overcoming his previous reluctance to arm blacks, on March 16, 1869, he signed a militia bill into law that organized the National Guard Service of South Carolina (NGSSC). All males between the ages of eighteen and forty-five were eligible, but most whites refused to serve with blacks. The result was the NGSSC quickly became a "black militia" that served as a counter to the white willingness to resort to force.[23]

At least one of Scott's motivations for creating the black militia was that its offices and pay represented another source of patronage that would win allies and votes. In spite of such incentives, disgust with the degree of corruption that had infested South Carolina caused a rift in the Republican Party. "Reform" Republications sought alliance with "moderate" conservatives, and a Union Reform Party emerged that nominated Richard Carpenter for governor. Former Confederate General Matthew Calbraith Butler was nominated as lieutenant governor.[24]

While reform was indeed an issue, Zuczek dismisses the Union Reform movement as an "elaborate song-and-dance" to camouflage the true conservative agenda of restoring white rule. Railing against corruption was merely a means to an end. Zuczek assesses that it "created an opening, a chance to secure a foothold in the government as a stepping stone to full control."[25] Indeed, the Union Reform Party is an example of Kelly Greenhill and Solomon

Major's assertion that actors "adjust their goals (but not their preferences) according to the prevailing opportunity structure."[26] Wade Hampton understood this dynamic, writing fellow Union Reformer James Connor, "We must by steady, patient, and persevering work, get possession of the State Government."[27] Such conditions did not yet exist in 1870, and the Union Reform Party suffered a series of state-wide defeats, including in the gubernatorial race.

With the failure of this attempt at "conciliation," conservatives turned to the Klan as the "method of dealing with Radicalism."[28] A series of disturbances erupted in the upstate, where the Democrats had carried the election of 1868. In 1870, however, Democrats received just forty-three percent of the vote in the twelve upstate counties, and Scott received 28,394 votes compared to 21,365 for Carpenter. Observers credited the reversal to the new presence of the black militia, and "the racists set out to put an end to a situation that threatened to leave no part of South Carolina secure for white supremacy."[29]

The violence began the day after the election in Laurens County, where Scott had tallied 3,022 votes compared to 1,967 for Carpenter. Democrats resolved to forcibly disarm the black militia, and a crowd of some 2,500 armed whites soon gathered in Laurens. In the aftermath of the violence, several Republicans were killed.[30]

The incident in Laurens ignited a wave of violence that spread through the upstate, particularly in Spartanburg, Union, and York Counties. C.L. Casey, deputy U.S. Marshall, estimated some 500 outrages were committed in Spartanburg. Two mass lynchings occurred in Union County. Major Lewis Merrill, commander of the Seventh Cavalry at Yorkville, estimated between three and four hundred incidents of violence in York County between November 1870 and July 1871.[31]

The increasing Klan activity attracted Congressional attention, and a series of three enforcement acts were passed to ensure that the provisions of the Fourteenth and Fifteenth Amendments were followed. The first act, passed on May 31, 1870, made it a federal offense to try to deprive anyone of his civil rights. A second act, passed on February 28, 1871, established federal supervision over elections. Neither of these measures had a significant effect on the situation, leading President Ulysses Grant to meet with Congressional leaders to urge the passage of stronger legislation. The result was the Ku Klux Klan Act, passed on April 20, 1871, which allowed the president to suspend the privilege of the writ of habeas corpus upon his own discretion in a defined area. This action would allow authorities to detain suspects without the need to present formal charges or indictments, saving time and personnel, and facilitating mass arrests.[32]

Armed with this new tool, President Grant dispatched U.S. Attorney General Amos Akerman to assess the situation in South Carolina. By October 16, Grant was convinced that there existed in Spartanburg, York, Chester, Union, Laurens, Newberry, Fairfield, Lancaster, and Chesterfield Counties, "combinations for the purpose of preventing the free political action of citizens who were friendly to the Constitution of the Government of the United States, and of depriving emancipated classes of equal protection." Grant estimated two-thirds of the white men in those counties were active in these organizations and that they had "the sympathy and countenance" of the majority of the remaining third. Grant identified these combinations as "Kuklux Klans" and described their objects as being "by force and terror to prevent all political action not in accord with the views of the members, to deprive colored citizens of the right to bear arms, and of the right of a free ballot, and to suppress the schools in which colored children were taught, and to reduce the colored people to a condition closely allied to that of slavery."[33]

President Grant had the information he needed, and on October 17 he suspended the privilege of the writ of habeas corpus in the nine upstate counties. United States Army troops and Justice Department officials immediately began apprehending suspects, and by April 1872, Attorney General Akerman reported 533 total arrests.[34]

As impressive as these results initially appeared, however, the anti–Klan effort ran into problems after prosecutions began in the federal circuit court in Columbia in late November 1871. Attorney General Akerman lacked the manpower, money, and other resources necessary to punish all the perpetrators. Moreover, chief prosecutor District Attorney David Corbin realized that most of the crimes "were committed prior to the Act of April 20, 1871," and therefore could be considered ex post facto charges. Akerman was forced to admit, "It seems to me that it is too much for even the United States to undertake to inflict adequate penalties through the courts."[35]

The results bore out Akerman's frustrations. When the first term closed, only fifty-four men had been convicted and sentenced. Of these, only five had been found guilty by trial. The other forty-nine had pled guilty. When the new term began in April, 278 cases carried over, involving over 400 people. This term proved eighteen men guilty, but hundreds of cases remained on the docket.[36]

The reality of the situation forced Akerman to settle for a policy of "selective prosecutions" that focused on those suspected of being Klan leaders and those involved in "deep criminality." Lesser suspects were released on light bail, and those Corbin determined to have played "a reluctant part" because of "compulsion" were released altogether. Eventually, space limitations led to the release of even many of the most dangerous suspects with the understanding that they would return for trial. In the final analysis, Zuczek concludes the serious offenders received "hardly more than a slap on the wrist."[37]

There was little hope for salvaging the deteriorating situation, and Akerman resigned on December 12, 1871. Among his reasons may have been a general frustration with waning popular interest in the prosecutions. "Such atrocities as Ku Kluxery do not hold their attention," he confided to a friend. "The Northern mind, being full of what is called progress runs away from the past." To others Akerman advised that "the Southern republicans must cease to look for special support to action" and that "our friends" in the South must learn "to stand on their own feet" and "not depend always on propping from Washington."[38]

Akerman was replaced by George Williams, who had no background in law enforcement, and his lack of experience in such matters served as a harbinger for the direction the federal government's offensive against the Klan would go. At the end of 1872, Williams reported 1,207 cases pending under enforcement acts and only ninety-six cases terminated. In April 1873, he suspended all cases already carrying indictments. Only four men were convicted in 1873, and 540 cases were dismissed. There were no convictions in 1874 and 555 dismissals.[39]

The last convicted South Carolina Klansman left prison in 1874. All others had been pardoned, had their sentences shortened, or already served their brief terms. By 1877, six years of prosecutions had convicted only 162 men in South Carolina while dismissing approximately 1,233 cases.[40] In spite of its seemingly dismal conviction record, Herbert Shapiro, an early scholar of the federal crackdown on the Klan in South Carolina, declared the effort a success. "The Ku Klux Klan of South Carolina was defunct," he declared. "The limited steps taken by the Federal Government were adequate to destroy the organization."[41]

Richard Zuczek offers an alternative analysis which reflects a much more aware, agile, and strategic Klan. By the spring and summer of 1871, Zuczek notes the Klan could already count significant achievements such as the disbanding of many of the black militias, the removal of Republican officials, and the general intimidation of the Republican population. At the same time, however, the arrival of federal cavalry in the state in March, the passage of the Ku Klux Klan Act in April, and the initiation of a congressional subcommittee's investigation indicated a growing interest in Washington that suggested a federal intervention might be in the offing. "Rather than risk losing what they had gained," Zuczek assesses, "conservative whites across South Carolina opted for peace."[42]

District Attorney Corbin seems to agree with Zuczek that the initiative lay with the Klan. He told Attorney General Williams that he had reports that "orders were given last summer" to stop the violence *"for the present."* According to Corbin's information, the Klan intended to lay low *"until the storms blew over"* and then "resume operations."[43]

The Mississippi Plan

Zuczek concludes that the lackluster federal action in South Carolina "revealed the inadequacies of the enforcement program for all to see—and for some in the South to use."[44] Indeed, the events in South Carolina were closely followed in Mississippi. In 1873, the state's Republicans had divided along carpetbagger and scalawag lines as respective supporters of either Adelbert Ames or James Alcorn. When Ames was elected governor, many white conservatives who had supported Alcorn migrated to the Democratic Party. The Republican split also allowed the Democrats to win several Congressional seats in the 1874 election. Encouraged and emboldened by these advances, conservative Mississippians saw a chance to seize control of the state's legislature in the 1875 election, ensuring Democratic senators would be sent to Washington and having the power to impeach Ames if necessary.[45]

The man who would engineer this Democratic renaissance was James George, the newly elected Democratic Party chairman. It would not be a peaceful process, and as the election drew closer, Mississippi was thrown into a crisis by a series of racial riots. The most serious erupted in Vicksburg in December 1874 when a white mob arrested Peter Crosby, the city's black sheriff. When a column of black militia marched to Crosby's defense, the heavily armed whites met them at a bridge at the southern edge of town. Actual casualty figures are hard to determine, but dozens of blacks were killed in what a congressional investigating committee declared "a simple massacre."[46]

With Vicksburg forcibly under white control, Governor Ames called the Mississippi legislature into a special session at which he described the riot as "insurrection in the fullest sense." On December 19, he telegraphed President Grant the text of a resolution passed by both houses of the legislature requesting federal troops be dispatched to restore order in Vicksburg. Ames had requested federal troops be sent to quell trouble mounting in Vicksburg prior to the August 5 city elections, but Grant had refused based on an inconclusive report sent him by an Army officer who had investigated the situation.[47] This time the case was clearer, and on December 24, Grant ordered Lieutenant General Philip Sheridan to report to New Orleans, take command of the Army's Department of the Gulf, investigate reports of disorders in Louisiana and Mississippi, and take whatever action was necessary. Sheridan wasted no time. On January 4, 1875, he telegraphed Ames from New Orleans, "I have to-night assumed control over the Department of the Gulf. A company of troops will be sent to Vicksburg to-morrow." Furthermore, he telegraphed Secretary of War William Belknap:

> I think that the terrorism now existing in Louisiana, Mississippi, and Arkansas could be entirely removed, and confidence and fair dealing established, by the arrest and trial of the ringleaders of the armed White Leagues. If Congress would pass a bill declaring

them banditti, they could be tried by a military commission. The ringleaders of this banditti, who murdered men here on the 14th of last September, and also more recently at Vicksburg, Miss., should, in justice to law and order, and the peace and prosperity of this southern part of the country, be punished. It is possible that if the President would issue a proclamation declaring them banditti, no further action need be taken except that which would devolve to me.[48]

In spite of Sheridan's adamancy, President Grant's cabinet, especially Secretary of State Hamilton Fish, was much less sanguine about the use of military force to enforce black rights. Recognizing how politically unpopular such a measure would be, Grant seemed to concur. In a January 13 proclamation, he said, "I have no desire to have United States troops interfere in the domestic concerns of Louisiana or any other state."[49] Nicholas Lemann concludes opponents of Reconstruction "would not have been wrong in detecting a wobble in the administration's support of [such heavy-handed measures as advocated by] General Sheridan."[50]

A congressional investigative report of the Vicksburg affair released on February 27 stated the matter very succinctly:

> One of two things this nation must do: it must either restrain by force these violent demonstrations by the bold, fierce spirits of the whites; it must, by the exercise of all its power, if needed, secure to every man, black and white, the free exercise of the elective franchise, and punish, sternly and promptly, all who violently invade those rights; or it must say to the enfranchised voters of the South—creatures of its own word, staunch, true, and faithful to its Government—we have made you men and citizens—we have given you the right to bear arms and to vote; now work out your own salvation as others have done; fight your way up to full manhood, and prove yourselves worthy of the endowments you have received at our hands. It is for the country to decide which is best. But the country must decide quickly.[51]

Although the report accurately framed the choice, President Grant remained "a cipher" as the November 1875 elections approached in Mississippi. White conservatives understood that brazen violence might lead to federal intervention, but if they pursued their objective of preventing the Republican Party from organizing the black vote "in a more shadowy manner, what Grant would do was not clear."[52] The pre-election environment in Mississippi thus became a game of cat and mouse in which the white conservatives experimented with their limits, always careful not to push so far as to warrant federal intervention.

One place those boundaries were severely tested was at a Republican gathering at the Moss Hill plantation outside Clinton on September 4. Some two thousand blacks gathered there for a barbeque and political meeting to which Governor Ames had been invited but declined to attend. The Republicans also invited a Democrat speaker to attend and engage in a debate. The speaker arrived, accompanied by a contingent of whites bearing concealed weapons. He delivered his speech without incident, but soon after Republican Henry Fisher started his, a white heckler interrupted him. An uproar ensued and a gun was fired. Some Republican attendees who had come armed grabbed their guns, and whites and blacks exchanged fire. In the end, three white men and seven or eight blacks were killed. The surviving blacks scattered.[53]

The violence then spread to the surrounding area as whites reacted to rumors that the blacks had reorganized for an attack on Clinton. Posses of unopposed whites began roaming the countryside terrorizing blacks. E.B. Welborn, a black Republican, recalled, "They just hunted the whole country clean out, just every man they could see they were shooting at him just the same as birds."[54]

As the rampage continued, Ames telegraphed President Grant on September 8 to report that "domestic violence, in its most extreme form, exists in certain parts of this State." After outlining the situation, Ames appealed "to the general government for the means of giving that protection to which every American citizen is entitled." "A necessity of immediate action," Ames pleaded, "cannot be overstated."

Instead of the "necessity of immediate action" urged by Ames, a triangular exchange among Ames, President Grant, and Attorney General Edwards Pierrepont consumed the week following the Clinton riot. Grant, who was vacationing at the time, was alarmed by the situation and instructed Pierrepont to prepare a proclamation for his signature answering Ames's call for help. In the meantime, Grant wanted Ames "to strengthen his position by exhausting his own resources in restoring order before he receives govt. aid." Pierrepont took advantage of Grant's absence to respond in a way consistent with the attorney general's personal anti-interventionist views. He prepared the proclamation as instructed, but left it in his office undated and unsigned. He then sent Ames a letter on September 14 wondering "why you do not strengthen yourself in the way the President suggests." Pierrepont counseled Ames to "take all lawful means and all needed measures to preserve the peace by the forces in your own state and let the country see that the citizens of Miss. who are largely favorable to good order, and are largely Republican, have the courage and the manhood to *fight* for their rights, and to destroy the bloody ruffians who murder the innocent and unoffending freedmen." Pierrepont concluded by gratuitously comforting Ames that "if there is such resistance to your state authorities as you cannot, by all the means at your command, suppress, the President will swiftly aid you in crushing these lawless traitors to human rights."[55]

Seemingly left to his own devices, Ames attempted to form a militia of white Republicans, but on September 22, he confided to his wife, "I have not been able to find even *one* man to cooperate with me." In desperation, he took the drastic step of putting "all the arms I have or can possess into the hands of colored people and shall demand that they fight." Such a move of course excited an emotional response from the white community, and the sight of an armed black militia company marching from Jackson on October 9 to deliver arms to another militia company in Edwards was seen by many as a deliberate provocation. As a result, W. Calvin Wells, secretary of the Hinds County Democratic campaign commission, reported that many local Democrats asked him "to allow a squad of men to enter Jackson, surround the [governor's] mansion at night, and take Ames and hang him to a post."[56]

Instead, cooler heads prevailed. George Chase, a New Yorker sent to Jackson as a personal emissary of Attorney General Pierrepont, arranged for a meeting between Governor Ames, Mississippi's Democratic Party chairman James George, and other white conservatives. George had already telegraphed Pierrepont, ensuring him that Ames's account of the situation in Mississippi was an exaggeration. As the Democrat told it: "There are no disturbances in this State now, and no obstructions to the execution of the laws. There has been an unexpected conflict at a political meeting, and some subsequent disturbances, but everything is quiet now. The governor's call for United States troops does not even pretend there is any insurrection against the State government, as required by the revision of *United States Statutes* of 1875, p. 1034. Peace prevails throughout the State, and the employment of United States troops would but increase the distrust of the people in the good faith of the present State government." George went on to repeat, "Perfect peace prevails throughout the state."[57]

The "peace conference" took place at the governor's mansion on October 13 with George dominating the discussion. In a little over two hours a plan was developed in which Ames agreed not to use the militia to restore to power Albert Morgan, the sheriff of Yazoo City, who had been forcibly ousted by a mob of Democrats on September 1, or to ship any more guns around the state. Ames balked at George's request to disband the black militias entirely, but agreed to collect their weapons and ask militia members to return to their homes. In exchange, George and the Democrats promised to ensure full voting rights for blacks in the November election.[58]

George's biographer Timothy Smith describes George's compromise with Ames and subsequent efforts to control more aggressive Democrats as reflective of George's fear that "open violence would draw the attention of the federal government which might send in troops."[59] Inevitably, hotheaded renegades inflicted violence on blacks in spite of George's promise, and with each instance George sent immediate assurances to Chase, who remained in Mississippi to monitor the situation, that all was well. Republican detractors felt George had "hoodwinked" President Grant about peace in Mississippi, and even Chase knew that some Democrats "intended to carry the election peaceably if they could, forcibly if they must."[60]

Indeed, one way or another, the election did end in a Democratic victory. They captured a majority in the legislature and soon began impeachment proceedings against Ames. Ames resigned amidst a campaign of humiliation and opposition, but before he did, the Democrats impeached black Lieutenant Governor Alexander Davis in order to ensure he not succeed Ames. Instead the next in line, president pro tem of the senate, Democrat John Stone, became Mississippi's governor.[61]

The Edgefield Plan and the Rise of the Red Shirts

The formula for the successful restoration of white conservative rule in Mississippi became known as the "Mississippi Plan," which Philip Dray describes as "intimidation just strong enough to keep blacks from the polls but subtle enough to avert any real protest from the North."[62] Seeing the success of this strategy in Mississippi, Democrats in other Southern states adopted similar strategies. Before long, Martin Witherspoon Gary developed a particularly detailed version of George's technique for use in South Carolina.[63]

Gary had begun his Civil War service as a captain in Wade Hampton's Legion and eventually rose to the rank of brigadier general. Although the two men had an inexorable wartime connection, they came to differ over postwar policies. Hampton advocated "bloodless coercion" through displays of power such as demonstrations and parades to intimidate black voters. Gary championed a more violent and aggressive approach. "The glorious Palmetto," he lamented, "has withered but not died." "Should it become necessary," he proclaimed, "it will be watered by the blood of the patriotic sons of South Carolina."[64]

At the helm of what Zuczek declares as "the most dangerous element in the Democratic party," Gary developed the "No. 1 Plan of the Campaign," also called the Edgefield Plan or the Shotgun Policy.[65] In so doing, he corresponded with Mississippi Democrats to learn lessons from their successful redemption of their state. Sam Ferguson, a native South Carolinian living in Mississippi, wrote letters to Democrats in South Carolina and was "brought to the state to give practical instruction in the 'Mississippi Plan' of carrying elections in the face of a hostile majority."[66] In a letter to Theodore Barker, Ferguson boasted of how Democrats carried the election in a Mississippi county of fewer than 1,200 white voters and over 6,000 black voters through superior white determination and willingness to use violence.[67] Gary also consulted with other South Carolina Democrats including George Tillman and Matthew Calbraith Butler. The result was a "policy of terrorizing the negroes at the first opportunity, by letting them provoke trouble and then having the whites demonstrate their superiority by killing as many of them as was justifiable."[68]

The Edgefield Plan was a list of thirty-three items Gary deemed necessary to win the election. Many were rather commonplace and innocuous, such as providing "transportation to old and helpless voters" to ensure "all Democrats turn out and vote" (item 10). Others were extralegal, such as "Every Democrat must feel honor bound to control the vote of at least one negro, by intimidation, purchase, keeping him away or as each individual may determine, how he may best accomplish it" (item 12). The most sinister and dangerous were left off the copies publicly circulated and distributed only in the privacy of Democratic club meetings. These included instructions for the arming and organization of "Democratic Military Clubs" (item 3), and the foreboding admonition, "Never threaten a man individually. If he deserves to be threatened, the necessities of the times require that he should die. A dead Radical is very harmless—a threatened Radical or one driven off by threats from the scene of his operations is often very troublesome, sometimes dangerous, always vindictive" (item 16).

Critical to the implementation of Gary's plan were the clubs he instructed "must be uniformed in a red shirt and they must be sure and wear it upon all public meetings and particularly on the day of elections" (item 29). The idea of such "Red Shirt" organizations began with the Mississippi Plan.[69] Journalist and Red Shirt member Alfred Williams believes their symbolic attire made its first appearance in South Carolina on August 25, 1876, at a parade in Charleston. The expression "waving the bloody shirt" was associated with attempts to arouse sectional emotion, and Democrats had recently intercepted a confidential letter from Judson Kilpatrick to Republican presidential candidate Rutherford Hayes that nothing but "money and the bloody shirt" could carry the Indiana Republican. Williams reports that "it was in derision of this that that red shirt was flaunted in Charleston and later adopted as uniform."[70] It quickly became the "badge of Southern manhood," memorializing the blood shed on behalf of the cause during the Civil War. Unlike the Ku Klux Klansmen, who hid their identities behind hoods, the Red Shirts were an open symbol to the entire population—black and white, Democrat and Republican—of their devotion to Democratic rule and white supremacy.[71] South Carolinian women went to great lengths to produce enough shirts to meet demand as "the fashion flashed through the state with the amazing swiftness with which ideas, changes or modifications of politics and methods of campaigning spread."[72]

The Red Shirts organized themselves into "rifle clubs" with a core membership of Confederate veterans, many of whom had served under Hampton during the war. They were well armed, experienced in military tactics, and most had written constitutions. Administrative control rested with Brigadier General James Conner, while Colonel Samuel Pickens commanded an "upper" division and Major Theodore Barker a "lower" one.[73] The clubs reflected the prowess, discipline, efficiency, and organization of the military heritage of their members. They were also disciplined enough, having learned the lesson of the excessive Klan violence earlier, to sufficiently manage conflict so as not to draw more federal troops to the state.[74]

Like the Klan before them, the rifle clubs were in effect the military arm of the Democratic Party. The political arm rallied behind Wade Hampton, who had become "the leading Lost Cause figure in [South Carolina]—the symbol of white suffering, for southern honor, and for vindication."[75] Hampton insisted the rifle clubs rely on presence rather than violence, and state Democratic chairman Alexander Haskell met often with county representations cautioning them to avoid initiating conflict.[76] Still the rifle club show of force was a critical part of Hampton's campaign for governor in 1876. As he made a grand march across the state, Red Shirts accompanied him every step of the way, leading impressive entries into each county and town, where Hampton would be welcomed with great fanfare. Zuczek describes the atmosphere of the tour as "the triumphant procession of a conquering hero," with the Red Shirts carrying the message: "You are powerless against us, and we will do as we please."[77]

Such a mobilization of manpower and strength allowed Democrats to turn out in large numbers at Republican meetings. Indeed, Gary's Edgefield Plan had mandated that "we must attend every Radical meeting that we hear of whether they meet at night or in the day time" (item 13). As it happened, armed, mounted, and uniformed rifle club members would surround the rally, creating such a commotion that the gathering would often be forced to disperse. A popular tactic was to demand "division of time" to allow a speaker to present the Democratic point of view. Republican refusals resulted in an uproar that left the candidate appearing weak, so the Democrat request was usually allowed. The Democratic speaker would then proceed to so abuse and discredit the Republican cause in front of would-be supporters that many Republicans simply ceased campaigning out of frustration. Such actions fulfilled Gary's plan: "Democrats must go in as large numbers as they can get together, and well armed, behave at first with great courtesy and assure the ignorant negroes that you mean them no harm and so soon as their leaders or speakers begin to speak and make false statements of facts, tell them then and there to their faces, that they are liars, thieves and rascals, and are only trying to mislead the ignorant negroes and if you get a chance get upon the platform and address the negroes" (item 13). Throughout these well-planned and orchestrated events, the Democrats were careful to stop their "hacking" techniques short of the outright violence that would invite federal intervention.[78]

In spite of such restraint and Hampton's emphasis on avoiding conflict, the campaign was one of the bloodiest in American history.[79] It is not surprising that in such a supercharged environment, the slightest misunderstanding, apprehension, or excess would escalate the already tense situation into conflict. Indeed, significant and deadly riots erupted in Hamburg, Ellenton, Cainhoy, and Charleston.

The Charleston riot is perhaps the most illustrative of both the impact and discipline of the rifle clubs. The violence erupted after J.R. Jenkins, a black Democrat, addressed a meeting of the Hampton and Tilden Colored Club of Ward Four on September 6, 1876. As Jenkins delivered his acerbic assault on Republicans, a crowd of hostile blacks ominously gathered to menace him when he left the meeting. An escort of whites managed to usher Jenkins and other black Democrats safely along King Street to the protection of the federal troops at the Citadel Green. In the process, a white fired his pistol in the air to push back the crowd. This escalation brought more hostile blacks to the scene. At first, the whites and the Charleston police were able to keep the crowd at bay, but soon black crowds were advancing unopposed through Charleston's streets, assaulting whites and destroying property.[80]

In 1875, Charleston had a population of 56,540 people, of which fifty-seven percent were black. In the surrounding county, blacks made up seventy-three percent of the population. In addition to these overwhelming numbers, black assertiveness was fueled by Charleston's history of a significant free black population during the antebellum period and the low country's history of black militancy exemplified by the Stono Rebellion of 1739 and the Denmark Vessey Conspiracy of 1822. These circumstances left the city's white population cowering in fear amid the present circumstances.[81]

If help was going to come for Charleston's white population, it would be in the form of the local rifle clubs. The Carolina Rifle Battalion mustered, but remained in ranks as blacks roamed the streets jeeringly decrying the rifle clubs' absence. The commander of the lower division of clubs, Theodore Barker, explained the clubs' inaction was not the result of fear, but of the overall Democratic strategy of avoiding giving cause for federal intervention. Noting that the riot was ebbing and that a white show of force might rekindle it, Barker "decided not to bring fight, under the circumstances, but to postpone this encounter, in order that, when made, it may be more effectual."[82] While Melina Meek Hennessey characterizes the rifle clubs as "caught ... by surprise" and "embarrassed,"[83] a more flattering assessment is offered by Alfred Williams, who concludes that had Barker unleashed a "slaughter of negroes," it "would have hardened the North against the entire South and South Carolina especially and assured election of a president who, from all we had reason to believe, would continue the Grant policy of fastening the Reconstruction government on the state more strongly and cruelly than ever." Instead, Williams lauds Barker for exemplifying the ability "to find and hold the delicate balance of enough show of strength and determination to give confidence and protection to friends, with the self-restraint and regard for life and law that would keep us the good will and support of the voting masses at the East and West."[84] If Williams's interpretation is correct, then Barker's actions are one of the most poignant examples of the strategic perspective and mastery of the Democratic side.

South Carolina Redeemed

The election was held on November 7. On October 9, Governor Daniel Chamberlain had ordered the rifle clubs to disband and cease to exist, but they merely reorganized themselves under some new and often absurd name. Thus on the eve of the election, the "Allendale Mounted Base Ball Club," "Mother's Little Helpers," and the "First Baptist Church Sewing Circle" continued to parade under arms and in their flaming red shirts.[85] It was a humorous but effective demonstration of the tactic the Democrats had by now perfected of ostensibly complying with the law.

As a result, in spite of the intent of Chamberlain's proclamation, on election day the Red Shirts seemed omnipresent. Williams reports in the middle and upcountry "Red Shirts were riding all roads." They kept up a steady stream of gunfire and yells and cheers for Hampton designed "to terrorize Republicans and encourage and hearten Democratic negroes." "At most of the polling places," Williams recalls, "the Red Shirts went into camp, built bonfires and remained on guard, prepared to take charge of the polls and hold the head of the line of voters so that the negro Democrats might be voted early and the Republicans delayed and held back as much as possible."[86] It was Gary's Edgefield Plan in action.

On the strength of the massive white mobilization, the intimidation of the rifle clubs, a sense of general frustration with Republican corruption among many South Carolinians, and an extremely efficient campaign, initial returns gave Hampton the victory. It was immediately contested, however, as supporters of Hampton's opponent, Republican incumbent Daniel Chamberlain, accused the Democrats of fraud. For five months, both men claimed to be governor, and two rival assemblies also claimed to be the legal state house of representatives. South Carolinian whites, however, were in no mood to let slip from their grasp "a victory years in the making."[87]

The Democrats had good reason to be confident and resolute in this struggle. Post-conflict scholars Kelly Greenhill and Solomon Major argue that "the most significant determinant in a peace initiative's ultimate success is the distribution of power among the competing factions on the ground and those implementing the peace."[88] By 1875 in South Carolina, this balance had shifted in favor of the conservatives. According to Zuczek, the change occurred because Hampton's backers controlled not just "the all-too-real threat of force" represented by the Red Shirts, but also capital and property. When Hampton declared a "Starve Them Out" policy by which taxes could only be collected by men he had appointed, white South Carolinians responded with enthusiasm. Zuczek concludes, "Without the power of compulsion, which the Republicans did not have, neither court rulings nor legislative acts could bring in white money."[89] Even President Grant acknowledged the reality, saying, "The whole army of the United States would be inadequate to enforce the authority of Governor Chamberlain. The people of that State resolved not to resort to violence, but adopted a mode of procedure much more formidable and effective than any armed demonstration. Unless Governor Chamberlain can compel the collection of taxes, it will be utterly useless for him to expect to maintain authority for any length of time."[90]

Electoral confusion reigned at the national level as well, where Democrat candidate Samuel Tilden defeated Rutherford Hayes in the popular vote, but the electoral count was in dispute over alleged voter fraud in Louisiana, Florida, and South Carolina. Following secretive deliberations and negotiations, a special commission declared Hayes to be president. It is impossible to determine the details, but many observers conclude the decision involved some "Bargain of 1877" by which Hayes, in exchange for securing the White House, would grant Home Rule to the South. Indeed, within two months of assuming office, Hayes ordered the federal troops surrounding the South Carolina statehouse to withdraw, and Hampton peacefully assumed office. By his actions, Hayes sent the clear message that the federal troops would no longer play a role in the political affairs of South Carolina and the rest of the former Confederate States. It was the final triumph of Redemption. The federal will and capability to compel compliance had steadily decreased as the conservative will and capability to resist had steadily increased. The conservative ascension to the superior position represented the federal failure to comply with Greenhill and Major's requirement: "If peace accords are to be sustained, the opportunity structure that prevailed during the negotiations must be perpetuated."[91]

The change was soon felt throughout the state. Between 1868 and 1871, before its terror campaign was checked by federal authorities, the Klan was most active in the upstate counties of York, Spartanburg and Union. In contrast, fear of inciting the large black majority to violence had served as a check on white aggression in the low country.[92] Even in 1876, Hampton had faced an openly hostile black crowd while delivering a political speech in Beaufort. Alfred Williams described it as "the one failure of the campaign" and could barely conceal his relief as the party withdrew from the place where they had "been made to feel hatred every minute and at every step."[93]

With Hampton in the governor's mansion, however, things were much different. In the closing days of the 1878 political campaign, black political icon Robert Smalls was surrounded at Gillisonville, just outside of his Beaufort County base, by "eight hundred red-shirt men, led by colonels, generals, and many leading men of the state."[94] In the subsequent election, the balance of power had shifted so decisively that Red Shirt units parading past polling places were able to intimidate enough Republican voters to hand Smalls his first defeat in what had previously been a "black paradise."[95]

"Spoilers"

The reversal of Reconstruction and the Redemption of South Carolina is an example of what Stephen Stedman describes as the challenge "spoilers" pose to post-conflict peace. Stedman defines spoilers as "leaders and parties who believe the peace emerging from negotiations threatens their power, worldview, and interests,"[96] as opposed to "custodians of the peace," who are "actors whose task is to oversee the implementation of peace agreements."[97] As the custodians of peace develop and implement effective strategies to manage spoilers, Stedman cautions they must pay close attention to spoiler position and type.

Stedman notes that "spoilers can be inside or outside a peace process."[98] Those positioned outside the process are willing to use overt violence to undermine the peace, while those operating on the inside use stealth to manipulate the peace process to their advantage.[99] The Ku Klux Klan and the Red Shirts were outside spoilers, and, as such, were able to operate with much fewer constraints than inside ones. According to Stedman, outside spoilers "use overt violence as a strategy toward undermining peace."[100]

The starkest example of outside spoilers' resort to violence was the Ku Klux Klan's willingness to use "all weapons at the whites' disposal with ... cold-blooded determination."[101] Zuczek argues the Klan in South Carolina "was a mounted, armed symbol of white authority that held unquestioned power of life or death in racial matters."[102] When the Klan became so violent that it brought unwanted federal intervention, a similar capability was provided by the Red Shirts, who, although still classified as outside spoilers, operated with enough savvy and discretion to masquerade as inside ones.

The white conservatives also were the type of spoilers Stedman describes as "total." Total spoilers "pursue total power and exclusive recognition of authority and hold immutable preferences."[103] In South Carolina, they demanded nothing less than the restoration of white political, social, and economic domination. The most militant representation of this group was the Klan's political purpose "to reverse the interlocking changes sweeping over the South during Reconstruction: to destroy the Republican party's infrastructure, undermine the Reconstruction state, reestablish control of the black labor force, and restore racial subordination in every aspect of Southern life."[104] Such totality was also present in Gary's Edgefield Plan call upon candidates to "if necessary lay down their lives to carry this election" (item 22), and his declaration that victory would come "at all hazards" under a campaign mantra to "fight the Devil with fire" (item 25).

Stedman identifies three major strategies to manage spoilers: inducement, socialization, and coercion. He notes custodians "can employ more than one strategy—either simultaneously (with different priority and emphasis) or in sequence," and, indeed, all three were tried in South Carolina.[105] Nonetheless, ultimate success was elusive.

Inducement involves "taking positive measures to address the grievances of factions who obstruct peace." In short, it hopes to secure spoiler cooperation by "meeting the spoiler's demands."[106] Republican accommodation of the Democrats' demands for equal time at political rallies was both a sign of weakness and an ill-advised attempt at inducement.

The strategy of socialization requires parties to comply with established norms, and "these norms then become the basis of judging the demands of the parties."[107] Congressional Reconstruction's requirement that states had to ratify the Fourteenth Amendment before being readmitted to the Union is an example of socialization.

Coercion "relies on the use or threat of punishment to deter or alter unacceptable spoiler behavior or reduce the capability of the spoiler to disrupt the peace process."[108] The federal crackdown against Klan activity in 1871 employed this strategy.

Following Stedman's argument, the overall failure of these combined strategies is best attributed to the custodians' failure to match the strategy to the type of spoiler.[109] Total spoilers were the main threat in South Carolina. Stedman explains that inducement and socialization are inappropriate counters to the total spoiler's "all-or-nothing terms," and instead recommends a coercive approach.[110] However, because the white conservatives applied Greenhill and Major's prescription of building capabilities until they became able "to unilaterally achieve a better deal than the one on the table," they were in a position to challenge a coercive strategy based on the declining federal willingness to use force.[111] President Grant's description of Chamberlain's impotency to challenge Hampton's claim to the governor's office testifies to this shift in power.

In the end, the custodians withdrew, a strategy Stedman cautions "backfires against a total spoiler, who has everything to gain if custodians abandon the peace process."[112] The only chance a strategy of departure has to succeed is if the custodians first "deprive the spoiler of resources—both capital and weapons."[113] Hampton's tax policy and the Red Shirts certainly demonstrated this condition did not exist.

In Reconstruction-era South Carolina, the spoilers excelled the custodians in strategy, tactics, resourcefulness, determination, and perseverance. The result, according to Zuczek, was that "in the end, Reconstruction did not fail; it was defeated."[114] While contemporary military authorities regarded the experience as an aberration from their normal mission and spent little energy codifying lessons learned, their experience was hardly unique.[115] In the post–Cold War explosion of nation-building efforts, the United States found itself in similar situations. The difficulty of achieving self-sustaining peace in the Balkans, Somalia, Iraq, and elsewhere was often attributed to total spoilers willing to wait for the shift in opportunity and capability that accompanied the inevitable waning of U.S. interest and will. Rather than a new phenomenon, this strategy appears to be one with which America has considerable experience, both as custodian and spoiler.

CHAPTER 7

Nation-Building at the Local Level: Vietnam

The over-centralization of power is commonly cited as a recurring problem in nation-building. One complaint is that international efforts tend to focus on the capital city and ignore the countryside, where the majority of people live. Instead, proponents of decentralizing power argue it creates more checks and balances and also helps to mobilize the local middle class to reach average people and spur grassroots political activity. Another benefit of decentralization is that encouraging local leaders is a good way to develop future political talent and shift power from functionaries of the old system. It also is often easier to track resources and hold people accountable on a local level.[1] Nonetheless, while "democratic theory tells us that decentralized government will improve democracy[,] development experience at times provides a less favorable view."[2] The nation-building activities that occurred at the local level in Vietnam beginning in the late 1950s are one such example of this reality.

This local-level focus was particularly relevant because in a "people's war" such as was unfolding in Vietnam, the center of gravity is obviously the people. As a result, the Americans and their South Vietnamese allies became enmeshed in a struggle with the North Vietnamese and communist forces to "win the hearts and minds" of the Vietnamese people. The democratic forces' pursuit of what became known as the "pacification campaign" demonstrates both the theoretical logic behind local-level nation-building and its practical difficulties.

After the defeat of the French at Dien Bien Phu, the 1954 Geneva Accords divided Vietnam into two halves, one led by Ho Chi Minh in the north and the other by Emperor Bao Dai in the south. Elections that would ultimately unify Vietnam were scheduled to occur two years later. In October 1955, Ngo Dinh Diem became the first president of the newly formed Republic of South Vietnam, and the U.S. established the Military Advisory and Assistance Group for Vietnam (MAAGV) to support the fledgling ally. When the date set by the Geneva Accords passed without the promised countrywide elections, Ho launched a protracted war to realize his vision of a united, communist Vietnam.

The communist effort followed the classic Maoist formula for protracted war. In its early stages, the insurgents organized themselves and conducted limited subversive activities of a selected rather than continuous nature. A select cohort of Vietminh soldiers who had remained in the south after the Geneva Conference of 1954 were able to attract thousands of supporters and establish a presence in numerous South Vietnamese villages. In December 1960, the insurgents formed the National Liberation Front (NLF), an organization led by communists but designed to unite all those disaffected by Diem by promising sweeping reforms and genuine independence. As a southern movement, the NLF allowed North Vietnam to claim it was not violating the Geneva Conference's provision against sending forces into the south. Nonetheless, the NLF took its orders from the politburo in Hanoi. Recognizing this association, the Diem government gave the NLF the pejorative label Viet Cong (VC), or Vietnamese Communists. Through the NLF, the communists had a leadership element available to direct the South Vietnamese population.

Using a combination of agitation and propaganda, NLF cadres aroused the people's dislike for the Diem regime. Diem was urban-oriented, which alienated him from the rural areas, where peasants were plagued by poverty, poor medical care, and harsh taxation. Officials were distant and often corrupt and offered little assistance. Land reform was a particular problem. Of all the arable land, forty-five percent was owned by just two percent of the total population, and the vast majority of the landowners were wealthy absentee landlords. Many especially resented Diem's refusal to redistribute more than 370,000 acres of land owned by the Catholic Church. This particular point highlighted an even bigger problem: Diem was French-educated and Catholic in a country that was eighty-five percent Buddhist. The end result was a vulnerable and alienated population ready for change offered by the communist insurgent movement.

The NLF created special organizations to recognize oppressed groups such as farmers, women, and children. They used songs, skits, and plays to explain their program in terms the people could understand. In 1958, there were an estimated 12,000 VC in South Vietnam. By 1963, NLF strength had grown to 300,000, creating a Viet Cong Infrastructure (VCI) that would enable Ho's insurgency.

The NLF also used terror tactics to expand their control. By the end of 1963 it was estimated that the VC had committed more than 13,000 assassinations. Between 1964 and 1967 over 6,000 more were killed. Many more were kidnapped. The victims were the natural community leaders such as hamlet chiefs, school teachers, and social workers that the VC eliminated to make the population more vulnerable and discourage cooperation with the South Vietnamese government. In response, rather than acknowledging an insurgency problem and instituting much-needed reforms, Diem merely increased his repressive style of government. The end result was that, while cruel, the VC's actions were effective in gaining control of much of the population.

Critical to this control was the existence of a VC "shadow government" throughout the South Vietnamese countryside. Whenever possible, communist cadres were secretly assigned positions as village chiefs, police officers, postal workers, and district-, province-, and national-level officers. These officials levied taxes, regulated trade, drafted men, and punished criminals on behalf of the communist cause. The VC hoped to have a complete government in place when their victory was finally won, and these individuals then could step forward and formally claim their offices. This infrastructure was critical to North Vietnam's control over the South Vietnamese peasant population.

In such an environment, American officials recognized that "all aspects of the nonmilitary nation-building process ... had to be closely tied with area security if the overall effort was to have any chance of success."[3] Therefore, a "pacification campaign" was developed to shield the peasantry from the VC threat while at the same time strengthening their commitment to the South Vietnamese government. While many military commanders like General William Westmoreland saw pacification as a distraction from the "Big War" of attrition, its proponents saw it as focusing on the true center of gravity in a "people's war."

Lieutenant General Victor Krulak, the Special Assistant for Counterinsurgency and Special Activities during the Kennedy Administration and a strong proponent of pacification, argued that protecting the South Vietnamese population must be "a matter of first business."[4] Likewise, Robert Komer pragmatically argued, "Until the GVN regained dominant control of the countryside and provided credible semipermanent protection to the farmers, it would hardly be feasible to proceed with other aspects of pacification."[5] In the same vein, Ambassador Maxwell Taylor stated, "We should have learned from our frontier forbears that there is little use planting corn outside the stockade if there are still Indians around the woods outside."[6]

These interpretations of the problem were reflected in "PROVN—The Program for the Pacification and Long-Term Development of South Vietnam," a U.S. Army report commissioned in 1965 and completed in March 1966 that called for a greater focus at local levels. The study argued that "the crucial actions are those that occur at the village, district and provincial levels. This is where the war must be fought; this is where the war and the object which lies beyond it must be won."[7] This conceptual emphasis was reflected, with varying degrees of sincerity, efficiency, and success, by local level initiatives involving Agrovilles, the Strategic Hamlet System, Revolutionary Development, and the Combined Action Program.

Agrovilles

Of all the situations that made the South Vietnamese rural population vulnerable to VC exploitation, perhaps the most frustrating was the critical need for land reform. The Agroville Program was an early pacification initiative intended to address this condition.[8]

Beginning in 1958, the Diem government used a combination of direct force and incentives to relocate peasants scattered throughout the countryside into large communities called Agrovilles. The initial focus area for the effort was the Mekong Delta, where the dispersed pattern of settlement exacerbated the security problem. Villages were strung out for miles along canals and waterways, making them vulnerable to communist infiltration. President Diem felt that it was this geographic isolation that made the peasants easy prey rather than considering that the VC might actually be appealing to the people by meeting their needs. Thus, in Diem's mind, relocation would free the people from the clutches of the enemy and the problem would be solved.[9]

While security was an important part of population relocation, Philip Catton also argues it was "the centerpiece of the government's plan to modernize the Republic of Vietnam (RVN) and simultaneously free it from dependence on the United States."[10] It was part of a vision of transforming South Vietnamese society from the bottom up through the doctrine of "Personalism," which emphasized a spirit of communal solidarity that would hopefully produce national loyalty.[11] A host of observers saw the potential of the strategy. Diem's American advisor Wesley Fishel believed that Diem's province and district chiefs would bridge the gap between the central government and the rural masses and "bring every district in the country into contact with its neighbors and with the capital."[12] Political development theorist Lucian Pye posited that the key to competing with a revolutionary insurgency lay in expanding the state structure from the capital to distant provinces and villages in order to meet the needs of the peasantry more effectively than the revolution could.[13] Economist and national security planner Walter Rostow saw the solution to the VC was to provide an alternative through a pattern of nation-building that replaced the institutions of the insurgency with those of the state in order to give the peasant, caught in the "transition" to modernity, a renewed appreciation of the potential for personal advancement.[14]

Fulfilling visions such as these would involve an exercise in nation-building at the local level.

Diem wanted to secure the people's allegiance at the local level by making them aware of their larger national identity in order "to bridge the traditional gulf that separated town and country in Vietnam." To accomplish this goal, he emphasized collective action, self-help, and hard work in a program of "Community Development" that aimed to promote group solidarity by teaching what the individual can accomplish through unified action. Diem saw another benefit in local initiative: by building the Agrovilles themselves, the peasants would help free Vietnam from foreign dependence. In the process, of course, Diem would be able to protect the project from the American oversight that he feared would limit his options.[15] Certainly from the perspective of the nation-building donor, this indigenous independence, made possible by local-level nation-building, may be cause for concern. Indeed, the Americans suffered from this condition in Vietnam.

Whatever may have been Diem's intentions, the Agroville program was plagued by a number of abuses and inefficiencies. Provincial officials conscripted thousands of peasants for construction work without pay, drafting many more than were actually needed. The construction interrupted the farmers' efforts to bring in their harvests, and a scarcity of construction equipment forced the projects to be completed largely by manual labor. Rather than correcting this problem, the government boasted that because of the absence of machines, "the people should feel that this was something they had done themselves."[16] Diem characteristically set a rushed pace for the Agrovilles in spite of providing only limited resources. The government allocated the equivalent of $13,000 for each settlement, although estimates for some centers were two-thirds greater than that. The pressure of limited time and money led to additional conscriptions as officials emphasized signs of physical progress rather than peasant satisfaction. Of course, these increased demands only served to alienate the peasants further, and ultimately the Agroville Program served more to exacerbate the problem rather than help it.[17]

Under pressure from the Americans, Diem finally agreed in March 1960 to slow down the construction of Agrovilles in order to alleviate the program's excesses, and this deceleration eventually turned into a gradual abandonment of the program. With only twenty centers having been built and further construction lagging far behind, Diem announced in September that the program would be halted. He explained his decision by citing monetary difficulties, but U.S. Ambassador Elbridge Durbrow, recognizing the program's lack of resonance with the peasantry, speculated that "perhaps [Diem] has finally been convinced that the 'real cost' is the loss of popular support for his regime."[18]

Strategic Hamlets

The failure of the Agroville program left the pacification effort somewhat adrift. Not only had the Agrovilles failed to stem the insurgency, they seemed to have contributed to it. Diem now found himself under increasing pressure to adopt the U.S.-styled policies he had hoped to avoid. In response, Diem's brother Nhu began plans for a successor to the Agrovilles that became known as the Strategic Hamlet Program. American officials found merit in Diem's proposal, and in early 1962, the program became what one observer described as "the centerpiece of [the American] nation-building efforts."[19]

Based on a program that had worked well for the British in Malaya, the idea was to concentrate the rural population in a limited number of fortified villages to provide them physical security against the VC. By focusing on existing settlements, rather than attempting to build new ones, the Strategic Hamlet Program hoped to avoid some of the construction problems that had plagued the Agrovilles. While each case was slightly different, the process generally involved a series of similar steps. First, South Vietnamese government "Rural Reconstruction" teams of ten to twenty men would take a census of an existing village and identify families and their apparent loyalties on a map. Villagers would then be organized into work groups to build fortifications for the new settlement. Houses outside the perimeter would be moved inside or destroyed, and a hamlet militia would be organized and trained. Finally, the peasants would be issued identification cards, photographs of family members would be posted on the walls of their house, a hamlet administrative center would track all population movements, and curfews would be enforced. While this security and surveillance distinguished the area inside the perimeter, the area outside would become a free-fire zone where all activity was assumed to be enemy. Once this security was established, social programs that would hopefully foster government allegiance were planned to follow.[20]

State Department intelligence chief Roger Hilsman emphasized the importance of this "civic action" phase of the Strategic Hamlet Program, hoping that teams of Vietnamese backed by U.S. advice and supplies would build an "essential socio-political base" by forging a new set of ties between the rural peasantry and Diem's regime. Hilsman's goal was to "set up village government and tie it into the district and national levels assuring the flow of information on village needs and problems upward and the flow of government services downward."[21] Government largess would help transform "traditional" loyalties to family and formerly isolated, largely autonomous villages to a "modern" identification with a specifically South Vietnamese nation-state.[22]

The U.S. military agreed. A Joint Chiefs of Staff report in early 1963 argued that the problem was that "historically the central government in Vietnam has not reached down and made itself felt to the peasant. Likewise, the peasant has not truly identified himself, his activities, or his future with his government nor has he thought in terms of national political issues as we know them." The Strategic Hamlet Program would reverse this situation by a "'rice-roots' program" whereby elected hamlet officials would "decide on projects for the improvement of the well-being and living conditions of the people" that would lay "the framework for a democratic political process."[23] Such an outcome is entirely consistent with twenty-first century expectations of decentralization. "By bringing government closer to citizens," proponents of this process argue that people can "participate more effectively in local affairs, including identification of community priorities. Local leaders can be held increasingly accountable for decisions that affect citizens' lives."[24]

According to this vision, nation-building in Vietnam "would steadily move forward: one hamlet at a time."[25] Instead, the Strategic Hamlet Program was largely a failure. Unlike the Chinese immigrant squatters who were the subject of the British relocations in Malaya, the indigenous South Vietnamese peasants had strong local roots and close family ties, and lived in socially cohesive communities.[26] Moving to another location interrupted their Buddhist practice of veneration of ancestors. Additionally, the relocations caused the peasants to abandon generations of hard work and took vital, arable land out of production, which hampered economic progress. In the new hamlets, the peasants had to start over from scratch, without compensation for their labor or loss. The ever-present security and surveillance measures left one observer wondering if he had "blundered into some sort of prison camp."[27] South Vietnamese peasants were naturally bitter in their resentment to the forced relocation, and "not much nation-building took place in such a repressive environment."[28] Like many groups, they chose to "resist nation-building because it means the destruction of their way of life."[29]

The result was a disgruntled population that was ripe for VC exploitation, a situation facilitated by the fact that many VC secretly relocated to the new hamlets with the rest of the population. Many peasants were so alienated by the entire ordeal that they slipped away from the hamlets and returned to their ancestral lands. This development greatly hindered one of the goals of the relocation, which was to create free-fire zones in the vacated areas based on the assumption that anyone there now was a VC.[30]

As part of the program, the VC-controlled areas that could not be penetrated by the government were subjected to random bombardment by artillery and aircraft in order to drive the people into the safety of the strategic hamlets. This process created tens of thousands of refugees, which Diem advertised as a show of political support—the population voting with its feet—as the people fled the VC to government-held territory. In actuality, the refugees were angered by this dangerous disruption to their lives, and they resented the government as the instrument of it.[31]

The relocations created other problems as well, including the perception that if relocation was necessary in the first place, then security must be weak. Many peasants were left with the impression that if the South Vietnamese government was not able to secure even its allies, fully supporting the government would be dangerous. Finally, by moving the population away from the countryside, a significant, if imperfect, source of intelligence was lost.[32] Summing up the Strategic Hamlet's failure to address the needs of the South Vietnamese people, Dave Palmer concludes the program was "executed with too little real feeling for the human beings involved."[33] An even more fundamental conclusion may have been that, for whatever merits Personalism may have conceptually held, the idea that the Diem "regime was not one that rural Vietnamese were interested in identifying with or participating in at all was rarely considered seriously."[34]

All these problems were exacerbated by reporting inaccuracies that served to further weaken perceptions of the program's legitimacy. By the summer of 1962, the Diem government claimed to have established 3,225 strategic hamlets, which held over four million people or one-third of South Vietnam's population. When the Diem regime collapsed in October 1963, it became apparent that many of these hamlets existed on paper only, and the reporting was part of a South Vietnamese misinformation campaign to deceive the Americans. As a case in point, the number of "secure" hamlets in Long An Province was revised downward from over two hundred to about ten after Diem's death.[35] Accurately measuring the success of the effort would be a common difficulty throughout the pacification program and a continual challenge to its legitimacy. As with the Agrovilles, the result of the Strategic Hamlet Program was "less rather than more security in the countryside."[36]

Revolutionary Development

Recognizing sufficient progress was not being made, President Lyndon Johnson convened a meeting with South Vietnamese leaders including new President Nguyen Van Thieu and Premier Nguyen Cao Ky in Honolulu in February 1966 to discuss the status of economic, social, and political projects for South Vietnam. President Johnson made it clear that he expected a massive increase in pacification productivity in the upcoming year, and he expressed his mounting impatience with the need to develop an effective American organization for pacification support. The Honolulu Conference sent a clear message that Johnson considered business as usual to no longer be sufficient.[37]

As a result of the meeting, the South Vietnamese decided to give a new face to the pacification program by calling it Revolutionary Development. Most contemporary definitions of Revolutionary Development were along the lines of "those civilian, military, and police actions taken to eliminate Viet Cong political and military activity and to enhance the economic, political, and social development of the community."[38] The program's objectives reflected its local-level emphasis:

—To provide sustained security against Viet Cong local forces, terrorists, and infrastructure to permit conduct of economic, social and political programs.

—To establish effective political structure at the local level with the participation of the people.

—To stimulate self-sustaining economic activity.[39]

The roots of this initiative can be traced to the expansion of the People's Action Teams that occurred in 1964–1965. Started under CIA sponsorship, these teams were trained extensively in political indoctrination and motivation. Significantly, they lived and worked among the South Vietnamese population whose loyalty was being vied for by both the communist and democratic forces. The South Vietnamese now vastly expanded the number of teams by absorbing some members of existing programs run by separate government ministries and also recruiting new members. This growth, however, created a competition for scarce South Vietnamese resources that became a major point of contention between American civilian agencies and the military. The result was a "sharpened ... dichotomy between military and civilian operations."[40]

Even with the reorganization, coordination remained a major problem. The Ministry of Revolutionary Development under General Nguyen Duc Thang provided broad administrative guidance for population security and nation-building programs. A hierarchy of Revolutionary Development councils, emanating from the National Central Revolutionary Development Council in Saigon through corps- and division-level councils to those in each province, implemented Thang's directives. On the American side, the U.S. Embassy's Mission Liaison Group, led by Deputy Ambassador William Porter, provided general guidance and supervision at the national level.[41]

Although Porter had no authority over the participation of the Military Assistance Command, Vietnam (MACV) in pacification, General Westmoreland designated his chief of the Revolutionary Development Division of the J-3, Colonel Joel Hollis, to serve as an advisor to Porter with an office in the embassy. By serving as MACV's single point of contact with the embassy on pacification, Hollis represented "an improvement in coordination." In fact, Hollis's office routinely produced staff work that bore Porter's signature.[42] Nonetheless, Porter was distracted from these duties because "he was already doing a 24-hour job as [Ambassador Henry Cabot] Lodge's Chief of Staff running the Embassy." As a result, Porter "understood what needed to be done[, but] his performance in getting it done was not very effective."[43] This arrangement continued until November 1966, when the MACV Headquarters effort was absorbed by the Revolutionary Development Support Directorate headed by Brigadier General William Knowlton. In the meantime, Robert Komer, who in March 1966 was named a special assistant for pacification matters to President Johnson, tried to unify support for these programs in Washington.[44]

At the core of the Revolutionary Development program were teams of fifty-nine South Vietnamese specially trained and financed by the CIA. Thirty of the team members were self-defense experts, equipped with light arms and tasked to perform security functions. The other twenty-nine were specialists in every kind of village need who set up a political structure within the villages and hamlets and supervised short-range development projects.[45] According to one Special Forces officer, the Revolutionary Development cadre's "efforts are directed at the people to gain their support and cooperation, to protect them, and to assist them in governing themselves."[46] It was a formula "consciously imitative of Vietcong techniques."[47]

The first Revolutionary Development cadre groups graduated from the National Training Center in May 1966. By the end of 1968, more than 700 cadre teams had been trained and deployed. Each team contained headquarters, security, and reconstruction elements. Dressed in peasant garb, they would move into a hamlet, identify and eliminate the VC secret political cadre, remove corrupt South Vietnamese officials from office, organize democratic institutions, and create a hamlet defense force. They also collected simple census data and built modest assembly halls where the local population could meet with district officials to initiate small improvement projects such as those involving education, land reform, financial credit, roads, irrigation, and health. Once these objectives were accomplished, the team would move on to another hamlet while the South Vietnamese government continued to develop the programs that had been started. To supplement these teams, several U.S. civilian agencies worked at various levels in information, agriculture, and public health programs.[48]

Nonetheless, while it appeared promising at first, George Herring concludes that Revolutionary Development "ran afoul of many of the problems that had frustrated earlier pacification programs." Poor coordination, "the creaking Saigon bureaucracy," difficulty in recruiting sufficient personnel, inadequate training, inconsistent funding, competition with other programs, and a lack of perseverance all contributed to disappointing results. Moreover, "having seen so many other programs come and go," Herring notes, "the villagers greeted the [Revolutionary Development teams] with a mixture of apathy and caution."[49] This was foreboding in light of one observer's assertion that "population support is the fundamental objective of revolutionary development. Without this support there can be no lasting success."[50] Perhaps even more damaging, there was little evidence that the South Vietnamese government was genuinely committed to the reforms that Revolutionary Development envisioned. In fact, many of the South Vietnamese political elites viewed a better educated and empowered peasantry as a threat to their power.[51]

Revolutionary Development also failed to provide the security that was prerequisite to success. The "justice, health programs, welfare activities, road maintenance, electricity, and agricultural assistance" envisioned by pacification could not "be brought into an area until protection has been provided to the population."[52] Instead, security was so tenuous that in many cases the Revolutionary Development cadres themselves were harassed and terrorized by VC. Many fled, and those who stayed did so at great risk. During a seven-month period in 1966, over three thousand Revolutionary Development personnel were killed or kidnapped.[53] In part as an effort to check such violence, the United States turned to the Phoenix program to eliminate the VC cadre. Phoenix was very successful in accomplishing this important security mission, but was not designed to include the subsequent civic action programs that were part of Revolutionary Development. To this end, Phoenix may be accused of violating the admonition that "improvement must go hand in hand with anti-infrastructure operations, or the population will likely regard government efforts as repressive."[54]

CAP

The program that probably came closest to the intent of PROVN, and the one that best adhered to the principles of both security and unity of effort, was the Combined Action Program, or CAP. Beginning as a small experiment to secure U.S. military bases around Phu Bai and Da Nang in 1965, CAP soon became the linchpin in the Marines' strategy for winning the war.[55] It also came to exemplify Westmoreland's negative attitude toward pacification.

A CAP platoon was a combination of a fourteen-man Marine Corps rifle squad and one Navy medical corpsman, all of whom were volunteers, and a locally recruited Popular Forces (PF) platoon of about thirty-five men. The resulting CAP was assigned responsibility for a village, which typically consisted of five hamlets spread out over four square kilometers with an average population of 3,500 people. The American Marines lived with their Vietnamese PF counterparts and became integral parts of the unit. The effect was synergistic. The Marines gained intelligence from the South Vietnamese soldiers' knowledge of the local terrain and enemy, while the PF benefited from the Marines' firepower, tactical skills, and discipline. The CAP was a solid and mutually beneficial combination.[56]

Perhaps most important, the constant Marine presence sent a powerful message that the Americans were there to stay. They did not fly in by helicopter in the morning and fly out at night to leave the villagers at the mercy of the VC. This continued presence was critical because the peasant who cooperated with the government had to carefully weigh the risk of VC reprisals directed toward himself, his family, his friends, and his community against the benefits of improved clothing, food, education, and medical assistance. When the Americans flew in and flew out, the risks to the Vietnamese villager often outweighed the benefits. However, under CAP, the Marines shared the same fate as the South Vietnamese soldiers and people. In fact, CAP Marines took 2.5 times the casualties of the PF in the CAP. The CAP was a strong testimony of American commitment and partnership, and gave the Vietnamese people a sense of enduring security.[57]

In the fall of 1966, a battalion from the 25th Infantry Division executed Operation Lanikai in the Hau Nghia province and learned the same lesson regarding presence and security. The battalion's report of the operation noted that U.S. units on pacification missions "must be prepared to live in the pacification area until the people have been made to feel secure and their cooperation has been won…. The full benefits of pacification type operations in an area can only be realized through vigorous and constant efforts to sustain the favorable conditions created until such time as the local Vietnamese officials and military leaders are prepared to accept the full gamut of civil and military responsibilities."[58] Reports such as this one recognized the importance of creating the secure environment that would enable local-level growth and development to occur.

The CAP program expanded steadily, and in 1966 there were fifty-seven CAP platoons. By the end of 1967, the number had grown to seventy-nine. Despite these increases and demonstrated success, Westmoreland was unwilling to adopt the program, arguing that he "simply had not enough numbers to put a squad of Americans in every village and hamlet; that would be fragmenting resources and exposing them to defeat in detail."[59] While there is some merit to Westmoreland's argument about numbers, his genuine objection lay more in a fundamental strategic difference. Westmoreland viewed the CAPs as static and defensive employments of his resources. Instead, he favored the aggressive pursuit and destruction of enemy forces. The focus of CAP at the small-unit level also violated Westmoreland's quest for the mass he needed to gain a conventional battlefield victory.

On the other hand, CAP advocates argued that the real battlefields were the villages, and the real enemy was the VC in them. Lieutenant General Krulak argued, "If the enemy cannot get to the people he cannot win." In an effort to "comb the guerrillas out of the people's lives," he urged that protecting the South Vietnamese population must be "a matter of first business."[60] Once the villages were secured, the repelling of enemy main forces would be an easy matter, given the American superiority in firepower and mobility. Furthermore, the main enemy forces would be severely weakened by denying them the logistical support they enjoyed from the unsecured villages. Such arguments fell largely on deaf ears.[61]

In the end, Westmoreland never put the CAP concept fully to the test and ultimately vetoed the strategic concept. Perceived as competition with "the Big War," CAP was never allocated the manpower resources it required, and, lacking a grand strategic direction, its local successes were never able to be replicated on a larger scale. For many, CAP showed that the Marines, building on their experience in Cuba, Haiti, the Dominican Republic, Nicaragua, and Panama, seemed to understand pacification better than their Army counterparts.

The philosophical difference between the two services is exemplified by Krulak and Army Major General Julian Ewell. Krulak insisted that the big force engagements "could move to another planet today, and we would still not have won the war because the Vietnamese people are the prize."[62] In contrast, Ewell, commander of the 9th Infantry Division and a major proponent of the body count, had his staff draw up a report that concluded, "The most relevant statistical index of combat effectiveness was the average number of Viet Cong losses inflicted daily by the unit in question."[63] Ewell explained, "I guess I basically felt that the 'hearts and minds' approach can be overdone."[64] "In the 9th Division," he wrote, "we always stressed the military effort."[65] By and large, the Army high command shared Ewell's point of view.

Measuring

Against such resistance, pacification officials attempted various ways to use statistics to not only measure results, but also to boost the program's legitimacy with an often-skeptical military command. Major General Lewis Walt, commander of the III Marine Amphibious Force, developed an early model based on five "progress indicators": destruction of enemy units, destruction of the Viet Cong infrastructure, South Vietnamese government establishment of security, South Vietnamese government establishment of local government, and degree of development of the New Life Program (a successor to the Strategic Hamlet Program). Current military doctrine uses the term *measures of effectiveness* (MOEs) for such criteria that are "used to assess changes in system behavior, capability, or operational environment that is tied to measuring the attainment of an end state, achievement of an objective, or creation of an effect."[66]

**A Department of Defense pamphlet, "Viet-Nam: The Struggle for Freedom,"
depicted this photograph of a guard patrolling a fortified village protected by sharpened bamboo stakes. "The hamlet programs," the pamphlet explained, "serve the
dual purpose of providing physical safety and a better life through enhanced Government services." (Courtesy Naval History & Heritage Command.)**

Each indicator in Walt's system represented a possible total of twenty
points and was broken down into related subdivisions. A village that accumulated sixty points reflected "firm South Vietnamese/U.S. Government influence," while a score of eighty points indicated pacification. Critics questioned
Walt's formula, arguing that it was possible for a village to gather enough
points to be declared "pacified" even if the VCI, the most important of the
indicators, remained virtually undisturbed.[67]

Calls to conceptualize pacification in terms of incremental results
continued to increase after the Honolulu Conference.[68] As a result, Komer
introduced a variety of means to measure the effort in order to determine
if pacification was producing "an acceptable rate of return for [the] heavy

investments."[69] One was the "Hamlet Evaluation System" (HES), which, while it "borrowed freely" from Walt's system, sought to "provide a uniform measure of progress throughout Vietnam."[70]

HES used a five-letter scoring system to assess progress via eighteen security and development indicators. Security indicators were in the categories of VC military activity, VC political and subversive activities, and security based on friendly capabilities. Development indicators were in the categories of administrative and political activities; health, education, and welfare; and economic development. An "A" hamlet was excelling in all areas of security and development. A "B" hamlet was still considered high-grade with effective 24-hour security, adequate development, and no VC presence or activity. A "C" hamlet was relatively secure day and night. Viet Cong military control had been broken, and there were no overt VC incidents, although VC taxation was perhaps continuing. Economic improvement programs were underway. In a "D" hamlet, the VC frequently entered or harassed at night, and VC infrastructure was largely intact. The South Vietnamese program was in its infancy, and control of the hamlet was still strictly contested. An "E" hamlet was definitely under VC control, and American and South Vietnamese officials entered only as part of a military operation. Most of the population in an "E" hamlet supported the VC.[71] When Komer began the HES, there were 12,600 hamlets. He was able to assign U.S. senior military advisors to 222 of the 242 South Vietnamese districts.[72]

Under HES, American advisors made monthly assessments on worksheets that were then sent to Saigon for computer processing into composite scores. Like Walt's system, however, HES was susceptible to challenges to its objectivity and legitimacy. The evaluations took place at the district headquarters, far away from rural hamlets. A senior advisor normally visited just one-fourth of the district hamlets in a month. Visits to individual hamlets usually lasted only a few hours, and during that time most advisors were completely dependent on interpreters. The result was evaluations based largely on surface appearances or historical data. To make matters worse, these advisory positions were not considered career-enhancing jobs. Thus, many military officers cycled through them as quickly as possible in pursuit of the more prized combat positions.[73]

The result was that, in spite of efforts to make the evaluation as objective and legitimate as possible, assessment was still subject to manipulation. For example, in October 1968 the United States faced the disconcerting prospect of being subjected to demands for concessions at the Paris Peace Conference based on a communist claim of representing a large segment of the countryside. To preempt this possibility, MACV inaugurated the Accelerated Pacification Program (APP) in November.[74] The APP modified the criteria, attempting now to establish a minimal government presence in as many hamlets as possible. Some 1,000 additional hamlets were earmarked, but to accommodate these increased quantities, the quality of the effort was diminished. Where cadres once stayed six months, they now only stayed six weeks. One American adviser said, "The name of the game is planting the government flag."[75] Using these new standards, the number of "relatively secure" hamlets shot up to 73.3 percent, an all-time high.[76] In the process, though, the legitimacy of the reports became questionable.

One criticism of HES was that because the advisors had a vested professional interest in the results, the system was prone to manipulation. When William Colby replaced Komer as head of Civil Operations and Revolutionary Development Support (CORDS), Colby built on his prior experience with the Strategic Hamlet Program to create a new evaluation system designed to remove some of the subjectivity that affected HES. As part of this process, the army contracted with Control Data Corporation to develop a new survey called "HES 70." HES 70 was billed as "a highly integrated man-machine interface" which would solve the problem of subjectivity by being "objective and uni-dimensional."[77] The new survey counted such things as TV sets, organized activities for youths, motorized vehicles, self-defense forces, and other key indicators of security and development. However, in a marked departure from the old system, advisers no longer did the rating, and all scoring was done in Saigon using a formula not known to the advisers. The idea behind this arrangement was to remove the impression that the advisers were actually evaluating themselves. While HES 70 improved the system, it remained better suited to measure quantifiable factors such as control and suppression of the opposition rather than the less tangible but more significant ideas of popular allegiance and the strength of commitment to the South Vietnamese government.[78] Since the original goal of Personalism's approach to local-level nation-building was to build communal solidarity as a bridge to national loyalty, the inability to measure such progress was a serious shortcoming of the effort.

Conclusion

The local-level nation-building effort in Vietnam failed for a variety of reasons. Designed to strengthen the bottoms-up connection between the peasantry and the central government, initiatives like Agrovilles and the Strategic Hamlet Program showed that the central government had little top-down connection to the peasantry and was out of touch with the situation at the local level. Revolutionary Development failed to provide the security that is the prerequisite for any future development. The Combined Action Program showed promise but fell victim to the tension between decentralized and centralized approaches.

Perhaps the reason that most explains the overall failure, however, is a lack of perseverance. Such local-level efforts "are lengthy processes of incremental institutional change."[79] The local-level nation-building in Vietnam never benefited from the long-term commitment that such a gradual approach requires.

Infantry officer Samuel Smithers recognized the problem, cautioning, "No one can say how long U.S. troops will be required to remain in any particular province before it can be declared capable of protecting itself." Writing in 1967, Smithers cited commentators who predicted a U.S. presence "may well be required in Vietnam for as long as 20 years."[80] Edwin Chamberlain, another of the hard-working American military advisors of Smithers's era, confessed, "There is little glory and much weariness in pacification."[81] America eventually reached the same conclusion about the Vietnam War in general and lost its will to continue the effort.

While the local-level nation-building effort in Vietnam failed in its implementation phase, the concept remains both viable and valid, and certainly has been a major part of the recent nation-building effort in Afghanistan. As Mark Sedra explained in 2002:

> In a country where strong central authority is traditionally viewed with suspicion and apprehension, it is not surprising that ... efforts [focusing on the creation of robust state institutions] have had only mixed success. This is not to say that programs to strengthen the central government are unnecessary. Quite to the contrary, they are imperative. However, they must be pursued in parallel with efforts to promote security and democratic development at the community and municipal levels. In Afghanistan, the village, and not the central government, was, and continues to be, the key unit of governance in the country. Accordingly, to achieve lasting peace and security, the international community should adopt a community-based approach to reconstruction that advances the rejuvenation of Afghan civil society from the bottom up.[82]

Such a vision manifested itself in the Provincial Reconstruction Teams (PRTs), which Kael Weston, who spent nearly two years on a PRT in eastern Afghanistan for the State Department, described as efforts to "bring government closer to the people" through "bottom-up diplomacy, bottom-up development, bottom-up counterinsurgency." In so doing, Weston noted the PRTs were filling a void in central government presence in many parts of Afghanistan. "I remember a couple of elders, sitting at 8000 feet," he noted in a 2013 interview, "who said the last time we had a representative of the central government was when King Zahir Shah sent the tax collectors, and that was half a century ago. And they came up once and never returned."[83]

Like the local-level nation-building efforts in Vietnam, however, the PRTs also had a mixed record in Afghanistan. Michael J. McNerney, the Director of International Policy and Capabilities in the Office of the Deputy Assistant Secretary of Defense for Stability Operations, explains, "Despite their potential and record of success, however, PRTs always have been a bit of a muddle. Inconsistent mission statements, unclear roles and responsibilities, ad hoc preparation, and, most important, limited resources have confused potential partners and prevented PRTs from having a greater effect on Afghanistan's future."[84] Provincial Reconstruction Teams and other aspects of the U.S. nation-building experience in Afghanistan will be discussed in greater detail in Chapter 10.

CHAPTER 8

Nation-Building at the National Level: Iraq

In March 2003, an American-led coalition launched Operation Iraqi Freedom (OIF), which eliminated the Ba'athist regime of then President Saddam Hussein in less than two months, leaving the United States and its operational partners to plan and implement post-conflict reconstruction and nation- and state-building efforts in Iraq. Regrettably, those processes proved markedly more challenging than was the case in defeating the Iraqi armed forces. In particular, from the outset of America's intervention, the U.S.-led application of a national-level approach to nation- and state-building in Iraq has been complicated by the myriad ethnic, religious, and tribal divisions that have torn that state apart for centuries. The many daunting challenges spawned by such divisions, in turn, are the focal points for analysis in this chapter.

History demonstrates that, above all else, thorough, effective advance planning is central to the success or failure of any nation- and/or state-building project. Regrettably, the lack of such planning was glaringly evident in the case of Iraq, with little emphasis given to what would unfold in the aftermath of a successful military operation removing Saddam's regime from power. Rather than prepare for the conduct of a long-term nation- and state-building project in Iraq, one likely to require a substantial military footprint for years or perhaps decades, the George W. Bush administration believed falsely that only limited commitments in manpower and time would be necessary. Then, when it became apparent that its assessment was incorrect, the administration had to scramble to develop and implement its approach to the project and adapt as needed in response to evolving circumstances on the ground.

As L. Paul Bremer, who headed the Coalition Provisional Authority (CPA) during the first year of the U.S.-led occupation of (and conduct of nation- and state-building efforts within) Iraq, recalls of his flight into that state in the aftermath of OIF in May 2003, "Baghdad was burning. As the Air

Force C-130 banked above the curve of the Tigris River, I twisted in the sling seat and stared out the circular window of the cargo bay. The capital of Iraq stretched north beneath the right wing, dusty beige, sprawled in the shimmering heat. Dark smoke columns rose in the afternoon sun. I counted three, four, five ... seven."[1]

The anarchic conditions Bremer observed developed soon after the fall of Saddam's Ba'athist regime, which collapsed quickly under U.S. pressure, with myriad members of the Iraqi Army simply choosing to fade into the population rather than fight a losing conventional war against far superior coalition forces. Saddam himself fled as well and remained on the loose until captured by American forces in December 2003. He was tried and convicted of crimes against humanity and executed by hanging in December 2006, at which point Iraq remained insecure and politically unstable as the United States and its coalition partners attempted to implement a "national level" approach to the reconstruction of Iraq.

With these introductory observations as a useful point of departure, the balance of the chapter assesses that approach to nation- and state-building efforts in Iraq through the presentation of eight sections that unfold in the following manner. The first section reviews and assesses the relevant literature on "national" approaches to nation- and state-building projects. The second section examines the diplomatic prologue to and subsequent conduct of OIF, which resulted in the elimination of the regime of President Saddam Hussein and start of nation- and state-building efforts in the spring of 2003. The third section examines the cultural challenges associated with the use of a top-down national approach to attempting to build an Iraqi nation and state from 2003 to 2011. The fourth section examines the economic aspects of the national approach to Iraqi reconstruction and stabilization from 2003 to 2011. The fifth section examines the military and security aspects of nation- and state-building efforts in Iraq from 2003 to 2011. The sixth section examines the political aspects of nation- and state-building efforts in Iraq from 2003–11. The seventh section suggests some significant insights that academics and policy makers and practitioners should draw from the case of nation- and state-building efforts in Iraq. And the eighth section presents a set of conclusions on the past, present and probable future of Iraq.

National Approaches to Nation- and State-Building: A Synopsis of the Relevant Literature

America's use of nation- and state-building operations to safeguard its interests and those of its allies abroad dates to the emergence of the United

States as a Western Hemispheric power in the nineteenth century and, more significantly, its ascent to the ranks of global players, following its victory in the Spanish-American War of 1898. That triumph demonstrated America's rising economic and military power and political power relative to its European rivals, most notably Britain, France, Portugal and, of course, Spain. It also led the William McKinley presidential administration to engage in nation- and state-building projects in the two territories the United States seized from the Spanish—Cuba and the Philippines.

The cases of Cuba and the Philippines are the first two instances of nation- and state-building operations carried out by the United States on foreign soil in its history. Iraq, the subject of this chapter, is the latest such example.[2] Like many such cases, understanding the Iraqi case demands that one begin with an explanation of the distinctions between the terms "nation" and "state" and "nation-building" and "state-building." The *Oxford English Dictionary* defines "nation" as "a large aggregate of people united by common descent, history, culture or language, inhabiting a particular country or territory," and "state" as "a nation or territory considered as an organized political community under one government."[3] The most significant distinction between the two is the centrality of cultural factors to the development of a nation, as opposed to the equal importance of clearly delineated borders and centralized governmental institutions to a state. In those instances where a country is able to develop and maintain both sets of attributes, it can credibly be referred to as a nation-state, which the *Oxford English Dictionary* defines as "a sovereign state whose citizens or subjects are relatively homogeneous in factors such as language or common descent."[4] The United States is one notable example of such a polity. Iraq, by contrast, is most certainly not.

As with nations and states, there are also very important distinctions between nation- and state-building. The Rand Foundation's *The Beginner's Guide to Nation-Building*, the central conceptual and terminological volume in the authoritative series of texts on the topic, describes the former in the following terms: "Nation-building, as it is commonly referred to in the United States, involves the use of armed force as part of a broader effort to promote political and economic reforms with the objective of transforming a society emerging from conflict to one at peace with itself and its neighbors."[5] Francis Fukuyama defines the latter as "the creation of new government institutions and the strengthening of existing ones."[6] Perhaps the most important difference between the two is the relative significance of culture and national identity, as opposed to the proverbial nuts and bolts of economic and political institution–building that shape nation- and state-building projects, respectively.

The fact that Americans have viewed the United States as a nation-state rather than just a nation or a state from the outset of its existence has led many scholars and policymakers, particularly those situated within (or influenced directly by) Washington and its institutions and public policy foundations, to mistakenly use the terms nation- and state-building interchangeably. As Fukuyama asserts, "This terminology perhaps reflects the national experience, in which cultural and historical identity was heavily shaped by political institutions like constitutionalism and democracy. Europeans tend to be more aware of the distinctions between state and nation and point out that nation-building in the sense of the creation of a community bound together by shared history and culture is well beyond the ability of any outside power to achieve. They are, of course, right; only states can be deliberately constructed. If a nation arises from this, it is more a matter of luck than design."[7]

The "national experience" to which Fukuyama refers also helps to explain the American affinity for a national-level approach to the reconstruction of states in the aftermath of, if not amidst, instances of inter- and/or intra-state conflict, especially those whose continued existence is not certain. Since the end of the Cold War, such entities have been branded in the nation- and state-building literature as "weak," "fragile," "failing," and, in the worst cases, "failed" states. These types of states share a range of destabilizing features, most notably governmental inability to provide the citizenry with basic necessities, such as physical security, economic sustenance, political freedoms of any sort, or a common national identity.[8] Notable examples include the cases of Afghanistan and Iraq, both of which have fallen in each of the above three categories, if not the fourth, at least once at some point since the start of the 21st century.

In considering "national" responses to the challenges that lead states to intervene and participate in nation- and state-building projects designed to address and ideally resolve the problems of weak, fragile, failing and failed states, it is appropriate to characterize such shortcomings in terms of five issue areas in particular, those associated with culture, history, economics, politics and security. Those issue areas, in turn, are often interconnected across multiple levels of analysis, whether local, national and/or international, which renders the application of national approaches and policies to more micro-level problems all the more challenging. As Larry Diamond, a Stanford University scholar and editor of the *Journal of Democracy* who served as a CPA advisor in Iraq in the winter and spring of 2004, recalls in a memoir in his time there, with its multi-ethnic and multi-religious society of Arabs and Kurds, Shi'ites and Sunnis, and Saddam's history of repression and slaughter of Kurds and Shi'ites, as well as those Sunnis deemed threats to his Ba'athist regime, "Iraq was ... a deeply divided society, and some even questioned whether it could be called a nation.... The Kurds were not the only aggrieved identity group in Iraq. So were the much smaller minorities of Turkomans and Christians, along with the Arab Shi'ites, who made up an estimated 60 percent of the Iraqi population. Since the founding of the modern Iraqi state in the 1920s, the Shiites had been marginalized and victimized, as the Arab Sunni minority monopolized power and wealth. Under Saddam's rule, the Shiites lived with a sense of ongoing subjugation and persecution."[9] Applying national approaches to nation- and state-building projects in states featuring ethnically, racially, religiously and tribally diverse and often polarized societies has always presented daunting challenges for the intervening states and institutions involved, whether states, intergovernmental organizations (IGOs) or nongovernmental organizations (NGOs).

The Road to American Intervention in Iraq, 2002–03

One can quite credibly date the political and military timetables counting down to the March 2003 U.S.-led intervention in Iraq to the conclusion of the Persian Gulf War in the spring of 1991, if not the prelude to that conflict in the summer of 1990. In August 1990 in particular, Iraq invaded, occupied and annexed—albeit without any legitimate international legal basis—the neighboring state of Kuwait, a series of events that prompted American President George H.W. Bush to demand that Saddam withdraw his troops immediately or face an American-led attack to compel him to do so. Over the ensuing four months, the United States secured a series of United Nations Security Council (UNSC) resolutions calling for Iraq to remove its forces from Kuwait or face military action from an ethnically, politically and religiously diverse coalition of states cobbled together under American diplomatic leadership.

When Saddam refused to comply with any of those resolutions, the United States spearheaded a two-stage war effort in January and February 1991 (a one-month air campaign preceding a 100-hour ground operation) that resulted in Iraq's surrender, which was formalized via its acceptance of UNSC Resolution 687. In the contexts of Resolution 687 and 16 subsequent UNSC resolutions—the last of which (Resolution 4112) was passed unanimously in November 2002—the UN demanded that Iraq make a range of behavioral modifications to ensure its reacceptance as a productive member of the international community. Saddam's regime failed to comply fully with each one of those resolutions.

In particular, Iraq defied UN mandates by declining to: (a) eliminate its biological, chemical and nuclear weapons of mass destruction (WMD) development programs in an unambiguously verifiable manner; (b) cease attempts to acquire ballistic missiles with ranges greater than 150 kilometers; (c) renounce all terrorist organizations and refuse to harbor any members of such groups within its borders; (d) return all foreign prisoners seized during its 1990 invasion of Kuwait and the subsequent Persian Gulf War; and (e) refrain from repressing its domestic opponents, most notably the Kurds and Shiites.[10]

The administration of President William J. Clinton took limited diplomatic and military steps—reliance on UN weapons inspectors and the conduct of Operation Desert Fox following Saddam's expulsion of those inspectors in December 1998, in particular—to enforce UN sanctions on Iraq. The George W. Bush administration, by contrast, insisted that Saddam comply with all of the aforementioned resolutions or relinquish power. When he refused to accede to repeated U.S. demands to do so, which were issued by Bush, Secretary of State Colin Powell, Secretary of Defense Donald Rumsfeld and National Security Advisor Condoleezza Rice between September 2002 and March 2003, American and British forces launched the attack that removed Saddam's regime and set the stage for the conduct of nation- and state-building operations in Iraq. That intervention came without approval of a final UNSC resolution explicitly authorizing the use of force against Iraq, which has resulted in the near-universal characterization of OIF as a unilateral initiative in the context of debates among scholars, political pundits and policymakers ever since.[11]

By intervening without UNSC approval to do so, the Bush administration produced one of the most significant ruptures in transatlantic relations since the establishment of the North Atlantic Treaty Organization (NATO) in April 1949. Among the most militarily powerful and politically influential of NATO, the United States and United Kingdom sat on the side of the transatlantic debate favoring intervention to achieve regime change, while France and Germany suggested a continuation of economic sanctions and UN inspections of suspected Iraqi weapons of mass destruction. Further, the Central and Eastern European member states of NATO, who sought and secured membership in that institution largely on the basis of American-led enlargement of the transatlantic community in the aftermath of the Cold War, supported the U.S. position on Iraq over that of Paris and Berlin in 2002–03.

As is true of most nation- and state-building projects, the U.S.-initiated and -led endeavor in Iraq featured interconnected cultural, economic, military/security and political components. Policies associated with each of those components were applied in multiple stages that have unfolded since the spring of 2003. The implementation of those policies, in turn, was constricted by myriad domestic and international impediments, which are examined in much greater depth in the ensuing four sections.

Cultural Challenges to National Approach
to Iraqi Nation and State Building, 2003–11

Any assessment of the cultural challenges associated with the conduct of a nation- and/or state-building project must begin with a discussion of the myriad definitions of the term "culture." As a point of departure for that discussion, the *Oxford English Dictionary* defines culture as "the customs, arts, social institutions, and achievements of a particular nation, people, or other social group."[12] Scholars with expertise in a range of academic disciplines have developed and promulgated a seemingly endless array of definitions (and, more importantly, applications) of that term as well. In the fields of political science generally and political theory and international relations specifically, the late Samuel P. Huntington started one of the most followed debates of the post–Cold War era by asserting that cultural factors play a central role in driving the behavior of states in the international system— first in a 1993 *Foreign Affairs* article entitled "The Clash of Civilizations?"[13] and again in greater depth in the 1996 book *The Clash of Civilizations and the Remaking of World Order*.[14] Most significantly, Huntington notes, "People define themselves in terms of ancestry, religion, language, history, values, customs, and institutions. They identify with cultural groups: tribes, ethnic groups, religious communities, nations, and, at the broadest level, civilizations. People use politics not just to advance their interests but also to define their identity. We know who we are only when we know who we are not and often only when we know whom we are against."[15] The sociologist Geert Hofstede acknowledges the importance of culture but defines it in slightly broader and subtly different and more flexible terms, explaining that it "is the collective programming of the mind distinguishing the members of one group or category of people from others."[16]

Both Huntington's and Hofstede's explanations of culture are applicable to nation- and state-building projects generally and those in the Greater Middle East, such as the cases of Afghanistan and Iraq, in particular. Each proposes a conceptual approach that emphasizes cultural factors as central to driving human behavior, which is influenced by the ways leaders and their followers at levels ranging from individual and communal to national and transnational see themselves and, more importantly, their adversaries. More pointedly, British historian Bernard Lewis asserts that the Greater Middle East and the states situated therein must navigate a latticework of identities to which members of the population profess allegiance, contingent on the circumstances involved at a given juncture, explaining:

> The primary identities are those acquired at birth. These are of three kinds. The first is by blood, that is to say, in ascending order, the family, the clan, the tribe, developing

into the ethnic nation. The second is by place, often but not necessarily coinciding with the first and sometimes indeed in conflict with it. This may mean the village or neighborhood, district or quarter, province or city, developing in modern times into the country. The third, often linked with the first or second, or both, is the religious community, which may be subdivided into sects. For many, religion is the only loyalty that transcends local and immediate bonds. The second broad category of identity is that of allegiance to a ruler, in the past usually a hereditary monarch. This identity is normally acquired by birth. It may be changed by annexation, by transfer of power, or, for the individual, by migration, and, in modern times, naturalization. It is expressed in the obedience owed by the subject to the sovereign and to his multifarious representatives at the various levels at which a subject lives his life—the head of the state or of a department, the governor of a province or city, the administrator of a district, the headman of a village. In most of the world, and for most of the history of the Middle East, these two identities—the involuntary identity of birth and the compulsory identity of the state—were the only ones that existed. In modern times, under the influence of the West, a new kind is evolving between the two—the freely chosen cohesion and loyalty of voluntary associations, combining to form what is nowadays known as the civil society.[17]

For his part, the late historian of the Arab world Albert Hourani acknowledges the complexity of identity in the Middle East, but also emphasizes the strains of continuity spanning the millennia of the region's history, describing it as

a world where a family from southern Arabia could move to Spain, and after six centuries return nearer to its place of origin and still find itself in familiar surroundings, had a unity which transcended divisions of time and space; the Arabic language could open the door to office and influence throughout the world; a body of knowledge, transmitted over the centuries by a known chain of teachers, preserved a moral community even when rulers changed; places of pilgrimage, Mecca and Jerusalem, were unchanging poles of the human world even if power shifted from one city to another; and belief in a God who created and sustained the world could give meaning to the blows of fate.[18]

All of these scholars' approaches to the development of identity in the Middle East broadly is certainly applicable to the Iraqi case. While Iraq is as diverse as any state in that region, in terms of ethnicity, religious denomination and interpretation, and variable political and tribal affiliations and allegiances, it has been at the heart of the evolution of Islam from the very genesis and rapid enlargement of the Muslim world in the seventh century and certainly exhibits some of the aspects of historical timelessness to which Hourani refers. Consider, for example, the period of the Rightly Guided Caliphs (632–61) following the death of the Prophet Muhammad, during which the Shi'ite-Sunni Muslim divisions that persist in Iraq and across the Greater Middle East to this day were born. That period lasted from 632 to 661 and spanned the regimes of Abu Bakr (632–34), Umar ibn al-Khattab (634–44), Uthman ibn Affan (644–56) and Ali ibn Abi Talib (656–61). Known by Muslims generally and Sunnis specifically as a classical period of Islamic theological development and implementation, it was during this span that Muhammad's followers recorded the Qur'an based on the revelations the Prophet passed along during his lifetime, and then began to enlarge the territory the caliphate controlled and the membership in the ummah. Regrettably, tensions between factions loyal and opposed to Ali led to that caliph's assassination in 661 and the division of the ummah into Shi'a and Sunni denominations. The original cores of membership of those two strains of the faith were composed of those Muslims who supported the late Ali and those who did not.[19] That Sunni-Shi'a divide continues to drive conflict in the Greater Middle East generally and Iraq specifically to this day. Most significantly, the Islamic State of Iraq and Syria (ISIS), a terrorist organization that is driven by extreme interpretations of the Qur'an and boasts many of the attributes of a traditional state, has used sectarian divisions to maintain control over much of Iraq's Sunni-inhabited Anbar Province since the spring and summer of 2014.

Economic Aspects of the National Approach to Iraqi Nation- and State-Building, 2003–11

Unlike many weak, fragile and failing states, Iraq is blessed with a valuable natural resource (a petroleum supply among the world's largest), one that has the potential to fuel strong and enduring economic growth at both the national and provincial levels, albeit only if the environment is secure enough for the consistent extraction, shipment and sale of that resource. Yet, as with any state overly reliant on any one resource, Iraq is particularly vulnerable to threats to control over its oil, whether posed by domestic and/or foreign actors. Essentially, it must supply the security necessary to continue to improve the physical infrastructure to use those resources productively and consistently so over a significant period of time. Assuming effective protection of its resources and systemic reforms, Iraq will be able to compete more effectively at both the regional and global levels. Such reforms include long-term safeguards against centralized state control over the economy and the accompanying fiscal profligacy, governmental corruption and income inequality. Regrettably, however, governmental corruption remains a significant problem for Iraq, which was ranked 161st of 168 in Transparency International's 2014 "Corruption Perceptions Index," with the highest number signifying the world's most corrupt state.[20]

The ongoing economic reconstruction of Iraq has proceeded irregularly, contingent on the extent of security and political stability at a given juncture from its very inception in the context of the 2003–04 CPA process. In terms of economic growth, Iraq's Gross Domestic Product (GDP) has fluctuated regularly since 2003, as has the degree of security and political and social stability in that state from one year to the next. For example, when the CPA was established with Bremer at the helm in June 2003, the most daunting economic challenges grew out of infrastructure that had either been damaged or destroyed during the prosecution of OIF or, more often, lay in need of repairs resulting from prolonged use and/or poor maintenance. As time progressed, concurrent with the conduct of nation- and state-building operations and combinations of multiple Iraqi domestic- and foreign-driven insurgencies that emerged in response, American and Iraqi leaders and officials and the institutions they run have resigned themselves to focusing on those economic achievements that the security environment allows at a given temporal juncture.

Temporally, it is best to organize the forthcoming examination of the extent and types of economic growth over four distinctive periods: 2003–04, under the auspices of Bremer's CPA; 2004–07, as sectarian conflict, primarily between Iraqi Shi'ites and Sunnis, but also including the foreign-fighter-led and -driven al Qaeda in Iraq (AQI), fostered anarchy, particularly in Baghdad and the adjoining Sunni Triangle; 2007–09, as the U.S. military "surge" of 30,000 additional troops in the Iraqi capital and a complementary alliance of convenience between American forces and Sunni tribal leaders in Anbar Province nearly destroyed AQI and restored order to much of the country; and 2009–11, as the U.S. force drawdown and final withdrawal unfolded under the leadership of President Barack H. Obama.

Above all, two related policies instituted by Bremer—the disbandment of the Iraqi Army and the broader purge of civilians associated with Saddam's regime, both of which fell under the banner of de-Ba'athification— undermined the prospects for economic recovery (and eventual growth) from the outset of the CPA's nearly year-long period in control of Iraq. First, the demobilization of the Iraqi Army left officers and enlisted men alike embittered and desperate for the means to support their families. Second, the broader de-Ba'athification process of the demobilization was just one component of a purge that permeated all parts of the Iraqi economic and political system, with disproportionately negative consequences for the Sunni minority.[21]

By the end of CPA rule, Iraq was on the brink of, if not fully embroiled in, a ferocious sectarian conflict pitting majority Shi'a Muslims against minority Sunnis and (to a lesser degree) Kurds, which left the state struggling to maintain the physical security and political stability necessary for economic recovery, let alone enduring growth. The insecurity that permeated Iraq from 2004 to 2006 presented understandable (but still daunting) economic challenges during that period. Most notable among such challenges were interethnic and -religious disputes over control of Iraq's oil fields and the violence that such disputes entailed, which disrupted production, reducing profits and contributing to ever greater political instability in the process.

The U.S. military "surge" of 2007–09 provided both a welcome respite from the sectarian violence that permeated Iraq from 2004 to 2006 and a renewed hope for eventual economic progress, if not prosperity. The surge was Bush's decisive answer to challenges presented by the sectarian violence that left much of Iraq in a virtual state of anarchy from 2004 to 2006. And, ultimately, that bold decision was his, and it came amidst a domestic political environment that led many of the president's advisors to recommend drawing down rather than expanding the American commitment to Iraq. As Bush recalls in his memoirs, "Years from now, historians may look back and see the surge as a forgone conclusion, an inevitable bridge between the years of violence that followed liberation and the democracy that emerged. Nothing about the surge felt inevitable at the time. Public opinion ran strongly against it. Congress tried to block it. The enemy fought relentlessly to break our will."[22]

The end of the highly successful "surge" strategy planned and implemented by the George W. Bush administration from 2007 through the end of Bush's final term in office coincided with the inauguration of President Barack H. Obama in January 2009. From there, Obama placed an immediate emphasis on a military drawdown that left U.S. economic interests in Iraq considerably less secure than would likely, if not assuredly, have been the case with the retention of a substantial American ground presence, even if only 5,000–15,000, as opposed to the December 2011 withdrawal of all remaining forces.

Military/Security Aspects of the National Approach to Iraqi Nation- and State-Building, 2003–11

When assessing the military aspects of U.S. intervention in Iraq, one must consider three related temporal periods and sets of events: the prosecution of OIF from March to May 2003, which successfully eliminated Saddam's regime; the subsequent conduct of U.S.-led nation- and state-building operations in Iraq from June 2003 to December 2011; and the time since the withdrawal of U.S. forces in December 2011 to the present. Notwithstanding the utility of the prosecution of OIF, the period since the elimination of Saddam's regime has clearly presented far more security challenges than the Iraqi dictator ever did.

With respect to military planning and strategy, it is difficult to find many weaknesses in the conduct of OIF itself, particularly given the achievement of the removal of Saddam's regime in less than two months. The rapidity of the victory of the United States and its coalition partners, most significantly the United Kingdom, was at least partially the result of a lack of resistance, as much of the Iraqi Army simply faded back into the population rather than mount a strong defense of Baghdad. However, those forces retained the option of rejoining the fight at a later date, and many did in fact end up confronting the United States and its coalition partners as they attempted to carry out nation- and state-building operations as effectively as possible.[23]

The most daunting challenges U.S. military forces faced after what little resistance Saddam's forces presented quickly faded away were associated with playing roles American servicemen and women were then largely unaccustomed to. Managing the anarchy of a society suddenly deprived of the Ba'ath Party system—which nearly all Iraqis feared; many, if not most, despised; but nearly everyone depended on in some ways—proved difficult in several ways. First, the immediate needs of the population had to be met, most notably so with respect to basic necessities such as water, food and sanitation. Second, an assessment of Iraq's infrastructure in that state's most economically significant sector (the petroleum industry) had to be made, followed by needed modernization. Third came the perpetual political challenges to determine who among Iraq's ethnic and religious groups would operate petroleum extraction facilities and how to distribute eventual revenues from sales of those extraordinarily valuable resources.

The initial challenges triggered by the implosion of the Iraqi armed forces, most notably the physical insecurity, political instability and societal strife that came quickly on the heels of the fall of Baghdad, were managed by the U.S. military units controlling that capital city on the Euphrates and Tigris Rivers. Over the longer term, those responsibilities were distributed among a broader array of American, coalition and Iraqi actors, which are best explored temporally in the following manner: the prosecution of OIF from March to May 2003, which successfully eliminated Saddam's regime; the subsequent conduct of U.S.-led nation- and state-building operations in Iraq from June 2003 to December 2011; and the time since the withdrawal of U.S. forces in December 2011 to the present.

From a battlefield perspective, the conduct of OIF went extraordinarily smoothly, with a "shock and awe" air campaign to soften Iraqi defenses, especially in Baghdad, preceding a ground invasion that began across the border in Kuwait, then proceeded rapidly north to the capital. Upon arrival in Baghdad, American forces from the Fourth Infantry Division found a city and surrounding area in chaos as a result of the abandonment of the fight by Saddam's government and army alike, which left a rudderless public service sector unable to support the citizenry. It was filled by default by American military forces trained for combat rather than the policing and public service duties the inhabitants of Baghdad now lacked.[24] As George Packer, who covered the war in Iraq for the *New Yorker*, notes, "The Iraqi state had collapsed, and there was nothing to take its place."[25]

One of the most significant shortcomings of U.S. military intervention in Iraq was a dearth of planning for the post-conflict reconstruction and broader nation- and state-building efforts that would necessarily follow the fall of Saddam's regime, over both the short and longer terms. The strategy for OIF emphasized a rapid advance of U.S. forces from southern Iraq north to Saddam's base of power in Baghdad, where the defeat of the regime was expected to occur expeditiously, which did indeed prove the case. The trouble is that the Bush administration misjudged the challenges it would face once the regime was gone and the deficiencies of the system and society over which Saddam presided became suddenly and glaringly apparent. As Francis Fukuyama suggests, "The U.S. administration seemed to think that democracy and a market economy were default conditions to which the country would automatically revert once Saddam Hussein's dictatorship was removed, and seemed genuinely surprised when the Iraqi state itself collapsed into an orgy of looting and civil conflict."[26]

To succeed, states and those who lead them must learn from their mistakes, which is often difficult to do, especially for individuals in positions of power and authority. The aforementioned surge and accompanying strategic alliances demonstrate that, notwithstanding its planning blunders prior to the removal of Saddam's regime from power and nation- and state-building struggles on the ground in Iraq from 2003 to 2006, the Bush administration did have the capacity and will to adapt and shift its strategic approach. It did so by coupling the increase in U.S. forces the surge entailed with strategic alliances with Sunni tribal leaders eager to rid Anbar Province of the AQI presence and the extreme interpretations of Islam it imposed. The resulting decreases in AQI power and influence restored a measure of stability to Iraq that remained in place until the American drawdown the Obama administration emphasized from 2009 to 2011.

So long as the United States maintained a substantial military presence in Iraq, it retained at least a measure of influence over the political direction and behavior of the Shi'a-led national government in Baghdad. Absent that presence, Washington's ability to ensure at least some relevant role for the minority Sunnis situated in Anbar Province in national policymaking has been severely curtailed, if not eliminated altogether. The end result of the reduction of the American military commitment to Baghdad is an Iraq in which Iran on one hand, and the Islamic State of Iraq and Syria that rose from the proverbial ashes of AQI in the early 2010s on the other, enjoy greater power and influence than the United States.[27]

Political Aspects of the National Approach to Iraqi Nation- and State-Building, 2003–11

Perhaps the most complicated of the components of U.S.-led nation- and state-building efforts in Iraq is the political one. That is the case primarily because of the ethnic, religious and tribal divisions that pervade Iraq and the difficulty in establishing and maintaining a cohesive state that serves the interests of such a diverse array of actors. As with the assessment of the military aspects of nation- and state-building operations in Iraq, the political aspects of such efforts are best examined in stages, beginning with the establishment of the CPA in June 2003.

Under Bremer's leadership, the CPA was responsible for the governance of Iraq over the ensuing year. The challenges the United States and its coalition partners faced were daunting, particularly with respect to achieving the requisite security to begin building and maintaining economic and political stability, let alone facilitating even marginal levels of cooperation between Iraq's diverse cultural, ethnic, religious and tribal groups. As Diamond explains, the Bush administration "lacked an effective political strategy for postwar Iraq.... Part of the problem was that [the CPA generally and Bremer specifically] failed to comprehend how Iraqis perceived them—and the entire occupation. Throughout the occupation, the coalition lacked the linguistic and area expertise necessary to understand Iraqi politics and society, and the few long-time experts present were excluded from the inner circle of decisionmaking in the CPA."[28]

In fact, an interim Iraqi government assumed political control from the U.S.-led CPA in June 2004, and elections for permanent representative institutions unfolded with participation levels near 70 percent in December 2004. The first two stages of that process also went forward smoothly, with more than 60 percent of Iraqis voting in January 2005 elections for a transitional government and an October 2005 referendum to approve a national constitution.[29] However, maintaining political stability has been a perpetually daunting challenge in Iraq since then. Examples include Iraqi struggles to form a stable government in the aftermath of the disputed 2010 parliamentary elections and contentious relationships between the ruling Shi'ites and minority groups, especially the Sunnis, but also the Kurds, which grew markedly more pronounced following the U.S. military withdrawal in December 2011. Ultimately, those intra-state tensions contributed to the fall of the Maliki government in favor of one headed by another Shi'ite, Haider al-Abadi, in the summer of 2015.

As with the economic and military factors assessed in the two previous sections, the political impediments to nation- and state-building efforts in Iraq are best examined temporally in the following fashion: the prosecution of OIF from March to May 2003, which successfully eliminated Saddam's regime; the subsequent conduct of U.S.-led nation- and state-building operations in Iraq from June 2003 to December 2011; and the time since the withdrawal of U.S. forces in December 2011 to the present.

The political impediments to the conduct of the U.S.-led nation- and state-building project in Iraq prevalent from the outset of such efforts following the collapse of Saddam's regime in April 2003 had both American governmental and Iraqi domestic components. The former grew out of domestic opposition to U.S. intervention in Iraq and subsequent occupation of that state from 2003 to 2011. The latter reflected the ethnic, religious and tribal diversity prevalent in Iraq and the ways the history of internal conflict and divisions rooted in such diversity complicated the political processes therein. Under the management of Bremer's CPA, Iraq's nascent political system evolved structurally to allow for the eventual passage of a constitution mandating free elections and the development of enduring national institutions headquartered in Baghdad. However, in practice, Iraq's innate ethnic, religious and tribal diversity and group differences have continued to present daunting political challenges in the near dozen years since the CPA's dissolution in June 2004.

The Iraqi political system evolved in three related stages under American occupation from 2003 to 2011. The first stage, which is detailed above, was managed by the CPA and laid the foundation (albeit an imperfect one) for the creation and subsequent evolution of at least somewhat democratic institutions and processes beyond June 2004. The second stage featured the initial sets of Iraqi national voting processes for a transitional government and approval of a new constitution in January and October 2005, respectively, along with regular parliamentary elections in December 2005 and March 2010. Nouri al-Maliki emerged from the former election as Iraqi Prime Minister at the head of a Shi'a multiparty coalition. Maliki maintained that post following the latter election despite a challenge from Iyad Allawi, whose party won two more seats than Maliki's but failed to assemble a governing coalition. Maliki eventually built his own such coalition and retained power. The third stage commenced with the transition from the Bush administration to the Obama administration in 2009, continued through the end of the American military withdrawal in 2011, and was punctuated by Obama's emphasis on concluding Washington's commitment to nation- and state-building in Iraq.

The departure of U.S. combat forces from Iraq in December 2011 afforded greater latitude to the Maliki regime to further consolidate Shi'a political control over the national government in Baghdad at the expense of the minority Sunnis concentrated in the Anbar Province. Absent an American military presence on the ground, the United States had less leverage over the Iraqi government generally and Maliki specifically. The end result was even greater political marginalization of the Sunni tribes the Bush administration had aligned with to push AQI out of Anbar during the surge of 2007–08. Maliki's marginalization of the Sunnis created an atmosphere that allowed ISIS an easy path to seizure of much of north central and western Iraq over the first six months of 2014. Ultimately, despite maintaining control of the Iraqi government through the May 2014 parliamentary elections, Maliki was forced out in favor of another Shi'ite, Abadi, in August 2015. Abadi has remained in that position since.

Drawing Insights from the Nation- and State-Building Case of Iraq

As with any case of nation- and/or state-building, one of the principal benefits of investigating the example of the national approach applied in Iraq from 2003 to 2011 is to develop insights that are applicable to other cases in the future. It is appropriate to structure that assessment in terms of insights applicable within the cultural, economic, military/security and political issue areas, as well across those areas. Perhaps the best place to begin that discussion is with an assessment of the costs and benefits of U.S. intervention in Iraq, both from the perspectives of intervening actors at the state, intergovernmental and nongovernmental levels and also the Iraqi domestic and Persian Gulf and Greater Middle Eastern regional levels.

Culturally, the most significant insight to draw from nation- and state-building efforts in Iraq is the very importance of developing a clear understanding of a state's domestic political actors and their identities prior to intervening, especially with respect to a nation- and/or state-building project, in order to help determine how to put that polity back together after the presiding regime has been eliminated. Put simply, not nearly enough serious thought was given to the ethnic, religious denominational, and interpretive and tribal diversity of the Iraqi state that Saddam and his minority Sunni Ba'ath Party regime simply suppressed, by force if necessary. That must change when, or given the costs of nation- and state-building efforts in Iraq, if the United States engages in such projects in the future. A dearth of understanding of the culture of a state under reconstruction is a sure (and potentially irreversible) start on the path to a failed endeavor.

Economically, the costs and benefits of rebuilding Iraq are interdependent. In short, those states, international organizations and NGOs participating in nation- and state-building operations in that state have paid significant financial costs in the short term—the United States, for instance, spent more than $1 trillion in Iraq from 2003 to 2011—that may or may not prove as beneficial as originally anticipated, over the longer term. In the end, the degree to which investment in both economic and political development in Iraq will hinge on the level of internal security, the durability of that state's infrastructure, and the capacity of its political actors to co-exist peacefully, if not cooperate fully.

From the U.S. perspective, the most relevant political costs and benefits of intervention and subsequent nation- and state-building efforts in Iraq are both domestic and international in orientation. Domestically, the economic and military costs of nation- and state-building efforts in Iraq consumed the George W. Bush administration's foreign policy and national security agendas from the intervention in Iraq in March 2003 through the end of his second term in office in January 2009. Ironically, Iraq also consumed the Obama administration, more after the withdrawal of U.S. forces in December 2011 than before, as a result of ISIS's seizure of more than one-third of that country and nearly all of the Sunni-dominated Anbar Province since the start of 2014. The human and economic costs of the occupation of Iraq produced a level of discontent in the American electorate that helped to sweep Obama into office via the November 2008 presidential election.

At the international level, the intervention led to most significant rupture in transatlantic relations in the history of the North Atlantic Treaty Organization, with the United Kingdom joining Washington, and France and Germany opposing intervention. With respect to Iraq itself, and perhaps the Persian Gulf and broader Greater Middle East, American credibility was at stake on two levels. First, Bush promised to replace Saddam's autocratic regime with enduring liberal democratic institutions, irrespective of the economic and physical costs (in dollars and lives, respectively). Second, he pledged to achieve that objective with or without economic and military assistance from American allies and the broader international community. The United States remained committed to those pledges through the end of Bush's second term in office. However, once Obama commenced his tenure in the White House, the U.S. emphasis shifted quickly to a drawdown and subsequent withdrawal of all remaining American forces by the end of 2011, which his administration did indeed achieve.

The end of the U.S. military presence contributed significantly to two related outcomes on the ground in Iraq. First, it reduced the extent of Washington's influence over the Iraqi government generally and Maliki specifically. Consequently, with the American military stick now absent and continuing support from neighboring Shi'a majority Iran, Maliki saw no reason to refrain from using all available means to marginalize the roles of Sunni communities relative to the majority Sunnis in the Iraqi political system. Second, relegation to the political periphery left the Sunnis embittered and fully removed from any sense of a common Iraqi national identity. As a result, many, if not most, Sunni majority areas of Iraq lacked the requisite degree of solidarity with the Shi'a-led national government in Baghdad to render those parts of the country dependable when ISIS swept through in 2014. Instead, there was minimal resistance to ISIS, whose members are Sunnis, albeit those supportive of extreme interpretations of Islam. Ultimately, at least in the short term, the Sunni tribes who aligned with the United States against AQI during the 2007–08 surge view the Shi'a-controlled government and its Iranian backers as graver threats than ISIS.

Conclusions

This chapter was designed to achieve seven related objectives. First, it presented a synopsis of the relevant literature on national approaches to nation- and state-building projects. Second, it examined the diplomatic prologue to the prosecution of Operation Iraqi Freedom in the spring of 2003. Third, it examined the cultural challenges associated with the national approach to nation- and state-building efforts in Iraq. Fourth, it examined the economic aspects of that approach. Fifth, it examined the military/security aspects of that approach. Sixth, it examined the political aspects of that approach. And, seventh, it drew insights from the case of Iraq that will help inform future U.S.-led nation- and state-building efforts broadly and those in the Greater Middle East in particular.

Above all, collectively, the preceding examinations of each of the above issues in depth in the main sections of the chapter reveal some basic truths about nation- and state-building projects generally and the case of Iraq specifically. Such truths are best identified and explained both contextually in the issue areas involved, whether related to cultural, economic, political and/or security factors, and also in terms of the relationships between actors in those areas as they interact, both diplomatically and in practical terms in carrying out initiatives and operations on the ground.

Culturally, Iraq is as diverse as any state in the Greater Middle East. That diversity grows out of differences in ethnicity, religious faiths, belief systems and theological interpretations, and, often most important of all, tribal affiliations. The principal three ethno-religious groups at odds over a variety of issues are the majority Shi'a and minority Sunni Arab Muslims, along with the Kurds, who also practice a variant of Sunni Islam but have marked ethnic, cultural and related political differences with the other two groups. Those differences, in turn, have permeated (and complicated) the relationships among all three groups in the issue areas of economics, politics and security, concluding assessments of which follow.

Economically, Iraq retains promise, if only because of the extensive petroleum resources with which it has long been blessed. The problem is that realizing that promise is by no means assured, given the internal and external challenges it faces, even if one were to focus exclusively on issues directly associated with economic development. That is, of course, not a realistic option, as it is not possible to consider the economic issues involved in isolation from those in the cultural, military and political contexts. The past dozen years of nation- and state-building efforts in Iraq, as well as the broader history of similar projects in other parts of the Greater Middle East and developing world, are illustrative of precisely that.

Politically, Iraq is divided and will all but surely remain so moving forward. The aforementioned cultural diversity, punctuated by deep ethnic, religious and tribal differences and competition over Iraq's oil, have produced political polarization between its distinctive groups. Such differences have been complicated further by the seizure and maintenance of control over significant swaths of Iraqi territory by ISIS since early 2014. Most significantly, ISIS has used the Sunni-Shi'a divide to its advantage in maintaining control over Sunni tribal territory in western Iraq by pitting tribal leaders against the Shi'a-controlled national government in Baghdad.

Ultimately, how the future unfolds for Iraq in each of the above three issue areas will be conditioned by security conditions on the ground in that state at a given temporal juncture. Those conditions, in turn, are sure to be driven by three related sets of internal and external factors: first, the extent to which the Iraqi security forces can maintain order, with the understanding that the challenges to that objective will often vary from one province and time period to another; second, the degree to which the Iraqi political system retains a structure that marginalizes the Sunni minority in ways that ISIS can use to its advantage in maintaining control over much, if not all of western Iraq; and third, the evolution of the roles of regional powers such as Iran, Saudi Arabia and Turkey, and global powers such as the United States and Russia. Given their geographic proximity alone, the regional powers specified have no choice but to remain involved in Iraqi political and security matters. This is particularly true for an ascendant Iran. Further, the level of U.S. involvement in Iraq, most significantly Washington's military commitment, will continue to help condition how much influence Iran and its ally, Russia, wield therein moving forward.

CHAPTER 9

Nation-Building and Civil Society: Mitchelville

Critical to the success of a local-level nation-building effort such as the one attempted in Vietnam is the development of civil society. Indeed, a handbook of the United States Agency for International Development asserts, "Advancing the capacity of local governments to act effectively and accountably *requires* promoting the desire and capacity of civil society organizations and individual citizens to take responsibility for their communities, participate in local priority-setting, assist in the implementation of those decisions, and then monitor their effectiveness."[1]

Modern-day nation-builders describe civil society as occupying "the political space between the individual and the government." It includes a variety of organizations and activities, all of which "contribute to a democratic society and nonviolent political transition from war to peace" by performing a multitude of functions.[2] Civil society "can help shape and focus the energies of concerned citizens"[3] and enable them to have an impact on government decisions without necessarily competing for political power or resorting to violence. It gives a voice to minority and other marginalized groups. It helps increase government transparency, accountability, and responsiveness.[4] Without civil society, "politics becomes a murderous grab for power" and "democracy may not take root."[5]

Civil society "is believed to be closely related to the successful emergence of democratic practice."[6] Indeed, nation-building experts point to civil society as being a critical component of development, and other scholars declare it "the bedrock of democracy."[7] Conversely, its absence during the communist era is generally credited as having been a major impediment to Russia's transition to democracy.[8] The experimental freedmen's village of Mitchelville that was founded on Hilton Head Island, South Carolina, in 1862 is an excellent example of the role played by civil society within societies in transition and the importance of the participatory approach to such developmental efforts.

The Federal Capture of Port Royal

Port Royal Sound, South Carolina, was the finest natural harbor on the Southern seaboard, and its possession was critical to the Federal Navy's ability to execute the blockade of the Atlantic coast. On October 20, 1861, Captain Samuel Du Pont led a "Great Southern Expedition" of seventy-four vessels, including transports for a land force of 12,000 men, out of Hampton Roads, Virginia, headed for Port Royal. The Confederates quickly ascertained Du Pont's intentions, and on November 6, President Jefferson Davis reorganized the coasts of South Carolina, Georgia, and north Florida into a single department, naming General Robert E. Lee as its commander.

In spite of these preparations, the Confederates remained at a tremendous disadvantage when Du Pont attacked on November 7. Port Royal Sound was big enough to allow maneuver, and Du Pont developed a brilliant plan to use his steam engines to keep his ships moving in an elliptical pattern which would keep the two Confederate forts, Fort Walker and Fort Beauregard, under continuous fire.

Du Pont quickly brushed aside a weak Confederate flotilla of three tugs, each mounting one gun, and a converted river steamer, and turned his attention to the forts. With each pass of the elliptical maneuver, Du Pont's squadron widened its course so as to bring its guns closer to the target. These constant changes in speed, range, and deflection made the Federal fleet extremely hard for the Confederate gunners to engage.

Confederate resistance did not last long. As Du Pont began his third ellipse, he received word that Fort Walker had been abandoned. Fort Beauregard, which was merely an adjunct to Fort Walker, surrendered soon thereafter.

The Federals lost eight killed and twenty-three wounded. The Confederates lost about 100 total. The victory gave the Federals an excellent harbor that became the home base for the South Atlantic Blockading Squadron for the remainder of the war. Moreover, it struck a blow in both the sentimental heartland of secession and in an important cotton-producing region.

The Port Royal Experiment

In the wake of Du Pont's victory, many coastal and Sea Island planters withdrew further inland to escape Federal occupation. Their sudden departure left behind some 10,000 now masterless slaves. While these black Sea Islanders obviously welcomed this unexpected development, many found themselves entirely unprepared for their new freedom.

Lacking a sufficient policy or plan for the Federal occupation of the Sea

Islands and the subsequent flight of the white population and abandonment of their slaves, Secretary of the Treasury Salmon Chase dispatched Boston attorney Edward Pierce to Port Royal to assess the situation. Pierce headed south on January 13, 1862, and upon arriving found the Reverend Mansfield French was also on the scene conducting his own exploratory visit at the request of the American Missionary Association. Both men agreed on the wisdom of sending missionaries and teachers to assist the development of the Sea Islands blacks and resolved to generate such support. In a January 19 letter to Chase, Pierce explained the need for such "persons of good sense who could mingle with their religious exhortations advice and counsel as to how these people should act in their new condition, that is, be industrious, orderly, and sober."[9]

Local military commanders agreed with Pierce's assessment and solution. On February 6, Brigadier General Thomas Sherman issued General Order No. 9 in which he stated, "The helpless condition of the blacks inhabiting the vast area in the occupation of the forces of this command calls for immediate action on the part of a highly favored and philanthropic people.... Never was there a nobler or more fitting opportunity for the operation of that considerate and practical benevolence for which the Northern people have ever been distinguished."[10]

Existing and newly formed religious and abolitionist organizations took up the cause, and an eclectic flood of Northern reformers, missionaries, abolitionists, and educators, collectively known as the "Gideonites," soon descended upon the Sea Islands, unleashing what became known as the "Port Royal Experiment." The novel freedmen's village at Mitchelville was a singular aspect of this broader initiative. Among the organizations most active at Mitchelville were the New England Freedmen's Aid Society (NEFAS) and the American Missionary Association (AMA). (The nation-building role of the modern-day successors of nongovernmental organizations such as these will be discussed in greater detail in Chapter 11.)

Before he left for his exploratory visit to the Sea Islands, Pierce gained the enthusiastic support of the Reverend Jacob Manning, assistant pastor of Old South Church in Boston.[11] In a January 19, 1862, letter from Port Royal to Manning, Pierce confirmed the need of "ministering to these lowest poor children," adding "the compensation and support of such [relief workers] should be derived exclusively from private purses."[12] Manning published Pierce's letter in the January 27 *Boston Transcript* while other prominent Bostonians began sending invitations to a meeting to discuss the matter at Manning's house on February 4.[13] A chairman and secretary were named at this initial meeting, and three days later, a second meeting of seventeen attendees was held at the local Young Men's Christian Association. This group formed the Boston Educational Commission (BEC) and adopted a constitution with the purpose of promoting "the industrial, social, intellectual, moral and religious elevation of persons released from Slavery in the course of the War for the Union." Reflecting the impressive stature of the membership, Massachusetts Governor John Andrew was selected to serve as the commission's president.[14]

About two years later, the BEC was reorganized as the New England Freedmen's Aid Society or simply the New England Society. In both their forms, the Bostonian groups were philanthropic organizations without sectarian or political affiliation. Among those who labored on behalf of the NEFAS at Mitchelville were Gilbert and Antoinette Pillsbury and Elizabeth Breck.[15]

The American Missionary Association was an even more influential organization at Mitchelville. The AMA was founded in 1846 in Buffalo, New York, with the initial focus of establishing Christian missions around the world. From its inception, the AMA was strongly against slavery and considered the gospel to be a powerful abolitionist weapon.[16] In many ways, the AMA occupied the important antislavery middle ground between the Garrisonian demand for immediate, universal abolition and the older church mission boards that were often dominated by men willing to be more accommodating to slaveholding. The AMA represented a decidedly antislavery yet practical approach.[17]

The AMA's understanding of education as an important avenue for black advancement was demonstrated by its establishment of Berea College in Kentucky in 1859, and with the opportunities created by the Civil War, the AMA "felt itself specially called for and providentially equipped for ... the instruction and elevation of the colored people."[18] For the evangelical AMA, religion and education were inseparable. "Christian schools," it declared, "know absolutely nothing of education which does not magnify the Bible and keep it foremost."[19] Armed with this philosophical approach, the AMA quickly withdrew its missionary efforts elsewhere and "concentrated its energies upon this new field in the South."[20] The AMA dispatched the Reverend L.C. Lockwood to Hampton, Virginia, which led to the founding of the "first day-school for the Freedmen" on September 17, 1861, under the direction of Mary Peake.[21] It was also at the request of prominent AMA members Lewis Tappan and George Whipple that the Reverend Mansfield French was sent to the Sea Islands to determine what contribution the New York area could make there.[22]

The scope of the situation on the Sea Islands as reported by French gave the pragmatic AMA pause, and it feared the dire conditions exceeded its existing capabilities. Tappan and Whipple concluded, "The emergency required some further instrumentalists," which would be "likely to enlist a constituency that the Association could not reach."[23] To address this issue they called a public meeting at Cooper Institute on February 20. As a result, the National Freedmen's Relief Association (NFRA) was formed on February 22. Even though the NFRA was a distinct organization from the AMA, the ties remained strong. French, for example, although an officer of the NFRA, continued to send reports to Whipple at the AMA.[24]

E. Allen Richardson considers the NFRA "an attempt to broaden the AMA's ability to encompass a variety of ecclesiastical and secular interests," and its work "was intended as a demonstration of free-labor ideology."[25] The free-labor ideology was a complex amalgam that emphasized the value of work in a competitive, free-market economy. It assumed the superiority of Northern business practices and saw them as a model for Southern economic development.[26] For many free-labor thinkers, the problem facing the former slaves was that slavery had caused the destruction of families and family "instincts," a tendency to lie and steal, and a lack of self-reliance. The free-labor ideology held that these deficiencies could be overcome by education and that the former slaves could be prepared to take their place as free laborers in the competitive marketplace.[27]

In addition to giving impetus to the NFRA, by 1863 the AMA was also sending its own representatives directly into the field. These missionaries maintained a strong evangelical fervor and a desire to transform the freedmen. W.J. Richardson, the AMA representative in Beaufort, considered, "The great work is to unlearn them and learn them from, the vices, habits, and associations of their former lives."[28] Such a statement reflected the free-labor ideology that was prevalent in the AMA.[29]

The AMA saw the creation of the Freedmen's Bureau in 1865 as a welcome mechanism for focusing its free-labor initiatives. According to E. Allen Richardson, the resulting relationship was "unique, for in no other instance was power so completely integrated between church and state in a complex, symbiotic pattern of dual appointments, mutual agendas, and shared perceptions about the nature of Reconstruction."[30] The AMA's ties with both the NFRA and the Freedmen's Bureau helped ensure the dominance of the free-labor ideology in the Port Royal Experiment.

Unlike the other organizations, the AMA was in existence at the time of the seizure of Port Royal. Its head-start, infrastructure, size, and connections gave it considerable influence and economies of scale, especially in promoting its belief in the free-labor ideology and being able to sustain a longevity that eluded other organizations. By 1866, it fielded a force of 327 teachers on the Sea Islands.[31] Among the stalwart missionary teachers who served under AMA supervision at Mitchelville were Elizabeth Hill, Martha Clary, Margaret Burke, Effie Gould, and Ellen Seymour.[32]

The Refugee and Housing Crisis

Before these philanthropic organizations could focus on their evangelical and educational missions, however, many very practical humanitarian needs had to be met. Refugees and internally displaced persons besieged the Sea

Islands and saturated the available infrastructure at a rate that exceeded the throughput capacity. At its peak, the overall population of Sea Islands blacks had increased by over fifty percent, and on some single days, refugees amounting to nearly nine percent of the prewar population arrived in the area.[33] Such quantities simply overwhelmed available resources.

In his initial survey dated February 3, 1862, Pierce estimated a population of some eight thousand blacks under Federal protection on Sea Island plantations. Already, however, additions such as "negroes who have fled to Beaufort and Hilton Head from places not yet occupied by our forces" had swelled to nearly twelve thousand, swelling the number "we must now have thrown upon our hands, for whose present and future we must provide."[34] Elizabeth Hyde Botume wrote that Beaufort was "overflowing," and people "were quartered in every available place, and packed as closely as possible,—in churches and storehouses, and in the jail and arsenals." Nonetheless, Botume lamented, "There was still a great throng houseless, with no resting-place."[35] The worst was yet to come, with Pierce noting the number of new arrivals was "rapidly increasing."[36]

In addition to outside refugees, internally displaced persons also added to the instability. An early instance occurred in July 1862 when Major General David Hunter ordered the withdrawal of Federal troops from Edisto Island in order to concentrate his defenses. "Edisto is evacuated!" Laura Towne exclaimed, "and all the negroes brought to these islands." Beaufort was already "overcrowded with refugees," and the 1,600 new arrivals from Edisto, "with their household effects, pigs, chickens, and babies 'promiscuous,'" were sent to St. Helenaville, once a health resort that boasted a dozen or more mansions.[37] Another category of people arrived as Colonels James Montgomery and Thomas Higginson launched coastal raids to liberate slaves from Confederate rice plantations. One of the more notable of these expeditions was the June 1863 raid on Combahee that brought to Beaufort eight hundred members of "as poor and destitute a class of human beings as could possibly be found."[38] As a result of all these sources, a steady stream of homeless blacks needing almost all manner of care and services soon found themselves in the midst of the Port Royal Experiment.

The problem dramatically worsened as Major General William Sherman marched across Georgia from Atlanta to Savannah in late 1864. In his wake, countless slaves fled to his lines while others dispersed into the countryside. Reports vary as to how many refugees actually arrived at the coast with Sherman, but Major General Henry Slocum, who commanded the left wing of Sherman's march, estimated that seven thousand were still with the army when it reached Savannah.[39] Along the way, the wayfarers had endured much hardship, and for these suffering, homeless masses, the beckoning of the Sea Islands was "as clear as the polar star."[40] Even as Sherman presented Savannah "as a Christmas gift" to President Abraham Lincoln, "seven hundred cold, shivering, and hungry freedmen … in the direst need of every human requirement" were arriving at Beaufort.[41] Others soon followed in similar straits. Towne reports, "Very many come sick: indeed, nearly all are broken down with fatigue, privation of food, and bad air at night."[42] Botume writes, "With the army came a great gang of contrabands to be housed and rationed and taken care of."[43]

The numbers were staggering. Even with today's improved technological capabilities, getting accurate refugee counts is problematic, and contemporary reports from the Port Royal Experiment were further complicated by inconsistencies in geographic area of the count. In broad terms, however, Willie Lee Rose estimates "the Negro population … swelled from less than ten thousand at the time of the Federal occupation to more than fifteen thousand, even before any Sherman refugees arrived."[44] After this growth of over fifty percent, how many of the perhaps seven thousand blacks who arrived in Savannah with Sherman then migrated north to the immediate area around Port Royal and how long they stayed are unknown.

A variety of housing initiatives attempted to solve the mounting crisis. In his initial survey, Pierce described the slave quarters as each being assigned to a family and measuring sixteen feet by twelve feet. They were generally open, although some interiors were divided into sections by a partition. While conditions varied, Pierce found between ten and twenty sets of slave quarters on the plantations he visited.[45] Many were in poor repair, such as the "wretched hovels" Towne found at the old Jenkins, Fripp, and Edding's Point properties.[46] Austere to begin with, these houses certainly offered little hope of accommodating large numbers of refugees. The abandoned planters' homes provided relief for a fortunate few, but certainly not enough to make more than a small dent in the overall demand.[47]

The shortage of available housing and shelter complicated the Sea Islands' ability to accommodate refugees, and with all existing housing in use, tents were used as a stopgap measure until barracks were built.[48] With the advance of Sherman, temporary camps that had been built on the docks at Hilton Head and Savannah were overwhelmed. Lacking necessary shelter and sanitation, thousands died at these locations.[49]

Typical of the newly constructed housing was the village built to accommodate the refugees from Montgomery's raids. Botume describes these houses as resembling "huge wooden boxes" divided into four rooms. Each room was equipped with a fireplace, an opening for a window with a shutter, a double row of "berths" built against the wall for beds, one or more low benches, a pine table, and homemade cedar tubs. Each of these rooms accommodated a family of between five and fifteen members.[50] Adult women made up a large percentage of the population, in this case because many of the men were now serving in Montgomery's regiment.[51] The women made the best of the situation that they could, and Botume, finding herself "face to face with life in the 'one-roomed cabin,'" was favorably impressed by the fortitude of the occupants of these meager dwellings.[52]

Ormsby Mitchel and the Founding of Mitchelville

Such conditions were obviously unsatisfactory, and as early as October 1862, critics had observed, "The present negro quarters—a long row of partitions into which are crowded young and old, male and female, without respect either to quality or quantity, such has thus far been the necessity—having become a sort of Five Points [an allusion to a dilapidated section of Manhattan], half style, half brothel."[53] Among those who saw a better alternative was Major General Ormsby Mitchel, a multitalented West Pointer who had been assigned to South Carolina after running afoul of Major General Don Carlos Buell during the Federal Army's occupation of North Alabama. Presaging Major General William Sherman's policy of "hard war," Mitchel found himself at odds with Buell's conciliatory approach to the Confederate population and was recalled to Washington, then briefly sent to the Midwest on recruiting duty, before being appointed commander of the Department of the South.[54]

In this new capacity, Mitchel selected the Fish Haul Creek Plantation on the north end of Hilton Head Island as the site of a unique "experiment in citizenship" to develop "an actual town" rather than the earlier camps and barracks.[55] Mitchel described the site as "a beautiful piece of ground fronting upon the beach."[56] It was the property of Brigadier General Thomas Drayton, who had over 100 slaves there in 1860.[57] Mitchel described his plan in an October 13, 1862, letter to Secretary of the Treasury Salmon Chase:

> My model plantation, with its fields, fences, seeds, tillage, implements, houses, furniture, &c., would be organized with as little delay as possible. I would commence the buildings, which will be required for the large accessions of population which will certainly come to us, when we break through the enemy's line on the main land, which we are determined to do. I would have all the blacks distinctly informed as to the plan by which they were to be governed, educated, and made industrious and worthy citizens. I would tell them that the fruits of their future toil would be consecrated hereafter to their own benefit; to each family on the plantation I would give a separate dwelling, with a patch for their own private cultivation as a little garden. From estimates which I have carefully made, I am quite certain that an industrious family of three persons will certainly save from $150 to $200 each year. In five years such a family will have laid up in the Plantation Bank an amount sufficient to make them independent. And

then with industrious habits, with religious instruction, with correct moral views and sentiments, with minds properly trained to self-dependence, they may erect their own homes if they so choose, and begin the world for themselves.[58]

Unfortunately, Mitchel did not live to see his vision take shape. Already ill when he reported to South Carolina, Mitchel died of yellow fever in Beaufort on October 30, 1862, just weeks after writing his letter to Chase. However, his model village was completed in March 1863 and named Mitchelville in his honor.

What Mitchel had in mind was consistent with what black spokesman Garrison Frazier expressed during Secretary of War Edwin Stanton's visit to Major General William Sherman's army in January 1865, that he would "prefer to live by ourselves [rather than interspersed among whites], because there is a prejudice against us in the South that will take years to get over."[59] To that end, the local newspaper, *The New South*, announced on August 22, 1863, that "all colored servants of sutlers and other civilians will be required to remove to Mitchelville forthwith, unless they obtain a permit."[60] By the same token, white access to Mitchelville was controlled and limited by the military. It was Mitchel's intention to create a living space for the black population to have as its own.

Mitchel shared the belief of the NFRA and AMA in the free-labor ideology and its insistence on self-help. At the dedication of Mitchelville's First African Baptist Church, he told the audience that while he would "watch everything closely respecting this experiment.... Upon you depends whether this mighty result shall be worked out."[61] According to such a philosophy, Mitchel insisted "the negroes are to be made to build their own houses, and it is thought to be high time they should begin to learn what freedom means by experience of self-dependence, they are to be left as much as possible to themselves."[62]

Under this philosophy, government sawmills turned out great quantities of pine siding and beams from Hilton Head timber, but the local population did the construction.[63] Mitchel described the process in his October 13 letter to Secretary Chase: "I have at work a gang of fifty negroes, with a black man as foreman, and a white superintendent. The work is perfectly systematized; the houses of very simple structure; their various parts divided among gangs who work only on these parts. One gang is employed upon the frames, in getting them out and putting them up; another in getting out the sidings; another in putting up the sidings; another in splitting clap-boards for the roof; another in putting on the roof. And these fifty hands, now working earnestly and with high hope, are actually building a house a day."[64] The result was a cooperative effort in which the U.S. government provided the materials and supervision, but the future residents of Mitchelville gained a sense of ownership and personal investment from building their homes.

Although the architecture may have been somewhat rudimentary, it progressed with a palatable sense of energy and potential. Amid comments on the modest construction, a variety of observers sensed that Mitchelville represented something much more than the buildings. For example, Charles Carleton Coffin, an army correspondent for the *Boston Journal*, visited Mitchelville around the time of its completion. "At that time," he wrote, "there were about seventy houses,—or cabins rather,—of the rudest description, built of logs, chinked with clay brought up from the beach, roofs of long split shingles, board floors, windows with shutters,—plain board blinds, without sash or glass. Each house had a quarter of an acre of land attached. There was no paint or lime, not even whitewash, about them. It was just such as place as might be expected in a new country, where there were no saw-mills or brick-kilns, a step in advance of a hole in the ground or a bark wigwam." Coffin knew, however, that this was not the sum of Mitchelville. Even in this formative stage he could recognize Mitchelville "was the beginning of the experiment of civilization on the part of a semi-barbarous people just released from abject bondage, and far from being free men."[65]

As this transformation continued, NEFAS missionary Antoinette Pillsbury was awed by what she found at Hilton Head over a year after Coffin's visit. The living quarters were still eclectic, as Pillsbury describes them: "Some are made of round poles chinked with oyster-shell lime; some of slats; and some of boards, picked up and bought, of every conceivable size, while others are 'pieced out' with old canvas on the chimneys and roof." Like Coffin, however, Pillsbury saw the bigger picture. "This post," she wrote in September 1864, "is the great gateway of Freedom."[66] Reflecting significant growth from the time of Coffin's observation, Pillsbury wrote that Mitchelville now had "a population of from twelve to fifteen hundred."[67]

With its neatly arranged streets and quarter-acre lots, Mitchelville certainly looked the part of a community, but beyond these esthetic improvements also lay the framework for the institutions necessary to transition its residents from slavery and dependence to freedom and self-sufficiency. Visitors flocked to Mitchelville both to observe and be part of this bold initiative. On April 13, 1865, abolitionists William Lloyd Garrison and Theodore Titlon visited and attended church. John Nicolay, former secretary to President Lincoln and then consul to Paris, also attended. Secretary of War Simon Cameron visited with a Congressional delegation after the war and contributed money to a chapel that the congregation then named St. Simon's in his honor.[68] In recording his favorable impressions of Mitchelville's school system on his tour of the South between May 1, 1865 and May 1, 1866, newspaper editor Whitelaw Reid noted, "General Mitchel was one of Cincinnati's contributions to the war. But is Cincinnati behind Mitchelville?"[69]

More important than these visiting dignitaries were those who came to

Hilton Head in general and Mitchelville in particular to work, often as missionary teachers. The result was an eclectic blend of blacks and whites, military and civilian, locals and refugees, and relief workers and those in need of assistance who all labored together to help improve society. As such, Mitchelville is an instructive case study of how what today are called "nation-builders" can partner with indigenous stake-holders to foster development based on an effective mix of government and private-sector outside resources and a local sense of ownership of the process.[70]

Mitchelville as an Experimental Model Civil Society

For many individuals and organizations associated with the Port Royal Experiment, civil society was built upon "the four corner-stones of the church, the school-house, the militia, and the town-meeting," because it was these institutions that provided for "the essential rights of religion, education, self-defense, and self-government."[71] These concepts provide a convenient model for chronicling the characteristics of Mitchelville and its development.

The Church and Religion

Nation-building expert James Dobbins notes, "In many postconflict societies, civil society organizations are at work prior to the war. When present, the international community should utilize already existing capacity and build on that foundation."[72] Such was the case at Port Royal, where Willie Lee Rose noted, "One form of leadership known to Negroes even in slavery had been the church."[73] Likewise, Edward Pierce, on his initial fact-finding visit in January 1862, found "natural chiefs" had emerged among the black population, in part "by virtue of religious leadership," and he felt these individuals, if "first addressed, may exert a healthful influence on the rest."[74] The Reverend Abraham [sometimes cited as Abram] Murchison [sometimes cited as Mercherson], for example, served both as a pastor and mayor and became "a pivotal figure" at Mitchelville.[75]

This expression of the church's leadership role continued after Reconstruction. As legal opportunities for blacks were rapidly diminishing, "the church became the legal foundation of the community." Indeed, churches built at Mitchelville were "the center of religious, social, political, and educational life."[76] Murchison personally emerged as "the religious and secular leader of local blacks."[77]

Pierce observed the regular and self-regulated church activity of the Sea

Islanders.[78] He wrote, "Religion contributes a large part of life's interest to the inhabitants of Port Royal," and it was in this pursuit that he believed "not only their soul, but their mind finds here its principal exercise."[79] Given this dominant position and head start, the Sea Islanders were quick to enlarge this aspect of civil society.

The August 30, 1862, edition of *The New South* reported "the organization of the First Baptist Church of Hilton Head and the ordination of its pastor ... on the Sabbath before last." The paper noted that of the church's 120 members, "nearly 70 were professing Christians under the rule of their late masters, while the others have been converted and baptized since our advent among them." Four Federal Army chaplains superintended the service, and Abraham Murchison was "duly installed as ... pastor."[80]

A *New York Times* correspondent visiting the Department of the South declared Murchison "a remarkable Negro ... of very considerable intelligence and ability ... [whose] influence over the negroes here is immense."[81] An example of Murchison's standing was his involvement in the recruiting of black soldiers. After a private interview with Department of the South commander Major General David Hunter, Murchison called a meeting of all black males on April 7, 1862. Only two white men—the superintendent and head carpenter at Hilton Head—were present, and it was Murchison who held center stage. With "a great deal of clearness and force," he explained "the obligations and interests" associated with military service. Murchison's appeal "rose to eloquence" as he described "the labors, hardships and dangers, as well as the advantages of soldier life." He "was listened to with the most breathless interest," and at the end of the meeting, 105 recruits were enrolled. Within a week the number of volunteers had reached 150.[82]

Murchison was equally dynamic as a preacher. A *New York Times* reporter noted Murchison's "sermon was marked by considerable originality and a closeness of logic that surprised me; and the evident sincerity of his ministrations gave it an interest which does not always attend more pretentious efforts." The reporter was also impressed by the congregation, whom he found "attentive and decorous" and "all ... decently dressed."[83] Murchison reportedly baptized over a thousand freedmen during the war.[84]

Murchison's personal influence was joined by that of the First African Baptist Church. Located at the intersection of what are now known as Beach City Road and Mathews Drive, the landmark was often referred to as "Crossroads Church." Its importance was such that it "gave birth to all the black Baptist churches on the island."[85] St. James Baptist, for example, was founded in 1886 by former members of the First African Baptist Church.[86] Other denominations also established churches, such as the Queen Chapel African Methodist Episcopal Church, founded by AME missionaries and Hilton Head residents in 1865. Local lore holds that the church's first service was held under a live oak, with entertainment "afforded by the Mitchelville section on Hilton Head in which began an early AME church mission."[87]

Although whites often played a role in helping the churches get established, by July 1865, Pierce noted, "Nearly the whole church management is now in the hands of the blacks, who have regular deacons and preachers."[88] This ascension of indigenous leadership, however, did not mean the outside developers viewed the church solely as a sterile instrument of civil society. From the start, Pierce's call was for "missionaries," and there would always be an evangelical and denominational component to this aspect of the Port Royal Experiment.[89]

The Schoolhouse and Education

Almost inseparably linked to religion during the Port Royal Experiment was education, but this aspect of civil society was buffeted from much of the conflict that sometimes hamstrung church efforts. The Gideonites may have quarreled over many things, but "they were as one on the question of education; this gift seemingly came with no strings attached."[90] As for the Sea Islanders, their appetite for learning was insatiable. One told William Gannett, "We pant for it, sir."[91] Another told Elizabeth Botume, "Us wants to larn, fur we've been in darkness too long, an' now we're in the light, us wants to larn."[92] Even as the Gideonites descended on Port Royal, they learned that slave Will Capers "while his master was here had run a secret night-school for men."[93] Superintendents found that "the Negroes ... will do anything for us, if we only teach them."[94] It was perhaps this mutual enthusiasm and shared purpose that made education "the most successful branch of the experiment."[95]

Even before Edward Pierce's visit to Port Royal, the AMA had rushed missionaries to start schools in the area. The Reverend Solomon Peck established a school at Beaufort on January 8, 1862. Barnard Lee opened another on Hilton Head later that month.[96] The AMA eventually reported five schools in Mitchelville.[97]

Attrition among the teachers associated with the Port Royal Experiment was high, but some, like Jane Briggs Smith, proved to be stalwart in their commitment. Smith taught at Mitchelville under the sponsorship of the NEFAS chapter at Cambridgeport, Massachusetts.[98] "An unsentimental Garrisonian abolitionist," Smith was a staunch advocate of the "social justice" she felt was due to the black people.[99] Completely devoted to her work with the freedmen, in 1866 she wrote to her future husband, "My duty is there, my inclination leads me there; a great noble work is there which I am fitted to help do; my heart is in it—why should I turn away?[100]

In addition to whites such as Smith, there were many black contributors to the educational effort at Mitchelville. One was Lyman Anders, who was able to build a twenty-by-forty-foot building that served as a church and school. Anders was apparently a remarkable personality, having come to Hilton Head from Key West, Florida. He was one of the many former slaves who had joined the ranks of the Union Army. Anders was educated, not only knowing how to read and write, but also possessing a library valued at some one hundred dollars.

Antoinette Pillsbury was among the missionaries who were impressed by Anders and his project. Describing Anders as "very gentlemanly and unassuming," Pillsbury solicited funds from the NEFAS to help him complete his plans to install a floor and a few windows in his building. Pillsbury also recommended that if "an addition of twenty feet square could be made at the end or side for the accommodation of teachers [to live in], it would be an excellent position for a school." Pillsbury challenged her readers, "Is there not some town which will take this matter in hand, build the addition, and send a teacher? The expense of a teachers' room has been computed at about $250."[101]

Pillsbury's request was honored, and the 1866 Annual Report of the Missionary Society, Sunday-School Union and Tract Society of the Methodist Episcopal Church described Anders as having "a Church of about fifty members, and a flourishing little Sabbath-school." It was built, according to Anders, "by subscriptions from the white and colored people." Of the $350 required, he reported "the colored have given $94, and the Thirty-second colored troops from Pennsylvania paid $87.35." The superintendent boasted that Anders "is doing all in Mitchelville that any other missionary could do." In fact, in addition to Landers's duties as preacher and teacher, he was also acting as a "Trial Justice."[102]

The Militia and Self-Defense

A host of nation-building experts agree that before subsequent development can take root, an initial sense of security must be established.[103] To meet this requirement, a fort was built just south of Mitchelville in the fall of 1864 to protect the town from the possibility of Confederate raids. Two main roads approached Mitchelville from the southwest, and the fort's northern bastion guarded the southwesternmost of these roads. Its south bastion covered the parallel road. The fort's priest-cap (an M-shaped feature made up of two redans) covered the approaches from the northeast.[104]

Captain Charles Suter served as the fort's engineer; troops from the 32nd United States Colored Infantry began the project, and the 144th New York Infantry finished it. The 32nd comprised free blacks from Delaware, Maryland, and Pennsylvania. Like other black regiments, the 32nd was officered by whites. Its commander was Colonel George Baird, who on August 19, 1864, was ordered to move his regiment "to a point just beyond Mitchelville and encamp on ground which will be designated by Capt. Suter Chief Engineer Dept. South near which a work is to be constructed under his direction." There Baird would "furnish daily as large a detail for this purpose as the strength of the Regiment will permit." Wielding shovels, spades, picks, and axes, Baird's men labored under the direct supervision of Captain Patrick McGuire of Company A, 1st New York Engineers.[105] On September 26, the fort was officially named for Colonel (posthumously Brigadier General) Joshua Blackwood Howell, who had briefly commanded the Hilton Head District and died from injuries incurred when his horse fell on him on September 12 while Howell was commanding a division near Petersburg, Virginia.[106]

Work on Fort Howell progressed slowly, and McGuire and Suter frequently complained of manpower shortages. On September 2, Suter groused to Brigadier General Edward Potter, commander of the Hilton Head District, "I think a regiment of this size ought to furnish at least from 250 to 300 for duty and in this I think you will agree with me." Instead, the 32nd often assigned that number to guard duty either in their camp or at Mitchelville, leaving Suter to lament "their camp guard … is absurdly large." As a result, only 150 to 200 soldiers were typically assigned to work on Fort Howell each day.[107]

Progress was further hamstrung in mid–October when the 32nd was split up and its companies ordered to various locations on Hilton Head Island and elsewhere in the Department of the South. The 144th New York Infantry assumed the work responsibilities on Fort Howell and completed the project from mid–October to late November 1864. The 1st New York Engineers continued to supervise the construction. By the time Fort Howell was finished, the Confederates lacked sufficient strength to pose a threat to the Federal presence on Hilton Head, and Fort Howell was never tested in combat.[108]

Fort Howell's importance to Mitchelville lies in the fact that development proceeded under the protection of necessary security measures. Mitchelville was allowed to grow and establish its civil, economic, and political institutions without being subject to continual attack from Confederate forces. Moreover, although the 32nd Regiment was made up of soldiers from Northern states, the fact that fellow blacks were facilitating the opportunities Mitchelville provided to its citizens no doubt contributed to a sense of pride, ownership, and unity of purpose.

The Town Meeting and Self-Government

In addition to providing security, the military also played an important but not exclusive role in Mitchelville's government. This relationship and the plan of governance for Mitchelville were spelled out in General Orders No. 3 issued by Brigadier General Milton Littlefield on February 16, 1865. Mitchelville was declared a "village" and would "be divided into districts, as nearly equal to population as practicable, for the election of Councilmen, Sanitary and Police Regulations, and the General Government of the people presiding therein." While the military commander appointed a mayor (called a supervisor in the General Orders) and treasurer, the black residents would elect a councilman to represent each district, along with a recorder and a marshal. The supervisor and the councilmen formed a Council of Administration with the recorder acting as secretary. This council was empowered to determine the duties of the marshal and recorder and to make rules for the conduct and record of its proceedings. It was also charged to "pass such ordinances as it shall deem best in relation to the following subjects":

> To establish schools for the education of Children and other persons.
>
> To prevent and punish vagrancy, idleness and crime.
>
> To punish licentiousness, drunkenness, offenses against public decency and good order, and petty violation of the rights of property and person.
>
> To require the observance of the Lord's Day.
>
> To collect fines and penalties.
>
> To punish offences against village ordinances.
>
> To settle and determine disputes concerning claims for wages, personal property, and controversies between debtor and creditor.
>
> To levy and collect taxes to defray the expenses of the village government, and for the support of schools.
>
> To lay out, regulate, and clean the streets.
>
> To establish wholesome sanitary regulations for the prevention of disease.
>
> To appoint officers, places, and times, for the holding of elections.
>
> To compensate municipal officers, and to regulate all other matters effecting the well-being of citizens, and good order of society.[109]

Littlefield's order also specified, "The Supervisor shall hold a court at such times as the necessities of the Village may require, for the hearing and determining of disputes and controversies between the inhabitants of the villages. The parties aggrieved by any final decision of the Supervisor's Court, shall have an appeal to the commanding Officer of the District, through the Superintendent of Freedmen." Whitelaw Reid found the course of justice to be somewhat "tortuous" under these proceedings, as he records in a rather condescending and probably embellished "story of a stolen hen." Nonetheless, even Reid noted "better practices" were fast manifesting themselves and "already we are assured that theft is comparatively rare."[110]

Mayor Murchison maintained a close liaison with military officials. On August 12, 1864, he wrote Major General John Foster, commander of the

Department of the South, to complain of three soldiers he believed to be of the 25th Ohio Regiment and "under the influent of Licor" who had raped a Mitchelville woman. Murchison reported, "We have been trubled very often by these officers & Sailers & I think a stop aught to be Put to it." Murchison went on to complain of recruiting officers who were plying Mitchelville residents with alcohol. Foster endorsed Murchison's letter and queried the provost marshal, "The rule is for no men to be allowed to visit Mitchelville at night. Why is this not carried out? And who gives passes for this purpose?" Murchison's complaints were taken seriously. On October 4, the provost marshal ordered the Mitchelville guards "to arrest persons whom *Father Murchison* (Magistrate) may designate for any riotous or disorderly conduct."[111]

Mitchelville's Decline

By October 1864, three thousand people lived in Mitchelville, and the town "was approaching or had surpassed the available space and/or material" it had.[112] In 1865, the population fell to 1,500. Many had arrived at Hilton Head as refugees and perhaps returned to their original homes when the Civil War ended. More left in 1868 when the Army and the jobs associated with it departed. Nonetheless, Mitchelville survived into the 1870s as a vibrant community that produced a "sizable 'black yeomanry' class."[113] Succumbing to a variety of pressures, however, in the early 1880s, Mitchelville lost its character as a town and became a small, kinship-based community.[114] Much of this demise can be traced to the federal land restoration policy that resulted in the Drayton Plantation's being returned to the heirs of its former owner in April 1875.

Although the federal government deed failed to provide any protection for Mitchelville, the Drayton heirs were not interested in planting the lands and put them up for sale. A successful black man named March Gardner succeeded in buying most of Mitchelville, which at this time also included a store, cotton gin, and grist mill. Gardner put his son Gabriel in charge of Mitchelville and also trusted Gabriel to have a proper deed made out. Instead, Gabriel took advantage of the situation and eventually obtained a deed in his own name and then transferred the property to his wife and daughter. This act was the beginning of further chicanery and mismanagement that led to "a sad end to what was the birthplace of freedom for many Sea Island blacks." White investors, including Roy Rainey of New York, increasingly bought tracts of Hilton Head land, and by the late 1930s, only 300 blacks remained of a population of nearly 3,000 in 1890.[115] Such a turn of events certainly represents a marked departure from whatever promise Mitchelville once had for its black residents.

Mitchelville's Lessons for Nation-Building

Mitchelville is important for a plethora of historical and cultural reasons, but for the purposes of this study it is relevant as a case study of how nation-builders and the local population can work together to build civil society. Almost all aspects of Mitchelville reflect a cooperative effort. The idea was General Mitchel's, but he insisted on black ownership of the process and result. The houses were built by the black residents with government resources and supervision. Northern societies provided missionaries and financial support, but the churches were pastored and run by their black congregations. Philanthropic organizations also provided teachers and funds for schools, but the blacks enthusiastically embraced the education process, and some, such as Lyman Anders, were teachers as well. The Army provided Fort Howell to protect Mitchelville, but it was built in part by black soldiers who also guarded the town. Mitchelville's government was partly appointed by the military and partly elected by the residents, but the elected councilmen had significant authority through the Council of Administration.

Such relationships are indicative of the participatory approach to development which requires consultation with the groups who are likely to be affected by the effort, considering them to be "stakeholders" capable of making a positive contribution to the effort and enhancing its likelihood of success, rather than mere objects of programs and policies determined by others. Andy Sumner and Michael Tribe argue, "The more sensitive a project, program, or policy is to stakeholder interests, particularly at a community level, the more likely is the participatory approach to reap dividends in the form of effective design, implementation, and operation."[116] As recent American nation-building efforts have shown, the participatory approach aims to strike a difficult balance, but the experience at Mitchelville gives a hopeful example of what can be achieved if that balance is realized.

CHAPTER 10

The American Government as Nation-Builder: USAID in Afghanistan

In October 2001, less than a month after al Qaeda's terrorist attacks against America on September 11, 2001, the United States launched Operation Enduring Freedom (OEF) against that Islamic extremist organization and the Taliban regime that had harbored it in Afghanistan since 1996. Effective collaboration between Central Intelligence Agency (CIA) operatives and American Special Forces teams on one hand, and the Afghan Northern Alliance on the other, in the context of OEF resulted in the fall of the Taliban regime and dispersal and flight of the leadership of al Qaeda by December 2001.[1]

Absent Taliban political control, notwithstanding the extreme, brutal and often bizarre nature of such governance from 1996 to 2001, the United States, along with its North Atlantic Treaty Organization (NATO) allies and other members of the nascent International Security Assistance Force (ISAF), were left in early 2002 with the daunting challenge of managing nation- and state-building operations in Afghanistan from 2001 to 2016. Further complicating matters was the existence of an understandable American emphasis on the hunt for al Qaeda head Osama bin Laden and other significant leaders of that group and its Taliban allies, relative to the parallel physical reconstruction and economic and political institution-building processes underway during that period.

While American military forces have necessarily focused on mitigating the threats presented by al Qaeda and the Taliban, the United States Agency for International Development (USAID) has played an equally significant role in the conduct of nation- and state-building operations in Afghanistan, particularly in facilitating physical infrastructure construction projects and economic and political development and institution-building processes. In doing so, USAID has necessarily engaged in collaborative initiatives with a variety of actors whose origins, interests and approaches are often dissimilar in many ways. Examples are wide-ranging, including national government ministries based in Kabul and ethnic and tribal group leaders situated in Afghanistan's many geographically remote regions, as well as U.S. and NATO military commands and officers, and civilians working with intergovernmental organizations (IGOs) and nongovernmental organizations (NGOs). Finding commonalities that lead to opportunities for such disparate actors to achieve progress on mutually beneficial projects, whether related to economics, politics, security and/or other related issues can be particularly challenging.

With these introductory observations as a useful point of departure, the balance of the chapter assesses the role of USAID in nation- and state-building operations in Afghanistan in eight sections that unfold in the following manner. The first section reviews the relevant literature on the American approach to nation- and state-building projects and roles the USAID plays in the contexts of such endeavors. The second section identifies and explains the series of events that resulted in America's eventual intervention in Afghanistan in October 2001. The third section examines USAID's contributions to economic developmental efforts in Afghanistan from 2002 to 2016. The fourth section examines USAID's contributions to political developmental efforts in Afghanistan from 2002 to 2016. The fifth section examines USAID's contributions to social and cultural developmental efforts in Afghanistan from 2002 to 2016. The sixth section examines the relationship between USAID and U.S. military forces in the contexts of nation- and state-building efforts in Afghanistan from 2002 to 2016. The seventh section examines the relationship between USAID and IGOs and NGOs in the contexts of nation- and state-building efforts in Afghanistan from 2002 to 2016. And the eighth section presents a set of concluding observations on USAID's past, present and likely future contributions to nation- and state-building efforts in Afghanistan.

USAID and the American Approach to Nation- and State-Building: A Primer

The effective conduct of any nation- and/or state-building project requires the participation of a range of actors, including states, IGOs and NGOs. Further, with respect to states in particular, multiple organizations and individuals, with often differing interests and perspectives, are involved in the planning and implementation of a variety of components of such projects in contexts that include physical reconstruction of infrastructure, economic restructuring and diversification, political institution-building, and reconciliation between multiple domestic groups and individuals possessing distinctive ethnic, religious and tribal identities and grievances.

Given the focal point of the chapter, the most appropriate way to begin is by specifying the ways scholars and policymakers define the American approach to nation- and state-building projects and how it compares with the perspectives of other Western and non–Western states. Any nation- and/or state-building project commences after a decision by one or more states and/or intergovernmental organization to intervene in the domestic affairs of another state. Before electing to intervene or refrain from doing so, whether unilaterally or multilaterally, a state must determine if it is in its national interest to do so. If the answer is yes, it must then fashion (and implement) an effective plan for the intervention and, more importantly, what follows. Where nation- and state-building operations are concerned, one must also be prepared for significant shifts in the facts on the ground between the planning and implementation phases of a particular project. As Ambassador James Dobbins, Seth G. Jones, Keith Crane and Beth Cole DeGrasse note in RAND's *The Beginner's Guide to Nation-Building*, the first of a definitive multivolume work on the topic:

> Most interventions are launched for some immediate, usually negative purpose, e.g., to halt aggression, civil war, famine, genocide, or the proliferation of weapons of mass destruction. This purpose might be achieved quite quickly, but the intervening authorities will then be left with the more difficult, time-consuming, and expensive task of refashioning the society in which they have intervened. The intervention itself will change power relationships within that society and among its neighbors. Those advantaged by the intervention may begin to abuse their positions. Those disadvantaged may move to frustrate the intervening authorities' purposes.[2]

Instances of U.S. military intervention abroad during the Cold War, of both the large- and small-scale varieties, grew out of the bipolar struggle between the United States and Soviet Union for global power and influence. Cases in point range from the substantial (and quite costly) commitments Washington made to the Korean War of 1950–53 and Vietnam War of 1954–75 on one hand, and the more pragmatic (and successful) operations to support the Afghan mujahideen against Soviet occupation forces from 1981 to 1989 and intervention in Grenada in October 1983 on the other. In each of these cases, U.S. military commitments were driven in part, if not fully, by perceptions of Soviet influence of variable types, whether direct or indirect, in a given region of the world or country therein.

With the conclusion of the Cold War through the fall of the Berlin Wall in November 1989, reunification of Germany in October 1990, and dissolution of the Soviet Union in December 1991, the structure of the international system changed markedly, from bipolar to unipolar, leaving the United States as the world's lone superpower and changing the motivations for American intervention abroad and the conditions under which Washington was likely to take such action. Rather than intervention conditioned by the bipolar confrontation with the Soviet Union, not surprisingly, U.S. interventions since the end of the Cold War have been driven by a variety of traditional and nontraditional security threats. Examples include U.S. intervention in Somalia in the winter of 1992–93, American-led NATO intervention in Bosnia-Herzegovina in the summer of 1995 and again in Kosovo in the spring of 2009, with humanitarian concerns playing significant roles in driving Washington's actions in each instance. However, they also feature the conduct of Operation Desert Storm in the winter and spring of 1991 and prosecution of Operation Iraqi Freedom in the spring of 2003; the former expelled from Kuwait the Iraqi forces that had seized that neighboring state at the behest of President Saddam Hussein, who was himself removed from power via the latter operation. The link between all of these cases: the centrality of American leadership. As Richard Haass, who served in high-level positions in the U.S. Department of State in both the George H.W. Bush and George W. Bush presidential administrations and is now president of the Council on Foreign Relations, suggested in the aftermath of what amounted to an American victory over the now defunct Soviet Union, "In the post–Cold War world, in the age of deregulation, the lion's share of the burden of preserving international order falls on the United States. It is a burden worth bearing, both for what can be accomplished and what can be averted. In many cases the United States will be best able to do this by assuming the role of international sheriff, one who forges coalitions or posses of states and others for specific tasks."[3]

A central challenge in the implementation of any nation- and/or state-building project is effective management of relationships between the military and civilian actors on the ground in a given state under reconstruction, both individuals and the branches, agencies and departments they serve. Those relationships are typically complicated further by the countries, IGOs and NGOs they represent. Afghanistan is an instructive case in point, with USAID playing the lead role in physical reconstruction and longer-term economic and political institutional building, but necessarily under the protective umbrella of American and NATO military forces, and often in collaboration with IGOs and NGOs on the ground. Given the centrality of security to progress toward achievement of all of the above objectives, USAID has essentially had to resign itself to playing a secondary role, one dictated more by hunting for al Qaeda members and countering insurgent Taliban forces than economic and political development for its own sake.

While daunting, the challenges USAID faces in Afghanistan are not unusual, in that it typically must surmount broadly similar hurdles in all of the projects in which it engages—and that has been the case throughout the organization's history. Established in November 1961 in the wake of congressional passage of the Foreign Assistance Act, USAID necessarily had to embrace the innate challenges impeding the achievement of economic and political systemic improvements in countries across the developing world from its inception. Such challenges are central to USAID's mission statement, particularly as pertains to the interconnected relationship between international development and security, both for the United States and the countries it assists. That statement emphasizes, "We partner to end extreme poverty and promote resilient, democratic societies while advancing our security and prosperity."[4]

The fundamental principles and interests that undergird USAID's mission are rooted in the post–World War II assistance program the Harry S. Truman presidential administration implemented in Western Europe, known then and since as the Marshall Plan.[5] Promulgated by American Secretary of State George Marshall in the June 1947 Harvard University Commencement Address, the plan provided for more than $12 billion in U.S. grants to provide critical assistance to the states of Western Europe to boost their post–World War II recovery from 1948 to 1952. Just as important as the economic assistance itself was the Western European and transatlantic unity it fostered, concurrent with the opening act of the Cold War from 1945 to 1950. Put simply, the Western Europeans accepted U.S. assistance, acceding to Washington's insistence that the Marshall Plan be distributed cooperatively through nascent economic and political institutions that also included the American, British and French Zones of Occupation in the defeated German state. The Western Europeans, in turn, demanded that the United States make an enduring commitment to European security, as a safeguard against the dual potential threats of future German resurgence and Soviet expansion. As America's preeminent Cold War historian, John Lewis Gaddis, explains:

> Washington's wartime vision of a postwar international order had been premised on the concepts of political self-determination and economic integration. It was intended to work by assuming a set of common interests that would cause other countries to want to be affiliated with it rather than to resist it. The Marshall Plan, to a considerable extent, met those criteria: although it operated on a regional rather than a global scale, it did seek to promote democracy through an economic recovery that would proceed along international and not nationalist lines. Its purpose was to create an American sphere of influence, to be sure, but one that would allow those within it considerable freedom.[6]

Less than a decade after the completion of the Marshall Plan, USAID was launched by the John F. Kennedy administration. It was an additional tool to assist in American engagement in the developing world, where the United States consistently sought influence, particularly relative to that of the Soviet Union, over the course of the Cold War. As Kennedy noted when he launched USAID, "There is no escaping our obligations: our moral obligations as a wise leader and good neighbor in the interdependent community of free nations—our economic obligations as the wealthiest people in a world of largely poor people, as a nation no longer dependent upon the loans from abroad that once helped us develop our own economy—and our political obligations as the single largest counter to the adversaries of freedom."[7]

Since its birth, USAID has evolved through a series of stages, the most recent of which places that agency as a central actor in the conduct of nation- and state-building projects in places such as Afghanistan and Iraq. There have been five such stages to date, unfolding temporally in the 1970s, 1980s, 1990s and 2000s forward. In the 1970s, USAID shifted from emphasizing capital and technical assistance programs to developing and implementing a "basic human needs" approach focusing on food and nutrition, population planning, health, education and human resources. In the 1980s, USAID attempted to help stabilize currencies and financial systems through the promotion of market-based principles to restructure developing countries' policies and institutions. In the 1990s, USAID transitioned to a sustainable development approach, through which Washington pursued the establishment of liberal democracies with "open, market-oriented economic systems and responsive social safety nets," most notably in the newly independent states of Central and Eastern Europe. Since 2000, USAID has focused primarily on the issue area of American-led nation- and state-building operations generally, and the conduct of such projects in Afghanistan and Iraq in particular.[8]

The Road to American Intervention in Afghanistan

Any discussion on the path to American-led intervention in Afghanistan through the conduct of OEF in the fall of 2001 must begin decades, if not centuries, before then. The history of Central and South Asia is replete with examples of states that intervened in Afghanistan but failed to produce any enduring change in that country, whether economically, politically or socio-culturally. The most notable such past cases include the British and Russian Empires in the context of the "Great Game" for regional dominance over the latter half of the 19th century, as well as the Soviet Union, which occupied Afghanistan from 1979 to 1989, but was eventually driven out by domestic and international mujahedeen forces supported by the United States, Pakistan and Saudi Arabia.[9]

Unfortunately, the Soviet withdrawal did not produce any lasting stability within Afghanistan. Instead, it was followed by a half-decade of perpetual conflict among rival warlords representing that state's myriad ethnic groups, each of which exercised military, if not formal political, control over a particular geographic region. By the mid–1990s, Afghanistan was a failing state, one that had been all but abandoned by the United States, its former Russian adversaries and the broader international community. It was at that juncture that an ultraconservative group of Islamic Studies students known as the Taliban began to exercise influence over the territory surrounding the southern Afghan city of Kandahar. Over the latter half of the decade, the Taliban extended its control to more than two-thirds of the country, including the capital of Kabul.[10]

Ironically, but not surprisingly, since launching OEF in October 2001, an operation that drove the Taliban from power in just over two months, the United States and its allies have faced challenges in Afghanistan comparable to those the Soviets struggled with during the 1980s, particularly in the contexts of nation- and state-building initiatives therein from 2002 to 2016. One significant reason the United States found itself in a position that required intervention in Afghanistan in 2001 was the lack of concern Washington and its Western allies expressed over the brutal internal conflict that produced a state of anarchy in that state during the 1990s. The United States spent nearly all of the ensuing decade working to accomplish two daunting objectives—tracking down al Qaeda leader bin Laden and developing effective and enduring democratic political institutions in Afghanistan.

On May 2, 2011, a team of U.S. Navy SEALs carried out an operation in Abbottabad, Pakistan, that resulted in the killing of the most wanted man in American history—bin Laden, who had been at large since the 9/11 attacks, evading capture despite the elimination of the Taliban regime in Afghanistan that harbored him and his followers via the conduct of OEF and nearly a decade of subsequent U.S. efforts to find him.[11]

Rooting out bin Laden and al Qaeda was the principal objective for intervention in Afghanistan in the aftermath of the 9/11 attacks. However, once the Taliban was removed from power, OEF quickly transitioned into a broader nation- and state-building project in Afghanistan, one that spanned two terms for American President George W. Bush and continued into the second term of his successor, President Barack H. Obama. It was in March 2009 that Obama took action on one of the most significant foreign policy promises he made during the electoral campaign of 2008, promulgating a new strategy to manage—and eventually wind down—that project, while continuing to address related political and security challenges in neighboring Pakistan.

Obama's plan differed from the strategic approach taken by the Bush administration toward Afghanistan, Pakistan and the broader Central Asian and South Asian regions in two ways. First, the Obama administration pledged to deploy an additional 21,000 American troops to assist in the training of Afghan security forces in 2009. This promise was related in part to a shift in emphasis from nation- and state-building operations in Iraq to those in Afghanistan, concurrent with a force drawdown in the former theater from 2009 to 2011. Second, Obama emphasized the importance of viewing security and stability issues in Afghanistan and Pakistan as interconnected challenges.

In shifting the U.S. approach, Obama focused on the importance of five issues in particular: (a) the disruption of interconnected terrorist networks in both Afghanistan and Pakistan, including (but by no means limited to) those run by al Qaeda; (b) the development of more capable and accountable Afghan governmental institutions; (c) the development of more self-reliant Afghan security forces, with the assistance of the United States and its allies in the North Atlantic Treaty Organization (NATO); (d) assistance with Pakistan's efforts to enhance civilian control of its governmental institutions; and (e) greater international communal involvement and leadership, particularly from the United Nations (UN) in addressing each of the above four objectives.

The Obama administration had to maintain its policy through several bumps in the road since 2009, including continuing concerns over alleged corruption within the government of Afghan President Hamid Karzai and multiple shifts in command of American forces in Afghanistan. Along with the command shifts, the overall foreign troop presence in Afghanistan grew to nearly 150,000 (including 100,000 U.S. forces) in October 2010. However, in the wake of the killing of bin Laden, Washington began drawing down its forces in advance of a near complete withdrawal slated for December 2014, a deadline that led to Obama's decision to leave in place a follow-on presence of no fewer than 8,400 through the end of the president's final term in January 2017.[12] The many challenges that remain will be left for Obama's successor in the White House to manage.

Role of USAID in Economic Developmental Efforts in Afghanistan, 2002–16

A necessary point of departure for an informed discussion of USAID's role in economic development initiatives in Afghanistan is the specification of clear definitions of (and distinctions between) the terms "economic growth" and "economic development," which can be applied to the examination of any state under reconstruction. The *Oxford English Dictionary* defines economic growth as "an increase in the amount of goods and services produced per head of the population over a period of time."[13] By contrast, according to the World Bank, economic development is best defined as "qualitative change and restructuring in a country's economy in connection with technological and social progress."[14] The most significant distinctions between the two is that manifestations of the latter often drive the extent to which the former rises and falls over a given period. Further, a country's domestic characteristics and capabilities typically drive the ways in which its economy evolves and, in turn, affects the population situated therein.

The most relevant impediments to both economic growth and economic development in Afghanistan are rooted in three sets of related issues, all of which pose significant challenges to USAID's mission and projects within that country. The first such set of issues—political and social instability—is associated with a security environment that is unstable at best and anarchical at worst. The second set—ethnic, religious and tribal differences and, ultimately, conflict—grow out of Afghanistan's cultural diversity. The third set— distinctions between interests and related approaches of individuals, states and organizations on the ground—are the result of the presence of myriad state-and non-state actors participating in nation- and state-building efforts in Afghanistan. And the fourth set—myriad cases of economic and political corruption exhibited by both internal and external actors—have complicated each of the previous three sets of issues.

With respect to the first set of the above issues, the extent of security (or the lack thereof) is central to determining the level of success or failure in any nation- or state-building project, and that is certainly the case with Afghanistan. Insecurity has driven challenges associated with progress in all aspects of nation- and state-building operations in which USAID has engaged in Afghanistan since 2002. The country's rugged geography and related isolation of rural villages from the hub of national governmental, as well as international authority and activity in the capital of Kabul, make for an environment in which the population values tribal affiliations over a broader sense of Afghan identity. It follows naturally that villagers will look to tribal rather than national leaders to solve local problems, whether associated with economics, politics, religion or security. Those conditions produced an environment ripe for the development of insurgencies led primarily by the Taliban, which has continually undermined Afghan central governmental influence, let alone control, over the villages.[15]

Ultimately, the extent of success of USAID initiatives in any issue area is driven by the level of security on the ground in the context in which it is attempting to implement a particular program. Examples include the construction of roads and schools and provision of medical treatment to those in need in remote villages across Afghanistan, as well as more capital-intensive projects such as power plants and water treatment facilities. The safer a given city or village remains, the more benefits USAID infrastructure projects can provide for the population situated therein. Further, in order to achieve long-tern progress through a particular project, the residents of the area must be convinced that security safeguards are permanent rather than transitory in character. As Seth G. Jones notes, "By 2005, there was growing Taliban penetration of rural areas in eastern and southern Afghanistan. Given sustained security and assistance, villages across this swath of territory might have sided with the government. But without that help, they moved toward the insurgents. The logic is straightforward: the Afghan government's inability to provide essential services and security to rural areas increasingly marginalized the population, and provided a target of opportunity for insurgents."[16]

With respect to the second set of the above issues, Afghanistan's cultural diversity affects economic development in three particularly significant ways. First, differing political objectives between the capital in Kabul and tribal communities across Afghanistan produces differing levels of progress in pockets across the country. That disconnect is not a new phenomenon; rather, it is one that has been evident throughout the history of Afghanistan, whether those involved have exclusively domestic roots or also include intervening external actors at a particular temporal juncture. Second, the options for villagers to support their families differ from one region of Afghanistan to the next, with decisions on which such options to choose typically falling to ethnic and tribal leaders, as opposed to input from national governmental officials in Kabul. Third, the extreme interpretations of Islam imposed by the Taliban in areas it controls outright or has significant influence over, can limit opportunities for economic development, in particular through the exclusion of women from educational and workforce opportunities.

With respect to the third set of the above issues, communication and coordination between internal and external actors who have some common (but also many distinctive) interests and objectives is central to the conduct of any nation- and/or state-building project. How well or poorly those leading such a project manage the complications growing out of differences between military and civilian actors on one hand, and states, IGOs and NGOs on the other, typically determines the final outcome of a particular initiative. Consider the Afghan case under examination here. In the wake of a largely, if not wholly, unilateral U.S. intervention and removal of the Taliban regime from power in the fall of 2001, the number of outside actors on the ground in Afghanistan expanded rapidly. The first (and most significant) opportunity to solicit the participation of states, IGOs and NGOs alike in nation- and state-building operations in Afghanistan came less than a month after the fall of the Taliban in the form of a donors' conference in Bonn, Germany. That conference, which brought together some 60 states and 20 IGOs and NGOs, produced donor pledges of $1.8 billion for 2002 and $4.5 billion, including an initial $296 million in American aid, targeted for use by USAID.[17]

With respect to the fourth set of the above issues, few factors produce more anti-government and anti-foreign sentiments among Afghans, particularly those situated in culturally distinctive regions (and villages therein), than cases of corrupt officials within the national government and also among outsiders working for intervening states and organizations of the inter- and nongovernmental types alike. Such corruption is widespread within Afghanistan, as evidenced by that state's perennially woeful status in Transparency International's annual "Corruption Perceptions" Indices released over the past decade in particular. Since 2007, Afghanistan has finished among the world's most poorly governed countries in the world in those indices, including third most corrupt in 2015, no better than fifth most corrupt in any year from 2007 to 2014, and most corrupt in both 2012 and 2013.[18] The administration of President Karzai in particular generated consistent domestic and international criticism throughout his time in office. Domestically, for example, public opinion polling has suggested significant distrust of the Afghan national government since it was first installed in the aftermath of U.S. intervention. Such distrust grew more pronounced in the wake of allegations of voting irregularities in the 2010 presidential race that resulted in Karzai's reelection to a second term, and remains a concern under the shared leadership of President Ashraf Ghani and Chief Executive Abdullah Abdullah since the 2014 presidential election.

Collectively, the above three sets of impediments have contributed to sporadic economic growth and development since 2002. According to the Brookings Institution's "Afghanistan Index," for instance, annual GDP growth in Afghanistan has fluctuated markedly over the past dozen years, shifting from 15.1 percent in 2003, to 8.8 percent in 2004, to 16.1 percent in 2005 to 8.2 percent in 2006, to 13.7 percent in 2007, to 3.6 percent in 2008, to 21 percent in 2009, to 8.4 percent in 2010, to 7.2 percent in 2011, to 11.9 percent in 2012, to 3.4 percent in 2013, to 1.7 percent in 2014, and 2.5 percent in 2015.[19] Further, with respect to economic, political and social/cultural development, Afghanistan ranked 171st of the 188 countries included in the 2014 United Nations Human Development Index.[20]

Role of USAID in Political Developmental Efforts in Afghanistan, 2002–16

As with the issue of political development, it is only appropriate to begin any discussion of USAID's role in political development efforts in Afghanistan with a definition of the term "political development," which can be applied to the examination of any state under reconstruction. According to Francis Fukuyama, political development is best defined as "change over time in political institutions. This differs from shifts in politics or policies: prime ministers, presidents and legislators may go, but it is the underlying rules by which societies organize themselves that define a political order."[21]

The most relevant political impediments to nation- and state-building efforts in Afghanistan are best assessed contextually, with emphases placed on the domestic and international levels, respectively. The former grow in large part out of Afghanistan's ethnic, tribal and religious interpretive diversity, which provide fertile ground for the development of fierce rivalries that permeate the domestic political system. The latter are a product of the interests and roles of states, international organizations and NGOs in Afghan reconstruction and political developmental efforts, which produce relationships that can be cooperative in some issue areas and conflictive in others.

Domestic challenges to the political stability and institutional continuity in Afghanistan are based in large part on the limited control the national government in Kabul (headed by Karzai from 2002 to 2014 and President Ashraf Ghani, in collaboration with Chief Executive Abdullah Abdullah, since then) exercises over the state's regions. To date, as a general rule, the NATO-led ISAF and Afghan security have provided the requisite security for residents of Kabul to maintain relatively productive lives, whether through the manufacturing of goods or the provision of services. However, that security does not yet (and may never) extend far enough beyond the capital for the national government to consistently collect revenues and distribute aid where necessary in Afghanistan's many insular, remote and often dangerous regions.

Those regions, for their part, are administered by a diverse array of tribal leaders and warlords interested primarily in personal enrichment—and the accompanying political power—rather than improving the lives of the people living within the territory over which they preside. In most cases, such leaders are concerned more about the profits to be reaped from the imposition of road and border tolls and the production and smuggling of narcotics than engagement with the central government in Kabul. Such economic and political machinations complicate many, if not all, of the infrastructure projects in which USAID has engaged across Afghanistan since 2002. For example, with respect to the construction of roads to connect Kabul to the regions where it built numerous schools and water treatment facilities, such projects have been effective only so long as travel between the capital and local communities is deemed safe.

Most international-level political complications in the conduct of nation- and state-building operations in Afghanistan are associated primarily with two issue areas. First, the reluctance of states to commit the resources needed to build and maintain the Afghan economy over the short and long terms. Per capita assistance in Afghanistan was less than $50 a head in the first two years of operations there, as opposed to approximately $325 in Bosnia from 1996 to 1999 and $275 in Kosovo from 1999 to 2001. Overall, nearly $96 billion in foreign aid was dispensed to Afghanistan from 2002 to 2015.[22] Second, the aforementioned differences in the missions of U.S. forces and the ISAF have hampered the extent of cooperation between the two, especially prior to the elimination of bin Laden in May 2011. Such coordination has improved marginally over the past several years, but only in fits and starts and with decreasing levels of success, concurrent with the decreasing U.S. military presence in Afghanistan from 2011 to 2014 in particular.

Role of USAID in Cultural and Social Developmental Efforts in Afghanistan, 2002–16

As with the previous two sections, it is best to launch this discussion of USAID's role in cultural and social developmental initiatives in Afghanistan with definitions of the terms "cultural development" and "social development," which can then be applied to the examination of any state under reconstruction. However, given the terms involved, it is important to begin with the caveat that there are no universally accepted and applicable definitions of either term. For the purpose of this chapter, the following definitions of those terms are the most contextually useful. First, with respect to cultural development, the United Nations Educational, Scientific and Cultural Organization (UNESCO) defines the term as "the process of development or progress in the cultural life of a community."[23] Second, according to the International Institute of Social Studies, "Social development is about putting people at the centre of development. This means a commitment that development processes need to benefit people, particularly but not only the poor, but also a recognition that people, and the way they interact in groups and society, and the norms that facilitate such interaction, shape development processes."[24]

Above all else, the many ethnic and related tribal impediments to the economic and financial reconstruction of Afghanistan are a product of its cultural diversity. The country is composed of a mix of majority Pashtuns (in the south), minority Tajiks and Uzbeks (in the north), and Hazaras (in the heartland). Collectively, the Pashtuns account for 42 percent of the Afghan population, the Tajiks 27 percent, the Uzbeks nine percent and the Hazaras nine percent. Rivalries among those and a variety of smaller tribal groups have already undermined nation- and state-building efforts at both the national and regional levels, and will likely continue to do so.[25]

The characteristics and roles of Sunni Islam in Afghan society are best summarized in terms of history, geography, demography, and theological interpretation and behavior. Sunni Muslims first appeared in substantial numbers in the heartland of Central Asia late in the seventh century C.E. and have constituted a clear religious majority in Afghanistan from the outset of its history as an independent state in 1747. Geographically, Sunnis account for 85 to 90 percent of the population and are prevalent across much of Afghanistan, particularly in the south and east of the country, which is dominated by ethnic Pashtun tribes, while Shi'a communities are concentrated primarily in the Hazara-heavy north and west of the country.[26]

In terms of theology, as is true of one-third of Muslims globally, most Afghans are adherents to Hanafism, the most practiced of the four schools of Sunni Islamic law. However, the cultural traditions of Afghanistan's close-knit tribal communities ensure that orthodox interpretations of that school are the norm. And a powerful minority tilts toward the much more puritanical Hanbali school and its most extreme and dangerous offshoots, Salafism and Wahhabism. Established by Muhammad ibn Abd al-Wahhab (1703–1792) in eighteenth-century Saudi Arabia, Wahhabism emphasizes an extraordinarily strict interpretation of Sunni Islam, one that places severe limitations on the public roles of women, prohibits any behavior perceived as idolatry, and mandates robust punitive measures such as the amputation of limbs for relatively minor criminal offenses like petty theft and death by stoning for females deemed to have committed adultery.[27]

Broadly, the roots of Salafism date to the succession battle that produced the Sunni-Shi'a divide but also led to the evolution of the four schools of Islamic law, the most orthodox of which, Hanbalism, provided a foundation for the development of more extreme interpretations of the faith. One of the most extreme such interpretive strains is Salafism. The Arabic word salafi translates as predecessor or ancestor, a reference to the rule of the Four Rightly Guided Caliphs (632–660). That historical period featured a decisive Sunni emphasis on the development of (and adherence to) seminal Islamic sources, most notably God's revelations to Muhammad in the Qur'an and the Prophet's instructions and deeds in the Sunna and hadith. A theologically puritanical approach to practicing Islam, Salafism left ample room for extreme interpretations.

A number of groups situated in Afghanistan have practiced and, in many cases, imposed tenets associated with Salafism on that country's people. The most recent three such groups have influenced politics, religion and security in Afghanistan since it was invaded and occupied by the Soviet Union in December 1979. First, an assortment of Afghan mujahedeen and Arab fighters opposed the Soviet occupation on the basis of the tenets of holy war (jihad) originally promulgated during the Muhammadan era and the subsequent period of the Rightly Guided Caliphs. Second, after the Soviets withdrew in

1989, the domestic anarchy that ensued produced the emergence of the Taliban, a group of Muslim students educated in Pakistani religious schools (madrassas) that emphasized Salafism. From 1995 to 2001, the Taliban imposed on Afghans a perversion of Islam that excluded girls from education and mandated that they wear head-to-toe burkas when in public, prohibited playing musical instruments, and demolished ancient cultural artifacts. The Taliban was removed from power through the American-led conduct of Operation Enduring Freedom in the fall of 2001, but has maintained an insurgency against successive U.S.-supported Afghan governments since. Third, since 2014, affiliates of one the most powerful and extreme Salafist organizations in Middle Eastern history, the Islamic State of Iraq and Syria (ISIS), have imposed their own brand of extremism on the pockets of Afghan territory they control.[28]

On balance, the initial composition of the Afghan national government since the fall of the Taliban reflects its ethnic diversity, with a Pashtun (Karzai) atop the political power structure from 2002 to 2014, and members of other minorities—especially individuals in positions of authority in the Northern Alliance when it occupied Kabul in December 2001—dispersed throughout the state's variegated legislative, economic and defense bodies.

Yet, while the government was launched in a relatively expeditious fashion (less than a year after the fall of the Taliban) and has made reasonable, although sporadic, progress toward the development of enduring representative institutions, inter- and intra-ethnic disputes remain a threat to economic and political stability in general, and the personal security of leading officials including, but by no means limited to, Karzai in particular.

The situation is considerably worse at the regional and local levels, where age-old ethnic and tribal divisions have been exacerbated by two sets of circumstances: (a) renewed growth in the cultivation of opium-producing poppy fields; and (b) the U.S. hunt for al Qaeda and Taliban members, whose ethnic backgrounds have enabled them to blend into tribal communities across Afghanistan and in the neighboring Pakistan, where support for both groups remains strong.

The principal religious hurdles that must be cleared in order to better facilitate the economic and financial reconstruction of Afghanistan in the 2010s are rooted in inter- and intra-denominational differences that often drive relationships between individuals, communities, states and institutions at the domestic and international levels. Such differences most often grow out of the Sunni-Shi'a divide that dates to the period of the "Rightly Guided Caliphs" in the initial three decades following the death of the Prophet Muhammad in 631 C.E.

Domestically, perhaps the most significant challenge is the continuing transition from Taliban rule to the secular government of the Karzai administration. Put simply, Mullah Omar presided over an Islamic theocracy within which his extreme interpretation of the Koran resulted in legal dictates ranging from the brutal (e.g., the amputation of the hands of thieves and stoning of women suspected of adultery) to the bizarre (e.g., prohibitions on photographing individuals and flying kites). Since Mullah Omar's death in 2013, both of his successors at the helm of the Taliban—Mullah Akhtar Mohammad Mansour until his death in a U.S. drone strike in June 2016, and Mullah Wawlawi Haibatulah Akhundzada after that—have maintained the group's founder's extreme Islamic interpretive perspectives. Given the nature of that regime, adjustment to a secular system that allows for freedom of religious expression and increases markedly the economic and political rights afforded to women will be a generational struggle.

While Kabul is more modern and cosmopolitan than ever before, security remains tenuous at best, and the transition will likely continue to proceed at a considerably slower pace at the local and regional levels for two reasons. First, in light of the limited practical authority the Karzai government and that of his successors, President Ghani and Chief Executive Abdullah, have been able to exercise regionally and locally, intermixed religious and tribal customs nearly always trump national dictates in the latter contexts. Second, some communities are still loyal to the Taliban, whether strictly to ensure their safety or for deeper religious and tribal reasons. Both issues have complicated USAID mission in Afghanistan, as it must operate in areas that view the national government and motives of its American allies with understandable suspicion.

Comparable international-level impediments to nation- and state-building in Afghanistan have grown out of the interest-based actions of three sets of religiously disparate actors: (a) the conduct of the war on terrorism (of which al Qaeda was the focal point until the emergence in 2014 of the Islamic State of Iraq and Syria, which ultimately proved a more dangerous threat) by the United States and its allies; (b) cooperation—or in some cases, lack thereof—from Afghanistan's neighbors (most notably Shi'a Iran and Sunni Pakistan) in that effort; and (c) the secular, Christian and Islamic NGOs attempting to provide humanitarian aid without appearing to side with any of the above actors.

Collaboration Between USAID and American Military Forces in Afghanistan, 2002–16

Prior to engaging in an examination of the types of (and challenges associated with) collaboration between USAID and American military forces in

Afghanistan from 2002 to 2016, a broader discussion of the evolution of the relationships between U.S. government agencies and departments generally, and those on the civilian and military sides of the institutional equation, is essential. That discussion has four related stages. The first examines the planning and conduct of OEF and the dual (but not always complementary) objectives of counterterrorism and nation- and state-building that followed the fall of the Taliban regime in November and December 2001. The second examines the period from 2002 through the end of the Bush administration's second term in January 2009, during which the U.S. military focused primarily on the hunt for bin Laden and the struggle against al Qaeda and the Taliban more broadly, with the NATO-led International Security Assistance Force providing support for nation- and state-building efforts. The third examines the Obama administration's successful completion of the hunt for (and ultimate elimination of) bin Laden and subsequent shift toward an American drawdown that remains as incomplete as a range of ongoing USAID projects in Afghanistan. The fourth assesses the likely future path for the nexus between American military and USAID efforts in Afghanistan moving forward.

With respect to the first stage, planning for OEF commenced in the immediate aftermath of the events of 9/11, with both the CIA and U.S. Special Forces Command playing prominent roles in developing a tactical approach suitable for the circumstances in Afghanistan in the fall of 2001. Given the unexpected nature, scope and implications of al Qaeda's 9/11 attacks, the United States had only limited time to assemble and then set into motion its response. The situation in the ground in Afghanistan, and American assets and allies (both existing and prospective), conditioned the U.S. response. Above all, it was essential for the United States to strike expeditiously in a post–9/11 contextual environment characterized by significant domestic pressure for action against (and global acceptance of the need to eliminate) a Taliban regime that had long been viewed as a pariah internationally. Beyond the removal of the Taliban, OEF had two complementary longer-term objectives: the conduct of counterterrorism operations, including the search for bin Laden, on one hand, and support for an American-led nation- and state-building project on the other.

These two sets of objectives remained interconnected in some ways and distinctive in others in both the second and third stages under Bush and Obama, respectively, with the latter following the hunt for bin Laden through to its conclusion via the killing of the al Qaeda leader in a May 2011 Navy SEAL assault on a complex in Abbottabad, Pakistan. The best place to begin identifying and assessing those similarities and distinctions is with an examination of the broader relationships between U.S. civilian and military actors and organizations in general, and those between USAID and both American and ISAF/NATO military forces on the ground in Afghanistan in particular. USAID's interactions with American military forces have grown out of the central role of nation- and state-building endeavors to U.S. foreign policy in the post–Cold War era, which has seen interventions leading to the conduct of such projects extending from East Africa to southeastern Europe to the Middle East and Central and South Asia. For the military, primacy is naturally ceded to hard security issues as opposed to support for development efforts, particularly in Afghanistan, where the principal motive for U.S. intervention was to counter al Qaeda's 9/11 attacks rather than to launch a long-term nation- and state-building project. Consequently, USAID had to focus on achieving what it could in terms of the provision of communal services to villages whose residents remained constantly fearful of the potential for Taliban retribution for cooperating with the Americans, whose military forces were tracking both Mullah Omar and his al Qaeda allies.

Given the security challenges in Afghanistan and related distinctions between the missions of U.S. military forces and domestic political and international geopolitical objectives of the State Department and the USAID in that context, three issue areas merit further exploration in closing this section of the chapter: first, the conduct of military operations with intentional outcomes that undermine the image of USAID within a given community; second, the conduct of military operations with unintentional outcomes that also undermine that image; and third, distinctions between practical USAID achievements on the ground that strengthen the organization's ties with the leaders of one or more villages at the micro level and progress and setbacks in the broader relationship between the American and Afghan governments.

With respect to the first issue area, one must begin by noting that the United States has conducted a range of military operations, particularly those associated with counterterrorism and counterinsurgency efforts targeting al Qaeda and Taliban targets in Afghanistan and across the border in parts of Pakistan, since 2002. Many of those operations have had direct effects on the security environment in villages and broader regions across Afghanistan, including areas where loyalties among the population are mixed, with some supporting the national government in Kabul and, by association, the U.S. military forces from which it draws support, and others supporting the Taliban and more globally oriented Islamic extremist terrorist organizations such as al Qaeda and ISIS. Insurgent and terrorist attacks by these three terrorist organizations and their affiliates in Afghanistan number in the tens of thousands, including highs of 1,600 per week in October 2010 and no fewer than 1,200 per month since the U.S. and ISAF force drawdowns at the end of 2011.[29] In areas where there is a significant presence of and/or support for those groups, it is extraordinarily difficult for USAID and the NGOs it often cooperates with to operate safely, to the detriment of the population of a given village or region overall.

Regarding the second issue area, the U.S. and broader coalition missions that create the most significant anti–Western (and, by association, anti–USAID sentiments) are those resulting in unintentional casualties among Afghan civilians, as well as individuals representing NGOs. In addition to the 2,377 U.S. servicemen and women and 1,128 ISAF forces killed in Afghanistan since 2002, 25,500 Afghan civilians lost their lives in incidents related in some way to the fighting between 2006 and 2013 alone.[30] Worse, the degree of continuity in USAID projects in a range of villages and regions across Afghanistan has been consistently undermined by marked increases in the number of internally displaced persons in Afghanistan, which rose from 150,000 in May 2008, to 275,945 in October 2009, to 329,000 in March 2010, to 352,000 in December 2010, to 631,000 in December 2013, to 805,409 in December 2014, to 947,872 in June 2015.[31]

As pertains to the third issue area, to start, it is critically important to recognize that the completion of USAID projects on the ground from one village or region to the next on a daily basis, have only marginal effects on American civilian and military strategic and policy objectives. Further, the achievement of objectives in one such issue area can undermine those in another, especially regarding the security factors addressed in the previous two paragraphs. Above all, U.S. policymakers and practitioners must recognize that any significant progress moving forward will be linked directly to the extent of American military and civilian economic support and political commitments to the development and maintenance of enduring Afghan institutions with the capacity to serve—and earn the respect—to be perceived as legitimate by the public.

Collaboration Between USAID and IGOs and NGOs in Afghanistan, 2002–16

Prior to engaging in an examination of the types of (and challenges associated with) collaboration between USAID and a range of IGOs and NGOs in Afghanistan, it is important to provide a contextual foundation specifying some basic terminological definitions. First, consider the term intergovernmental organization. With the *Oxford English Dictionary* as a point of reference, it is perhaps best to tackle the words one by one. The former is "of, relating to or conducted between two or more governments."[32] The latter is "an organized body of people with a particular purpose, especially a business, society, [or] association."[33] Notable examples applicable to the case of nation/state building in Afghanistan include NATO, the UN and the World Bank.

Second, consider the term nongovernmental organization, which the UN's Rule of Law Website defines as "a not-for-profit group, principally independent from government, which is organized on a local, national or international level to address issues in support of the public good" that can "perform a variety of services and humanitarian functions, bring public concerns to governments, monitor policy and programme implementation, and encourage participation of civil society stakeholders at the community level."[34] Examples of NGOs applicable to the case of Afghanistan include Amnesty International, Doctors Without Borders, the Global Partnership for Afghanistan, International Red Cross and Red Crescent Movement, International Rescue Committee, Human Rights Watch, Oxfam and Transparency International.[35]

Interaction and cooperation with multiple IGOs, most notably ISAF/NATO and the UN, is and has been central to USAID's work in Afghanistan since early 2002. Two sets of similarities and distinctions in such relationships merit further investigation here: first, those that occurred under the auspices of the Bush administration from 2002 to 2009; and second, those that occurred under the auspices of the Obama administration from 2009 to 2016.

With respect to the Bush years, the principal focus on U.S. military operations in Afghanistan was on the hunt for bin Laden and the challenges of a stubborn Taliban insurgency that was never brought under control. Further impeding progress in reconstruction efforts in which USAID and its IGO and NGO partners participated during Bush's two terms in office was the disproportionate emphasis that administration placed on nation- and state-building efforts in Iraq, as opposed to those in Afghanistan, in terms of both civilian and military funding and commitments (please see Chapter 8 for a comparison). Those distinctions in emphasis limited the potential for progress in Afghanistan in two ways. First, in practical terms, the resources available in Afghanistan were always limited, which meant only so many projects could be attempted, let alone completed, by USAID on the ground. Second, such limitations created legitimate perceptions among Afghans, as well as America's Taliban adversaries, that the United States lacked a long-term commitment to Afghanistan.

With respect to the Obama years, from the outset, there was a significant shift in emphasis from Iraq to Afghanistan, one that grew more pronounced with the drawdown of the U.S. military presence in Iraq from 2009 to 2011, which was punctuated by the withdrawal of all American combat forces from Iraq at the end of 2011. That drawdown was accompanied by substantial increases in funding and force presence in Afghanistan, which helped to foster greater economic and political stability in that state. However, those funding and commitment levels declined rapidly in the aftermath of the elimination of bin Laden in May 2011. As a result, by the end of the Obama administration, the security and related economic and political situations in Afghanistan were as tenuous as under the Bush administration before that.

Collaboration between USAID and a range of NGOs on the ground in Afghanistan commenced soon after the fall of the Taliban regime in December 2001, albeit in a particularly challenging environment. The end of formal Taliban political and religious authority in Afghanistan did little to produce a more secure environment in that country, particularly for provinces and villages therein situated far from the seat of power in Kabul. Consequently, the risks associated with participating in development projects of all types have remained high since the United States intervened. Such risks range from Taliban insurgent targeting of NGO workers for kidnapping or killing, to accidental injury or death when munitions fail to strike the proper targets. Collectively, they present three sets of related challenges to collaboration between USAID addressed in greater depth below: insecurity; distinctive organizational interests and agendas; and local, national and international political complications, some connected and some not.

With respect to the first such issue area, insecurity comes in multiple brands and affects both USAID and the IGOs and NGOs with which that American agency works in the field in Afghanistan. The most prevalent security concern is the Taliban insurgency, which is especially strong in rural areas in the south and east of the country, particularly along the Afghanistan-Pakistan border. Regarding the second such issue area, all organizations have interests and related political agendas, no matter how noble their motivations and accomplishments in a given region of the world and country therein. And those motivations and the related interests associated with them drive the behavior of those organizations. For example, above all, in Afghanistan and in countries across the developing world more broadly, NGOs were on the ground prior to intervention by outside actors such as the United States and expect to be there after such external actors have withdrawn. Consequently, they must retain a significant measure of neutrality, so that they can continue to operate and avoid association with aspects of an intervention that have hurt rather than helped those residing in a particular Afghan village or region. As pertains to the third issue area, ultimately, American engagement in Afghanistan under both the Bush and Obama administrations was driven primarily by the ongoing U.S. struggle against transnational terrorist organizations rather than economic, political or social/cultural developmental efforts in that country, a reality that is unlikely to change under the presidency of Donald J. Trump.

Conclusions

This chapter was designed to achieve seven related objectives. First, it reviewed the relevant literature on America's approach to nation- and state-building projects in general and how USAID in particular fits into that approach. Second, it examined the path to U.S. intervention in Afghanistan in the aftermath of al Qaeda's 9/11 terrorist attacks against America through the prosecution of OEF and planning of subsequent nation- and state-building efforts therein. Third, it examined USAID's contributions to economic developmental efforts in Afghanistan from 2002 to 2016. Fourth, it examined USAID's contributions to political developmental efforts in Afghanistan from 2002 to 2016. Fifth, it examined USAID's contributions to social and cultural developmental efforts in Afghanistan from 2002 to 2014. Sixth, it examined the relationship between USAID and U.S. military forces in the contexts of nation- and state-building efforts in Afghanistan from 2002 to 2016. And, seventh, it examined the relationship between USAID and IGOs and NGOs in the contexts of nation- and state-building efforts in Afghanistan from 2002 to 2016.

The issues addressed and assessed in the aforementioned main sections of the chapter lead to the identification of four related sets of conclusions to be presented in the closing observations that follow. The first set is associated with the conditions and motivations that produced the initial U.S.-led intervention in Afghanistan in October 2001. The second is associated with the transition from a sole emphasis on tracking and attempting to eliminate the remaining threats posed by al Qaeda and the Taliban in the aftermath of the prosecution of OEF to the conduct of nation- and state-building operations in Afghanistan. The third is associated with the roles USAID has played to date in economic, political, and social and cultural developmental efforts in Afghanistan since 2002. And the fourth is associated with the prospects for the future roles of the United States generally and USAID specifically in Afghanistan moving forward.

The principal motivation for intervention in Afghanistan in the aftermath of al Qaeda's 9/11 terrorist attacks against the United States was extraordinarily straightforward: punish the perpetrators of those strikes and their Taliban hosts. Washington delivered a clear message by eliminating the Taliban regime as Afghanistan's predominant ruling authority and replacing it with a democratic, if not always incorrupt, central government under President Karzai's management in Kabul from 2002 to 2014 and under President Ghani's and Chief Executive Abdullah's leadership since 2014. However, fully dismantling al Qaeda, let alone eliminating its leader, bin Laden, while countering a Taliban-led insurgency, proved to be more daunting longer-term challenges. While the United States did indeed eventually kill bin Laden in May 2011, his removal certainly did not end the threats posed by al Qaeda and its affiliates, the latter of which are now even more powerful and dangerous than the group's core.

From the outset of period of post–Taliban governance in which Afghanistan still remains, the United States and its allies have followed a two-track strategy, with Washington focusing on the related counterterrorism and counterinsurgency side, and a combination of NATO member states and their development equivalents of USAID managing nation- and state-building efforts. On the counterterrorism front, the United States concentrated primarily on the hunt for bin Laden, while also adapting in an effort to manage the evolving (and interconnected) terrorist and insurgent threats posed by the Taliban. On the nation- and state-building front, notwithstanding the expenditure of significant resources of the economic, military and political types, progress has proceeded at a glacial pace, with no guarantees of the maintenance, let alone expansion, of local developmental achievements in a given issue area.

As is often the case with its endeavors across the developing world, USAID has been engaged in interconnected endeavors across myriad issue areas in Afghanistan, most notably developmental efforts of the economic, political and social and cultural types, all of which are conditioned by the security environment at a given juncture. In the economic issue area, USAID efforts have suffered from a common weakness of foreign aid in general: disproportionate expenditures relative to enduring achievements, particularly with respect to infrastructure projects. In the political context, USAID has had to manage the often shifting relationships between (and influence wielded by) Afghan central government agencies and regional power brokers in planning and implementing its projects in a range of localities. In the social/cultural issue area, the principal challenge has been (and remains) the development of enduring democratic institutions that conflict with the religious and tribal values and traditions of Afghanistan's diverse mixture of peoples. None of these challenges will be easy to manage moving forward, and the extent to which they can be mitigated has been and is sure to remain a product of the security environment on the ground at a given temporal juncture. Should the existing limited remaining U.S. and broader Western military commitments to Afghan security diminish further, so will the changes of the maintenance of even a semblance of economic, political and social stability in Afghanistan and the surrounding region in the future.

CHAPTER 11

NGOs and IGOs as Nation Builders: Bosnia

In the summer of 1995, the United States and its North Atlantic Treaty Organization (NATO) allies intervened militarily in Bosnia-Herzegovina to end the ongoing slaughter of Bosnian Muslims therein by Serbian forces supported by President Slobodan Milosevic's regime in the neighboring state of Serbia. That intervention came in the form of U.S.-led NATO airstrikes targeting Serbian forces ringing the Bosnian capital of Sarajevo, positions they had used to attack both military and civilian targets, including the February 1994 shelling of the city's main market square.

The Sarajevo market attack, which killed 68, was one of a series of tragic events that characterized a brutal 1992–95 intra-state conflict in Bosnia-Herzegovina, driven both by ethnic and religious differences between Catholic Croats, Muslim Bosniaks and Orthodox Christian Serbs, and by the political machinations of neighboring Croatia and Serbia and their leaders, President Franjo Tudjman and Milosevic, respectively.[1] The market bombing increased international pressure on both the United States and its European Union (EU) and NATO allies to intervene. So, too, did an ethnic cleansing campaign orchestrated by Milosevic, the most significant manifestation of which was the Serb massacre of some 7,000 Muslim Bosniak men and boys from the town of Srebrenica in July 1995. That tragic development left the administration of American President William J. Clinton little choice but to exercise the requisite political leadership to press NATO intervention on behalf of the Bosnian Muslim population.

Not surprisingly, NATO's superior military capabilities eventually forced Milosevic and the Serbs to the negotiating table at an American air force base in Dayton, Ohio. Essentially, the use of force by NATO against the Serbs set the diplomatic stage for the negotiation and subsequent implementation of the U.S.-brokered Dayton Peace Accords, the provisions of which included the creation of a tripartite Bosnian administration (a Serb Republic in one half;

a Muslim-Croat federation in the other) and the prosecution of war criminals under the auspices of the International Criminal Tribunal for the former Yugoslavia (ICTY). Ultimately, Milosevic himself was indicted and tried before the ICTY, although the proceedings were still ongoing when he suffered a fatal heart attack in his jail cell in The Hague in March 2006.[2]

With these introductory observations as a useful point of departure, the balance of the chapter assesses the roles of intergovernmental organizations (IGOs) and nongovernmental organizations (NGOs) in the conduct of nation- and state-building efforts in Bosnia since the negotiation of the Dayton Accord in the fall of 1995 through the presentation of eight sections that unfold in the following manner. The first section reviews the relevant literature on the roles of IGOs and NGOs in the conduct of nation- and state-building projects in states in the developing world since the end of the Cold War. The second section reviews the developments that led to NATO intervention in Bosnia in 1995 and the subsequent involvement of the EU, United Nations (UN) and a range of NGOs in nation- and state-building efforts therein since. The third section examines the roles of IGOs and NGOs in economic developmental efforts in Bosnia from 1995 to 2016. The fourth section examines the roles of IGOs and NGOs in political developmental efforts in Bosnia from 1995 to 2016. The fifth section examines the roles of IGOs and NGOs in transitional justice efforts in Bosnia from 1995 to 2016. And the sixth section presents a set of closing observations on the roles of IGOs and NGOs in nation- and state-building efforts in Bosnia from 1995 to 2016 and in the future.

IGOs and NGOs in Nation- and State-Building Efforts in Bosnia: A Literature Review

Given the centrality of IGOs and NGOs to nation- and state-building efforts in Bosnia and, of course, the discussion and analysis in the main sections of the chapter to unfold below, it is certainly sensible to begin the discussion by specifying some basic definitions of those terms. First, consider the term intergovernmental organization. With the *Oxford English Dictionary* as a point of reference, it is perhaps best to tackle the words one by one. The former is "of, relating to or conducted between two or more governments."[3] The latter is "an organized body of people with a particular purpose, especially a business, society, [or] association."[4] Couple the two and the incisive end result is an organization whose members are the governments of multiple states. Notable examples applicable to the case of nation/state building in Bosnia include the EU, NATO and the UN. Second, consider the term nongovernmental organization, which the UN's Rule of Law Website defines as "a not-for-profit group, principally independent from government, which is organized on a local, national or international level to address issues in support of the public good" that can "perform a variety of services and humanitarian functions, bring public concerns to governments, monitor policy and programme implementation, and encourage participation of civil society stakeholders at the community level."[5] Examples of NGOs applicable to the case of Bosnia include the Danish Refugee Council, the International Center for Transitional Justice (ICTJ), Transparency International, and the United Methodist Committee on Relief.

There is a robust literature on the roles of IGOs and NGOs in the international system generally and in the case of Bosnia during (and since) the mid–1990s specifically. Conceptually, the most appropriate place to begin the presentation of a necessary primer on that issue area is with a discussion of the ways the principal schools of international relations theory view the roles of states and institutions, whether of the inter- or nongovernmental variety, in the international system. There are two mainstream strains of such theoretical approaches—those associated with realism and its evolutionary offshoots (most notably neorealism, offensive realism and neoclassical realism) on one hand, and liberalism and its most prominent modern offshoot (neoliberal institutionalism) on the other. The former cluster focuses primarily on the importance of self-interest in driving the behavior of states in the international system and the ways the structure of that system affects interaction between the states interacting therein at given temporal junctures. The latter emphasizes the willingness of states to cooperate, even if the benefits are greater for one or more of their rivals in that system. Seminal thinkers and works in each of these theoretical clusters include realist Hans Morgenthau's *Politics Among Nations: The Struggle for Power and Peace* (1948),[6] neorealist Kenneth N. Waltz's *Theory of International Politics* (1979),[7] offensive realist John J. Mearsheimer's *The Tragedy of Great Power Politics* (2001),[8] liberal John Locke's *Two Treatises of Government* (1690),[9] and neoliberal institutionalists Robert O. Keohane and Joseph S. Nye's *Power and Interdependence: World Politics in Transition* (1977).[10]

For neoliberal institutionalists in particular, IGOs such as the UN, EU and NATO, as well as a range of NGOs, are extraordinarily important actors in the international system. While members of this theoretical school agree with the neorealists that the system is anarchical and draw on some realist precepts, such as the importance of state power, interests and behavior in the international system, they also believe that institutions temper the effects of that anarchy by facilitating cooperation between states. As Keohane explains, "Institutionalists do not elevate international regimes to mythical proportions of authority over states; on the contrary, such regimes are established by states to achieve their purposes. Facing dilemmas of coordination and collaboration under conditions of interdependence, governments demand international institutions to enable them to achieve their interests through limited collective action."[11] The strategic approaches and actions of policymakers and practitioners in the aftermath of the Cold War in the 1990s afforded scholars plenty of opportunities to test the theoretical provisions Keohane specifies.

During the bipolar confrontation between the United States and the Soviet Union (and, for that matter, the countries aligned with Washington and Moscow, whether by choice or imposition) that unfolded between 1945 and 1991, on balance, realism, neorealism, liberalism and neoliberal institutionalism were the principal theoretical lenses to explain both state and institutional behavior in the international system. The former strain was particularly effective in explaining how both the United States and Soviet Union viewed interests on the basis of power and security and perceptions of the relative strength of the other side and behaved accordingly. While the latter strain was largely ineffective in assessing American-Soviet relations, it did help to explain the unprecedented intra–European integration processes that grew out of the Marshall Plan, through which the United States provided more than $12 billion in grants to its Western European allies from 1948 to 1952 in exchange for the multilateral distribution of that aid via institutional frameworks that included West Germany. The initial such institutions involved were the European Coal and Steel Community and European Economic Community (EEC), which were established in April 1951 and March 1957, respectively. The EEC then evolved through multiple stages of deepening and widening, the latter resulting in the enlargement of that institution from its original membership of six (France, Germany, Italy, Belgium, Luxembourg and the Netherlands) to 12 by the end of the Cold War and 28 in the current EU.[12] While the EEC (and, ultimately, the EU) were built on a foundation of economic and political bonds, the Western Europeans also required a security guarantee against potential threats of German resurgence or Soviet expansion. The guarantee came in the form of a permanent American commitment to European security through the establishment of NATO through the Washington Treaty in April 1949.[13] As prominent historian of U.S. national security strategy John Lewis Gaddis explains, "NATO was very much a joint venture. Europeans proposed it and the United States permitted them a surprising amount of influence over its structure and strategies. European integration for years has flourished, independently of the Americans, but it could hardly have arisen had Washington not insisted upon European cooperation in return for economic and military assistance during the late 1940s. Only then did the process become self-organizing, with a character very much its own."[14]

The end of the Cold War left just one of the world's two superpowers— the United States—standing. That country, in turn, had to determine how best to define and pursue its national interests, in light of the transformation of the international system signaled by the implosion of the Soviet Union (1989–91). It was a topic stirring considerable discussion and debate among scholars and policymakers alike when Clinton took office in January 1993. Members of the aforementioned mainstream theoretical schools applied their traditional approaches to the reconfigured post–Cold War system, some suggesting that the United States had a unique opportunity to shape the future of that system, given its position as a global hegemon at a "unipolar" historical moment. On balance, the consensus among those on the realist/neorealist and liberal/neoliberal sides of the equation was that their respective models remained quite capable of explaining the post–Cold War world. Others disagreed. Three of the most significant alternative approaches, for example, were promulgated by prominent strategic thinkers Francis Fukuyama, Samuel P. Huntington and Robert D. Kaplan.

All three of the above figures broke in at least some ways with the mainstream thinkers, with Huntington putting forward the most novel such approach—his culturecentric "clash of civilizations" model—first in an article titled "The Clash of Civilizations?" in the Summer 1993 issue of the influential policy journal *Foreign Affairs*,[15] and then in a book on the same topic, *The Clash of Civilizations and the Remaking of World Order*, in 1996.[16] In both the article and the book, Huntington asserted that cultural factors, often rooted in ethnicity, language and religion, would drive the behavior of states and, more broadly, civilizations in the post–Cold War international system. Further, he suggested that those civilizations (and the states therein) were likely to clash over differences in their cultural attributes.[17] Fukuyama's vision of the emerging systemic order, by contrast, was decidedly more optimistic. He saw the conclusion of the Cold War as a signature global triumph for democracy over autocracy as a guiding principle for governance and order, expressing those views in his 1992 work *The End of History and the Last Man*.[18] Like Huntington, Kaplan expressed a far dimmer view of the prospects for the post–Cold War world than was true of Fukuyama. Most significantly, he suggested that a variety of sub-state factors would drive conflicts that destroy states from within, unveiling his assessment in a February 1994 article in *The Atlantic*, which was appropriately titled "The Coming Anarchy: How scarcity, crime, overpopulation, tribalism, and disease are rapidly destroying the social fabric of our planet."[19]

Individually, each of the aforementioned approaches provide useful ways to examine the systemic changes and resulting challenges evident since the end of the Cold War. However, rather than settle on one such approach, it is best to draw on aspects of them all to develop a clearer understanding of the nascent post–Cold War era that emerged during the 1990s. The George H.W. Bush presidential administration both brought the bipolar confrontation between the United States and Soviet Union to a close and managed the multilateral expulsion of Iraqi forces from Kuwait through the successful conduct of the Persian Gulf War in 1991. Together, these developments represented the end of an era in which traditional state-based challenges posed the greatest threats to American and broader Western interests. The quarter-century since then, by contrast, has featured the types of nontraditional intra-state and transnational conflicts and crises Huntington and Kaplan warned about. Responding effectively to such problems, in turn, typically requires action by both states and international organizations, issues that still leave room for interpretations from the mainstream realists, neorealists, liberals and neoliberals.

The Road to NATO Intervention
in Bosnia, 1992–95

The Bosnian intra-state conflict of 1992–95 was the first significant common security challenge the United States and its Western European allies faced in the aftermath of the Cold War, the final act of which featured the fall of the Berlin Wall in November 1989, collapse of communist regimes across Central and Eastern Europe in the winter of 1989-90, reunification of Germany in October 1990, and dissolution of the Soviet Union in December 1991. With the departure of the Soviet Union as a global superpower (its successor, the Russian Federation, has yet to restore the level of power, prestige and international influence Moscow enjoyed during the Cold War, although one could argue that President Vladimir Putin has made progress on those fronts in recent years), the United States had to recalibrate the resulting changes in relative power it possessed in the international system and the types of threats Washington and its allies would face moving forward.

Any credible assessment of the Balkan conflicts of the 1990s generally and the Bosnian civil war in particular must begin with a basic history lesson. The sources of those conflicts date back to the Middle Ages and are rooted in ethnic, religious and related cultural and political distinctions between the inhabitants of the region. Such distinctions have changed little over the centuries. Above all, the factors that contributed most to the eruption of intra-state violence in Bosnia in 1992 can be traced to the creation of the state of Yugoslavia via the Treaty of Versailles of 1919.[20] Above all, Yugoslavia was built on a rocky multiethnic and -religious foundation, one that required a strong leader to manage politically, the absence of which left that state vulnerable to internal conflict and division. Over the course of all but the final act of the Cold War, Yugoslavia had such a leader in place in Josip Broz Tito, who presided over that state's authoritarian political system from the end of World War II through his death in May 1980. Within a decade, the stability prevalent under Tito's authority, rooted in part in the nationalism engendered by the World War II Yugoslav resistance and maintained through its relative freedom of action within the Soviet sphere of influence during the Cold War, had broken down.[21]

In the wake of the fall of communist regimes across Central and Eastern Europe and the dissolution of the Soviet Union itself from 1989 to 1991, the geographically, ethnically and religiously distinctive segments of Yugoslavia quickly began to break away from what quickly became a political relic of the Cold War. Croatia and Slovenia were the first parts of Yugoslavia to break away, with both declaring independence in June 1991. Bosnia followed soon thereafter, and the brutal intra-state conflict that followed lasted from 1992 to 1995; the fighting raged on until NATO intervened in the summer of 1995. Regrettably, that action came only after fighting between Bosnian Muslims and Serbs in particular left more than 400,000 dead, the vast majority of whom were Muslims, in large part as a result of the military and political support Serbian President Slobodan Milosevic provided to the Serbs. Ultimately, the Srebrenica massacre provided the final trigger for NATO intervention, followed by the American-brokered Dayton Peace Accord that settled the conflict and provided the initial framework for the nation- and state-building efforts that followed.

The Dayton Peace Accord represented the first step toward the development of a stable and secure Bosnia and broader Balkan region. The accord, which was orchestrated primarily by American diplomat Richard Holbrooke, resulted in the establishment of a power-sharing political system that provided for a rotating Bosnian presidency headed, in turn, by a Catholic Croat, Muslim Bosniak and Orthodox Serb. The implementation of the Dayton Accord was managed first by NATO and then by the EU, with assistance from the UN and a range of NGOs in both cases. That implementation process and its aftermath involved several issue areas, with each progressing through multiple stages, synopses of which are presented in the closing paragraphs of this section, followed by more in-depth examinations unfolding in the subsequent sections of the paper. Those sections, in turn, address the roles of IGOs and NGOs in the contexts of the issue areas of economic development, political development, social/cultural development, and transitional justice efforts in Bosnia from 1995 to 2016.[22]

Economic development efforts in Bosnia have unfolded in the following three stages since 1995. The first stage progressed over the course of Clinton's two terms in office (January 1993–January 2001), during which his administration placed emphases on the reconstruction of Bosnia's infrastructure and economic system on one hand, and the implications for the dual European and transatlantic enlargement processes on the other. The second stage progressed over President George W. Bush's two terms in office (January 2001–January 2009), during which the U.S. shift in focus to the global war against terrorism contributed to a transition to EU rather than NATO leadership of nation- and state-building efforts in Bosnia. The third stage progressed over President Barack H. Obama's two terms in office (January 2009–January 2016), during which the lead roles in Bosnian economic development efforts were managed by Western European and international bodies, most notably the EU, UN, International Monetary Fund and World Bank.

Political development efforts in Bosnia have unfolded in the following three stages since 1995. The first stage progressed over the course of Clinton's two terms in office, during which the United States used implementation of the Dayton Accord in Bosnia to launch the first post–Cold War enlargement of NATO. The second stage progressed over President George W. Bush's two terms in office, during which the U.S. shift in focus to the global war against terrorism contributed to a transition to EU rather than NATO leadership of nation- and state-building efforts in Bosnia, with complementary efforts undertaken by the UN and a range of other IGOs and NGOs. The third stage progressed over President Barack H. Obama's two terms in office, during which America's emphasis remained on nation- and state-building efforts in the Greater Middle East, with only a marginal role in Bosnia's continuing political development process.

Transitional justice efforts in Bosnia have unfolded in the following three stages since 1995. The first stage progressed over the course of Clinton's two terms in office, with his administration emphasizing the UN's International Criminal Tribunal for the former Yugoslavia as the most effective means to pursue both justice and reconciliation in Bosnia. The second stage progressed over President George W. Bush's two terms in office, with his administration leaving the Bosnian justice and reconciliation processes to its EU allies and the global community more broadly. The third stage progressed during President Barack H. Obama's two terms in office, with his administration acting much as the Bush administration had done, particularly in light of continuing American commitments to nation- and state-building efforts in the Greater Middle East, along with the development of the Islamic State of Iraq and Syria (ISIS) and the threats it poses.

Roles of IGOs and NGOs in Economic Development Efforts in Bosnia, 1995–2014

A necessary point of departure for an informed discussion of the roles of IGOs and NGOs in economic development initiatives in Bosnia is the specification of clear definitions of (and notable distinctions between) the terms "economic growth" and "economic development," which can be applied to the examination of any state under reconstruction. The *Oxford English Dictionary* defines economic growth as "an increase in the amount of goods and services produced per head of the population over a period of time."[23] By contrast, according to the World Bank, economic development is best defined as "qualitative change and restructuring in a country's economy in connection with technological and social progress."[24] The most significant distinctions between the two is that manifestations of the latter often drive the extent to which the former rises and falls over a given period. Further, a country's domestic characteristics and capabilities typically drive the ways in which its economy evolves and, in turn, affects the population situated therein.

NATO intervention and the subsequent negotiation of the Dayton Accord brought the requisite break in intra-state conflict to allow for the conception, launch and implementation of economic recovery and deeper economic development initiatives in Bosnia. Those efforts and initiatives are best addressed temporally and in terms of organization types and issue areas during a given period, with the following four in particular to be examined: the prologue to NATO intervention (1992–95); the Clinton administration era (1993–2001); the George W. Bush administration era (2001–09); and the Obama administration era (2009–16). In each case, one must focus on the motivations for intervention for each of the actors involved, whether states, IGOs and/or NGOs, their contributions to economic development in Bosnia and the outcomes of such efforts.

The prologue to NATO intervention in Bosnia in the summer of 1995 had both political and military components. Politically, international organizations and their members alike had to determine the conditions, if any, under which to intervene and how best to do so if deemed essential. Discussions among EU members at both the state and institutional levels began in the immediate aftermath of the final act of the Cold War from 1989 to 1991. Unlike its immediate predecessor and successor (the administrations headed by the elder Bush and his son), the Clinton administration had to manage the military intervention in Bosnia, the settlement of the intra-state conflict that prompted that course of action via the Dayton Accord, and the economic and political developmental processes that followed.

Of the past three presidential administrations, Clinton's had the most direct role in assisting economic development efforts in Bosnia, both in terms of American foreign assistance via a range of government agencies and departments, including the Departments of Defense and State and the United States Agency for International Development (USAID), and in pressing for the requisite NATO intervention and presence to ensure a secure environment conducive to effective IGO and NGO efforts on the ground. With respect to the former, the United States has contributed nearly $3 billion in foreign assistance to Bosnia since 1995, including no less than $179 million per year between 1997 and 2001 and no less than $44 million in any year since then.[25] The vast majority of that assistance was provided by USAID, including much toward economic development initiatives. With respect to the latter, myriad IGOs and NGOs were quick to join nation- and state-building efforts in Bosnia in the aftermath of the NATO intervention that ended the intra-state conflict raging therein in the summer and fall of 1995. Numerous IGOs and NGOs have continued to contribute to economic development efforts in Bosnia since 1995, including the EU and UN, as well as the International Monetary Fund (IMF), Organization for Economic Cooperation and Development, and the World Bank. Overall, according to UN Development Program estimates, Bosnia has received some of the highest levels of development assistance ever recorded by a state, ranging from 12.1 percent of GDP in 2000 to 102 percent in 2001, to eight percent in 2002, to six percent in 2003, to 6.3 percent in 2004, to 4.3 percent in 2005, to 4.2 percent in 2006, to 3.8 percent in 2007, to 2.4 percent in 2008, to 2.3 percent in 2009, to three percent in 2010, to 2.3 percent in 2011.[26] The EU is the largest contributor of economic assistance to Bosnia since 1996, with its investments there over the past two decades accounting for $3.5 billion.[27] For its part, the World Bank has funded 68 economic development projects in Bosnia since 1996 for a total of $1.7 billion. At present, it is implementing 11 investment projects in that state worth a total of $420 million.[28]

By contrast, out of necessity given the demands of the struggle against Islamic extremist groups, such as al Qaeda, the Islamic State of Iraq and Syria (ISIS) and their affiliates, supporters and sympathizers, the Bush and Obama administrations have left economic development initiatives in Bosnia to the EU and many of the same IGOs and NGOs that commenced their efforts during their Clinton years. U.S. foreign assistance provided to Bosnia before and since the events of 9/11 are illustrative of the shift in Washington's focus away from the Balkans and Europe more broadly toward the Greater Middle East during those temporal periods. While U.S. aid to Bosnia never dipped below $179 million annually prior to the 9/11 attacks, it has never exceeded $82.7 million in any year since.[29] Much of the difference went to Afghanistan and Iraq, which had received little prior the U.S. interventions in the former in the fall of 2001 and the latter in the spring of 2003.

There are three principal insights for academics, policymakers and practitioners alike to draw from the economic development efforts of IGOs and NGOs in Bosnia. First, the more secure and stable an environment that exists politically and socially, the greater potential for economic development efforts to take hold and produce enduring positive outcomes. Second, ethnic and religious diversity often produces political differences that can quickly become difficult to contain and descend rapidly into violent conflict between opposing groups. The deeper the fissures these factors produce, the greater economic development shortcomings left in their wake. Ultimately, Bosnia faced precisely that set of circumstances from 1992 to 1995, exacerbated by NATO intervention that would have left a firmer foundation for progress had it come before the summer of 1995. Third, notwithstanding at least subtle, if not more glaring, differences in institutional agendas and objectives, steady assistance from multiple IGOs and NGOs, most notably the EU, IMF, UN and World Bank, relatively positive economic outcomes are possible, if not probable, as evidenced by advancement toward standards needed for eventual EU membership.

Roles of IGOs and NGOs in Political Development Efforts in Bosnia, 1995–2016

As with the issue area of economic development, it is only appropriate to begin the discussion of the roles of IGOs and NGOs in political development efforts in Bosnia with a definition of the term "political development," which can be applied to the examination of any state under reconstruction. According to Francis Fukuyama, political development is best defined as "change over time in political institutions. This differs from shifts in politics or policies: prime ministers, presidents and legislators may go, but it is the underlying rules by which societies organize themselves that define a political order."[30]

NATO intervention and the negotiation of the Dayton Accord that followed brought the requisite break in intra-state conflict to allow for the conception, launch and implementation of political development initiatives in Bosnia. Those efforts and initiatives are best addressed temporally and in terms of organization types and issue areas during a given period, with the following four in particular to be examined: the Clinton administration era (1993–2001), the George W. Bush administration era (2001–09), and the Obama administration era (2009–16). In each case, one must focus on the motivations for intervention for each of the actors involved, whether states, IGOs and/or NGOs, their contributions to economic development in Bosnia and the outcomes of such efforts.

As with economic development, of the past three presidential administrations, Clinton's had the most direct role in assisting political development efforts in Bosnia, both in terms of American foreign assistance via a range of agencies and departments, including the State and Defense Departments and USAID, and in pressing for the requisite NATO intervention and presence to ensure a secure environment conducive to effective IGO and NGO efforts on the ground. With respect to the former, USAID helped build a foundation for democratic progress growing out of the tenets of good governance enshrined in the Dayton Accord. The EU played an even more significant role over the longer term, affording Bosnia an opportunity for progress toward eventual accession to that institution. With respect to the latter, myriad NGOs joined nation- and state-building efforts in Bosnia in the aftermath of the NATO intervention that ended the intra-state conflict raging therein in the summer and fall of 1995. A range of those NGOs have continued to operate in and/or provide reports on political developmental progress in Bosnia since, including Amnesty International, Freedom House, Human Rights Watch, Reporters Without Borders and Transparency International.

Freedom House tracks the extent of democratic freedoms afforded to the citizens of states across the world each year in the context of its annual "Freedom in the World Report," which has divided countries into three categories—Free, Partly Free and Not Free—since 1998. Scores in the index range from one at the "Most Free" end of the scale and seven at the "Least Free" end of the scale. From 1996 to 2016, Bosnia's rankings in that index have remained in the "Partly Free Category." However, its aggregate scores in the index, which measures the extent of political freedoms enshrined in a range of governmental and nongovernmental political and broader civil society institutions, demonstrated gradual improvement from five in 1998 and 1999, to 4.54 from 2000 to 2002, to four in 2003 and 2004. Bosnia first achieved a score of three in 2005 and has fluctuated in the 3–3.5 range since then, with a score of 3.5 in the most recent index, which was released in 2016.[31]

Similar to the Freedom House rankings, Transparency International tracks perceptions of the environment for economic and political interaction in countries across the world by assessing the extent of governmental and business corruption therein. Scores in the Transparency International Corruption Perceptions Index, which has been issued annually since 1995, range from 0–10, with zero and 10 designating "Highly Corrupt" and "Most Clean," respectively. Bosnia was first rated in the in index in 2003, with a score of 3.3. That score has since fluctuated between lows of 2.9 in 2005 and 2006 and highs of 4.2 in 2012 and 2013. It score in the most recent index, which was compiled in 2015, was 3.8.[32]

The most significant political development initiatives in Bosnia since the NATO intervention in 1995 have been left to the EU, which has worked to assist that state in achieving slow but steady progress toward eventual membership in that supranational organization. Bosnia's progress through the path to membership has proceeded through multiple stages to date. It commenced with EU efforts to help stabilize Bosnia and build a foundation for the development of democratic political institutions over the latter half of the 1990s. It continued with the EU formally naming Bosnia as a potential candidate for membership at the Thessaloniki European Council Summit of June 2003. Since then, a number of agreements between the EU and Bosnia and Herzegovina have been negotiated and come into effect, including visa facilitation and readmission agreements (2008), Interim Agreement on Trade and Trade-related issues (2008), and the Stabilization and Association Agreement (SAA) that was ratified and entered into force in June 2015.[33]

There are three principal insights for academics, policymakers and practitioners alike to draw from the political development efforts of IGOs and NGOs in Bosnia. First, as with economic development, a consistently secure environment on the ground is central to the development and maintenance of liberal democratic political institutions. Any lapses in security will always undermine progress as far as political developmental issues are concerned. Second, as a general rule, political development is a long-term process, regardless of the country and broader region involved in a given case. In places lacking a significant tradition of democratic governance, as with Bosnia, the timeline lengthens. Third, the degree to which progress can be achieved is contingent on security and stability that are in large part determined by the extent to which reconciliation can be achieved between opposing sides in the 1992–95 conflict. Progress in that area to date, in turn, was driven in part by the IGO and NGO transitional justice efforts under consideration in the next section.

Roles of IGOs and NGOs in Transitional Justice Efforts in Bosnia, 1995–2014

As with the previous three sections, it is best to launch this discussion of the roles of IGOs and NGOs in transitional justice initiatives in Bosnia with definitions of the terms "justice" and "transitional justice," which can also be applied to the examination of any state under reconstruction. The *Oxford English Dictionary* defines "justice" as "behavior or treatment that is morally right and fair," or, more pointedly, "the administration of law in a way that is fair and morally right."[34] The ICTJ defines "transitional justice" as "the set of judicial and non-judicial measures that have been implemented by different countries in order to redress the legacies of massive human rights abuses. These measures include criminal prosecutions, truth commissions, reparations programs, and various kinds of institutional reforms."[35]

Modern transitional justice efforts date to the post–World War II reconstruction and reconciliation processes in Western Europe following the Allied victories over National Socialist Germany and Imperial Japan in May and August 1945, respectively. In both cases, those surviving military and political figures atop the German and Japanese regimes at the conclusion of the war were brought to justice before international tribunals. Those trials and broader punitive measures targeting those associated with the wartime regimes helped to bring a sense of closure for the West German and Japanese societies, respectively. That proved the first step toward the necessary reconciliation between West Germans and their former adversaries in Western Europe in particular. Further, both West Germany and Japan became close American allies against the Soviet Union during the subsequent Cold War era.

Over the past two decades, two types of legal processes have been developed to exact justice for war crimes committed during the civil wars in Bosnia and Kosovo: those administered within—and outside of—the Balkans. The most significant examples of the former and latter, respectively, are the ICTY and the judicial branch of UN Mission in Kosovo (UNMIK), which are headquartered in The Hague, Netherlands, and Pristina, Kosovo, respectively.

The ICTY was created by a 1993 UN Security Council resolution in response to a growing humanitarian disaster in Bosnia, where Serb nationalists supported by the Milosevic government were routinely committing atrocities against Muslim and Croat civilians. However, no indicted war criminals were brought to trial under ICTY auspices until after NATO intervened following the July 1995 killings of some 7,000 Bosnian Muslim men and boys in the supposed UN "safe area" of Srebrenica by Serb troops under the command of General Ratko Mladic. The Srebrenica massacre was the principal reason that NATO ultimately intervened in Sarajevo in particular at the Clinton administration's request. However, regrettably, holding those responsible for the Bosnian genocide proved a considerably longer-term proposition.

Mladic, Karadzic and Milosevic were indicted in connection with the Srebrenica slaughter, but the former two managed to avoid capture until July 2008 and May 2011, respectively. In 2001, the UN succeeded in securing Milosevic's extradition from Belgrade to The Hague. ICTY proceedings against Milosevic commenced in February 2002 and came to a close without a verdict as a result of his death in captivity in his jail cell in March 2006. As denoted above, Karadzic and Mladic were also eventually captured and brought to trial before the ICTY. Karadzic was convicted of genocide in March 2016 after a 497-day trial and sentenced to 40 years in prison. Mladic's trial at The Hague commenced in 2014 and was still in progress as of early 2017.

Concurrent with the unfolding ICTY process, UNMIK officials established an internationally administered court in Pristina to try alleged perpetrators of war crimes in Kosovo. To date, it has conducted trials for both Serbs and Albanians, including a set of 2003 proceedings that resulted in guilty verdicts for four former Kosovo Liberation Army soldiers for beating, torturing and killing civilians on both sides of the ethnic divide. However, efforts to help facilitate reconciliation efforts between civil war adversaries through the development of truth and reconciliation commissions, akin to those conducted previously in South Africa and multiple countries in Latin America, stalled in Bosnia as well as Kosovo and other states across the Balkans.

There are three principal insights for academics, policymakers and practitioners alike to draw from the transitional judicial efforts of IGOs and NGOs in Bosnia. First, IGOs and NGOs can play central roles in funding and facilitating transitional judicial processes in states under reconstruction. They can do so with a combination of punitive and reconciliatory measures, including war crimes trials for high-level nationalist political figures such as Milosevic and Karadzic. Second, the judicial processes to bring war criminals to justice under international auspices typically proceed at a glacial pace, in terms of law enforcement and military efforts to track and capture suspects, who are then brought to trial. The cases of Milosevic, Karadzic and Mladic are illustrative of that pace. Third, truth commissions are by no means universally applicable paths toward reconciliation. They are effective in some cases, most notably that of South Africa in the 1990s, and stall in others, as is true of the Balkans generally and Bosnia specifically.

Conclusions

This chapter was designed to achieve seven related objectives. First, it reviewed the relevant literature on the roles of IGOs and NGOs in the conduct of nation- and state-building projects in states in the developing world since the end of the Cold War. Second, it reviewed the developments that led to NATO intervention in Bosnia in 1995 and the subsequent involvement of the EU, UN and a range of NGOs in nation- and state-building efforts therein since. Third, it examined the roles of IGOs and NGOs in economic developmental efforts in Bosnia from 1995 to 2014. Fourth, it examined the roles of IGOs and NGOs in political developmental efforts in Bosnia from 1995 to 2014. Fifth, it examined the roles of IGOs and NGOs in social and cultural developmental efforts in Bosnia from 1995 to 2014. Sixth, it examined the roles of IGOs and NGOs in security affairs in Bosnia from 1995 to 2014. And, seventh, it examined the roles of IGOs and NGOs in transitional justice efforts in Bosnia from 1995 to 2014.

The issues addressed and assessed in the aforementioned main sections of the chapter lead to the identification of four related sets of conclusions to be presented in the closing observations that follow. The first is the extent to which Bosnia represented a test case of sorts, one on how best to manage both U.S. military interventions and the post-conflict reconstruction and nation- and state-building projects that have followed in the evolving post–Cold War world. The second is the extent to which intra-state conflicts present distinctive challenges, relative to those commonly experienced in traditional inter-state conflict environments. The third is the degree to which managing, if not fully resolving, such conflicts demands significant breaks from past approaches and tools employed by states, IGOs and NGOs. And the fourth is the extent to which insights drawn from the political developmental process in one state under reconstruction can be applied effectively to another.

U.S.-led intervention in Bosnia represented a significant turning point with respect to America's role in Europe in the wake of the final act of the Cold War. In the aftermath of the George H.W. Bush administration's masterful orchestration of the peaceful conclusion of that global confrontation on American terms, punctuated by the reunification of Germany in October 1990 and implosion of the Soviet Union in the fall and winter of 1991, there was no peace dividend in the Balkans. The euphoria of the bloodless conclusion of the Cold War in favor of the democratic West over the communist East faded quickly as Yugoslavia split into multiple parts along ethnic and religious lines, including in newly independent Bosnia, where intra-state conflict erupted in 1992 and continued until NATO intervention and American-brokered negotiations produced the political blueprint for the path forward. That plan, which was negotiated and mandated in the Dayton Accords in the fall of 1995, resulted in the establishment of a power-sharing system through which a Catholic Croat, Orthodox Christian Serb and Muslim Bosniak rotated as president. NATO intervention stabilized Bosnia to the extent necessary for a negotiated resolution of the conflict that afforded both the alliance and later the EU, UN and other organizations myriad opportunities to assist in the reconstruction of that fragile state. It also gave the Clinton administration a chance to use an effective response to a significant crisis as the foundation for the enlargement of NATO into Central and Eastern Europe. NATO enlargement, in turn, created the security blanket the Central and Eastern European and Baltic states needed to move forward with the EU application and accession negotiation processes.

While preoccupied with events in Afghanistan and Iraq during their collective four terms in office, the George W. Bush and Obama administrations also provided the requisite leadership and support to extend the NATO and EU enlargement processes into the Balkans. Both administrations recognized that limited support for economic and political development efforts headed by the EU in Bosnia made sense, especially when coupled with political leadership on NATO enlargement and consolidation projects that eventually extended deep into the Balkans, with the potential to bridge the EU member geographic gap between Italy and Greece. Steps toward the achievement of those objectives include the acceptance of Albania and Croatia as members of NATO in April 2009 and Croatian accession to the EU in July 2013.

Beyond those accepted as members of NATO and the EU, Bosnia and other Balkan states have made progress toward both objectives over the two decades since Western intervention. That intervention itself made such positive outcomes possible, which was not previously the case, but certainly did not ensure their occurrence. That required determination from within states across the region, most notably Bosnia, the one most deeply torn by the intrastate conflicts of the 1990s. The willingness of the United States and its Western European allies to intervene to bring that conflict to an end and make and fulfill further commitments to the creation and maintenance of security and stability in Bosnia allowed for follow-on efforts from NATO, the EU, IMF, UN and a host of NGOs to take hold. The end result is a state that, while not perfect, has a much clearer path to a peaceful, prosperous future in Europe.

CHAPTER 12

The Future of Nation- and State-Building

At its core, this book was designed to achieve six related objectives, all of which are central to understanding the issue areas of nation- and state-building, from a range of national, international and institutional perspectives and as demonstrated in both theory and practice. First, it presented an overview of the history of nation- and state-building as a field of academic study on one hand, and as an issue area in which Americans have been involved directly as policy makers and practitioners on the other. Second, it examined the conditions under which outside actors, whether states and/or inter- and nongovernmental organizations (IGOs and NGOs) should intervene and then carry out nation- and/or state-building projects in weak, fragile and failing states, especially in the developing world, and assessed the typical costs and benefits of such endeavors. Third, it assessed the characteristics of a series of case studies of nation- and/or state-building projects driven by two distinct types of motivational factors—altruism and national interests. Fourth, it examined the challenges of conducting nation- and/or state-building projects amidst, or in the aftermaths of, inter- and intra-state conflicts. Fifth, it examined the similarities and distinctions between the use of local and national approaches to the conduct of nation- and/or state-building projects. And sixth, it examined the roles of (and interactions between) outside actors, whether states, IGOs or NGOs in the conduct of nation- and/or state-building projects.

The six aforementioned points were expressed in the contexts of 11 chapters, with the evidence presented serving as a necessary foundation for the analytical conclusions drawn and policy recommendations put forward in this closing chapter. The first of those 11 chapters presented an overview of the academic disciplines associated with the study of nation- and state-building projects and a synopsis of the relevant literature on that topic. The second assessed the conditions that typically determine when states, IGOs and NGOs choose to participate in nation- and state-building projects. The third examined the case of Somalia in the 1990s as an example of altruistic motivations for the conduct of a nation- and state-building project. The fourth examined U.S. management of policy toward the states of Latin America by the administration of President Theodore Roosevelt from 1901 to 1909, in large part through the Roosevelt Corollary to the Monroe Doctrine, which mandated American (rather than European) intervention in states in that region in danger of economic failure. The fifth presented the cases of nation- and state-building projects in the Philippines following Washington's victory in the Spanish-American War of 1898 and in the Western Zones of Occupation in the aftermath of World War II from 1945 to 1949 as examples of such initiatives motivated by U.S. national and international security interests. The sixth examined a case that exemplifies the security challenges of nation- and state-building projects in which the victor in an intra-state conflict must then attempt to reconstruct whatever of the state is left at the end of hostilities: the American South during Reconstruction following the end of the U.S. Civil War in 1865. The seventh examined a case of nation- and state-building at the local level: Vietnam during the conflict pitting the United States and South Vietnamese against the North Vietnamese and Viet Cong during the 1960s. The eighth examined a case of nation- and state-building at the national level: Iraq from the U.S.-led intervention and prosecution of Operation Iraqi Freedom in the spring of 2003 through the withdrawal of all American military forces from that state in December 2011. The ninth examined the challenges associated with developing a vibrant civil society in the context of a nation- and state-building project in the case of Mitchelville, South Carolina, a city for escaped slaves during the American Civil War. The tenth examined the use of a governmental agency to play one of the lead roles in the conduct of a nation- and/or state-building project through an assessment of the case the United States Agency for International Development (USAID) in Afghanistan from 2001 to 2016. And the eleventh examined the roles of IGOs and NGOs in conducting nation- and state-building projects via the case of Bosnia-Herzegovina from 1995 to 2016.

With these introductory observations as a useful point of departure for the ensuing conclusions, the balance of the chapter has four sections, which unfold in the following fashion. The first section examines the parallels and distinctions between the types of nation- and state-building projects the United States and its allies have participated in over the course of American history—those following inter- and intra-state conflicts in particular. The second section assesses the types of insights drawn from past nation- and state-building projects that are most and least likely to prove useful in planning and implementing such projects in the future. The third section assesses the conditions under which the United States is likely to intervene and participate in nation- and state-building projects or refrain from doing so moving forward. And the fourth section presents a set of closing observations on the prospects for the planning and implementation of nation- and state-building projects in the future and the most prudent and effective policies to employ along the way.

Historical Typology of Nation- and State-Building Projects

Playing the lead role in the conduct of nation- and state-building projects has been central to the formulation and implementation of policies on behalf of U.S. national security interests at a range of American historical junctures, with the circumstances distinctive to at least some degree in each case. Broadly, four basic sets of circumstances and types of actors have led the United States to intervene and then participate in a nation- and state-building project in another country. The first set features cases where the United States defeated an adversary in a global war and then rebuilt that defeated state's domestic economic and political systems in America's image, while leaving it with extraordinarily limited military forces in exchange for Washington's protection (e.g., West Germany and Japan in the aftermath of World War II). The second set features cases where the United States refrained from intervening in a regional inter- and/or intra-state conflict and participating in nation- and/or state-building efforts therein despite international pressure to do so (e.g., Rwanda in the spring of 1994 and East Timor in the fall of 1999). The third set features cases where the United States intervened in a regional inter- and/or intra-state conflict primarily on behalf its allies and/or international humanitarian concerns rather than its own national interests, then engaged in nation- and state-building efforts (e.g., Bosnia in the summer and fall of 1995 and Kosovo in the spring of 1999). The fourth set features cases where the United States intervened in a regional inter- and/or intra-state conflict primarily to safeguard its own national interests rather than just those of its allies, then engaged in nation- and state-building efforts therein (e.g., Afghanistan in response to al Qaeda's September 11, 2001, terrorist attacks against America). Each one of these four sets of cases has been at least touched on, if not examined fully, in a separate chapter in the book and bears revisiting below.

The United States engaged in its most significant (and also most effectively planned and conducted) nation- and state-building projects following an inter-state conflict in the aftermath of the Allied victories over Germany and Japan in World War II. The former project commenced in earnest following the National Socialist German regime's unconditional surrender in May 1945 and the same action by Japan's Emperor Hirohito in the wake of the American atomic bombings of Hiroshima and Nagasaki three months later. The United States played the lead role in managing the military control of the Western Zones of Germany on one hand and all of Japan on the other. In each case, American generals served as military governors and played very hands-on roles in reconfiguring the economic and political systems of the states under reconstruction under Western democratic and free-market auspices—Lucius Clay in Germany and Douglas MacArthur in Japan—in essence foreshadowing the roles U.S. servicemen and women would play in places like Bosnia, Kosovo, Afghanistan and Iraq from the 1990s to the 2010s.

The post–Cold War era began with the promise of the triumph of liberal democracy, punctuated by the collapse of communist regimes across Central and Eastern Europe in the winter of 1989-90, the reunification of Germany in October 1990 and the implosion of the Soviet Union in December 1991. Such hopes faded rapidly amidst such culturally distinctive and geographically far-removed instances of intra-state conflict as the tribal wars of Somalia (1992–93) and Rwanda (1994) in east and central Africa, and the breakup of Yugoslavia and subsequent civil wars in Bosnia (1992–95) and Kosovo (1998–99). The William J. Clinton administration inherited the Somalia imbroglio from the George H.W. Bush administration and maintained the U.S. military commitment to the ongoing humanitarian mission there, which ended tragically with the killing of 18 U.S. Army Rangers in an ambush by tribes loyal to warlord Gen. Mohammad Farrah Aideed in October 1993.

Ultimately, the disastrous ambush in Mogadishu, punctuated by television footage of the bodies of some of the American servicemen killed in the ambush paraded through the streets of the Somali capital by Aideed's forces, rendered the Clinton administration extraordinarily reluctant to engage in any further interventions abroad. That reluctance was most evident in Clinton's decision not to intervene in the face of an unfolding genocide in the spring of 1994 in the Central African state of Rwanda, in the context of which the Hutu-led government slaughtered some 800,000 ethnic Tutsis.

When the United States pressed for and then led military intervention by the North Atlantic Treaty Organization (NATO) in Sarajevo in the summer of 1995, it saved the Muslim Bosniaks from a comparable brand of annihilation at the hands of Bosnian Serb forces. Those forces were inspired and supported by Serbian President Slobodan Milosevic and led directly by Radovan Karadzic and Gen. Ratko Mladic, the political and military leaders, respectively, of the Bosnian Serb component of the population. The U.S. decision to act, which came in the absence of collective Western European capacity or will to stop the Serb onslaught, was indispensable for the Balkans, as well as a useful means to launch NATO's enlargement into Central and Eastern Europe.

Ultimately, Bosnia proved just the inaugural one of multiple American-led nation- and state-building projects in the post–Cold War era, with others to follow in the context of a global struggle against terrorist organizations driven by extreme interpretations of Islam, first in Afghanistan and then in Iraq. These latter iterations of nation- and state-building have faced some comparable challenges to those in the Balkans. However, there are also many distinctions, most notably the markedly higher economic, physical and political costs the United States and its allies have sustained in Afghanistan and Iraq, but also the decreasing willingness of the American electorate to tolerate comparable initiatives in the future.

Past as Prologue: Identifying and Applying Nation- and State-Building Insights

Historians and political scientists have long debated the extent to which one can draw lessons from past events and then apply such insights to the development of a clearer understanding of the present, and perhaps anticipate, if not predict, the future. The former are typically cautious when applying specific lessons from one historical context to another, given the inherent unpredictability of the behavior of individuals and the states they lead, although they acknowledge the potential to learn from the past in order to better understand the present and meet the future. The latter, by contrast, choose to employ theoretical models to explain common relationships between variables equally applicable to different historical events or combinations of events from one temporal period to the next.

With respect to the identification of insights associated with one nation- and/or state-building project that can be applied to other broadly comparable, if not structurally identical such projects, both historical and theoretical approaches have merit. History provides an instructive frame of reference to trace the evolution of approaches to nation- and state-building by the United States. Theories add frameworks to assess challenges to nation- and state-building projects from multidisciplinary and interdisciplinary perspectives, with emphases on the fields of anthropology, economics, geography, political science and sociology. Drawing on those approaches, this section identifies policy making and implementation insights in four issue areas, those associated with planning, implementation, adaptation and resilience.

The first step in any nation- and state-building project is planning. The earlier such planning can be undertaken in advance of a decision to intervene in state already (or soon to be) in need of reconstruction, whether of the economic, judicial, military, physical, political and/or social-cultural variety, the better. However, by itself, starting early is not enough to ensure a thorough and objective planning process. That requires multiple steps to be done properly. First, it is essential to appoint a planning team with as much prior expertise on (and practical experience within) the state targeted for intervention as possible. Excluding those who are wary of the distinctive cultural challenges that a given project may present in order to reinforce preconceived notions of a particular presidential administration or government department or agency is especially dangerous. Second, never ignore the past. Although each case is different in at least some ways, one can always draw insights from one case that are helpful in planning for others in the future. What was done right? What mistakes were made? What challenges were the most daunting? Such information is always helpful. Third, leaders must be willing to consider innovative options they run counter to the majority opinion on a given issue. Fourth, building space for adaptation into any plan is a prudent approach, particularly given the recent history of U.S.-led nation- and state-building efforts in Afghanistan and Iraq specifically.

Once a plan is in place, it is left to the civilian and military representatives of the states and organizations involved on the ground to implement that plan and collaborate with their leaders at home to respond to any obstacles that emerge along the way. The most challenging phase of a nation- and state-building project is often, albeit not in every case, the opening one. There are two principal reasons why. First, nation- and state-building initiatives are typically launched in countries emerging from, if not still in the midst of, conflict, whether of the inter- or intra-state variety. The extent to which the transition away from conflict and toward constructive economic, political and social/cultural development is necessarily conditioned by the levels of security and stability intervening actors are able to maintain. Second, it is likely, if not certain, that only a limited number of the military forces participating in nation- and state-building efforts do so with the benefit of significant on-the-ground experience in the state under reconstruction and thus familiarity and comfort with its distinctive cultural characteristics.

Adaptation is central to conducting any nation- and/or state-building project effectively. Even with thorough planning and preparation, which does not always occur (as the case of U.S. intervention in Iraq illustrates), one must be wary of (and prepared to respond as expeditiously as possible to) the unknown. The sudden fall of a regime, for instance, can leave intervening military forces to assume tasks they are unaccustomed to performing. Rather than leading a military assault on an opponent, a general and his staff may be forced to provide public medical and policing services until enough order can be restored for that need to be met with natives of a given country. Similarly, in attempting to counter an insurgent movement and/or terrorist organization, officers may need to conduct negotiations to woo a tribal leader into an alliance against one or both of the aforementioned two, which demands the rapid accumulation of local cultural knowledge.

In order for a state under reconstruction to progress in multiple issue areas, whether associated with economics, justice, politics, security or any other matters, resilience is essential. States on the brink of failure rarely, if ever, recover quickly. Instead, most advance in an irregular fashion, with setbacks of a variety of types the norm. Consequently, a state often must rebound multiple times in response to the inevitable challenges it faces in building enduring governmental institutions. Shocks to the system can come in the form of terrorist attacks by insurgent groups one year and economic setbacks the next. Ultimately, how well a nascent state and its economic and political institutions respond to the uncertainty that security threats foster determines whether a nation- and state-building effort produces lasting progress, transitory change, or reversion to the system that sparked conflict in the past.

To Intervene or Not to Intervene?

As a general rule, it is prudent for the leader of a state to consider past events and historical legacies when determining whether to intervene in another state in the present or consider doing so in the future. Consequently, it is best to begin any discussion of American intervention abroad with a review of the types of factors that have contributed most to past instances of planning and implementation of such U.S. actions. Those factors are best categorized in terms of threats posed to the United States in the following four issue areas. The first set of threats features those directly affecting the security of the American homeland. The second set features those that affect U.S. national interests abroad, including dangers to U.S. military and civilian assets dispatched to bases and embassies on behalf of those interests across the world. The third set features those that affect the interests of U.S. allies in regions of the world deemed vital to American interests. And the fourth set features those that raise broad-based humanitarian concerns within the international community but are otherwise not critically important to U.S. interests. The ensuing discussion assesses U.S.-led interventions associated with the eventual conduct of nation- and/or state-building projects in the developing world in particular since the end of the Cold War.

With respect to direct threats to the American homeland, one must begin with the nation- and state-building operations associated in some way with safeguarding the United States from terrorist threats emanating from the Greater Middle East since the events of 9/11. There are two such projects to consider, one in Afghanistan and the other in Iraq. The former was the more justifiable of the two in terms of American national security concerns, given that al Qaeda members planned, trained for and coordinated the prosecution of the 9/11 attacks against the United States under Taliban protection within Afghanistan. Striking back at al Qaeda and its Taliban hosts was an easy decision for Bush to make, in terms of both domestic and international support for that course of action. The latter, justified largely on the premise that Iraq possessed significant stockpiles of biological and chemical weapons, as well as an active nuclear weapons developmental program, with potential for use against the United States and its allies, is considerably more difficult to justify in hindsight. While some chemical munitions were uncovered, along with evidence of planning for a nuclear program, those findings did not match the Bush administration's emphasis on the extent of the WMD threat that drove the United States to war in Iraq.

As pertains to threats affecting American interests abroad, the post–Cold War era is particularly instructive. Absent the bipolar confrontation with the Soviet Union, the United States found itself in need of an adaptation of its strategic approach, concurrent with a shifting threat environment in the international system. Rather than base its interventions abroad on concerns and threats associated with American power and influence relative to the Soviet Union, the United States had to focus on less familiar, but critically important, challenges posed by the emergence of weak, fragile and failing states and transnational terrorist networks. The first such challenges came across a broad swath of the developing world stretching from East and West Africa to the Balkans.

Given the broad range of American interests across the world (and myriad allies to consider from region to region), determining when, where and how to intervene, what economic, military and political tools to use in the process, and the risks warranted along the way, has been particularly challenging since the end of the Cold War. The easier decisions are those involving vital U.S. interests, such as unfettered access to the vast petroleum supply of the Persian Gulf, preventing those adversaries who do not possess nuclear weapons from obtaining them, and containing the ones that have already acquired them.

Closing Observations

In order to develop an informed understanding of any issue area, it is best to gather evidence drawn from a range of cases that are temporally and geographically distinctive. By doing so, scholars, policymakers, and practitioners can identify challenges to the implementation of a given policy or strategy approach that recur from one case and temporal context to the next and those that relate more to the particulars of the environment involved at a given juncture. That analytical approach is certainly quite applicable to the history of nation- and state-building. The section that follows considers the afore-mentioned insights drawn from the range of temporal and geographic cases explored in the evidentiary chapters of the book, using those insights to assess the prospects for the future organization and implementation of nation- and state-building projects around the world. It addresses that uncertain future in three contexts: those associated with the choice to intervene and participate in nation- and/or state-building projects, plan such projects, implement them and determine when external actors should withdraw.

Determining when to intervene and participate in any nation- and/or state-building project in another country requires the leaders of the govern-ments and organizations to consider the circumstances in each case and assess the effects on their national and/or institutional interests. With respect to intervention (and subsequent participation in such operations) by states, the issue of security is typically of predominant importance. Consequently, the greater the probability that failing to intervene raises the extent of security threats to a state, especially on the home front, the more likely intervention becomes. Further, the nature and degree of urgency of security threats are driven by the characteristics of the strategic environment at a given juncture. Consider, for instance, the changing nature of the strategic environment faced by President George W. Bush over the course of his initial term in office. Bush began that term convinced that the nation- and state-building operations in Bosnia and Kosovo in which the United States played a central role were ini-tiatives of the past that his administration would not repeat elsewhere in the world. Yet the Bush administration wound up leading the two costliest nation- and state-building projects in American history, first in Afghanistan and then in Iraq. The most significant reason for the shift: a post–9/11 perception by Bush and his national security team that replacing autocratic regimes with liberal democratic ones was a viable strategy to reduce the pool of recruits for terrorist organizations generally and al Qaeda specifically.

The marked costs and ongoing implications of the operations the Bush administration launched and the Obama administration continued in both Afghanistan and Iraq will likely ensure that future administrations are guarded at best and extraordinarily reluctant at worst to commit the United States to participation in, if not leadership of, comparable endeavors in the future. Above all, the cases of Afghanistan and Iraq have demonstrated how challenging the construction of stable and enduring economic and political systems under Western auspices in countries lacking comparable histories and cultural norms can be. In the former case, the impetus for intervention was understandable, legitimate and necessary in the wake of the 9/11 attacks. In the latter case, the principal rationale for intervention (the elimination of weapons of mass destruction) was dubious at best in hindsight. Despite the differing rationales and justifications, the two cases are most comparable in that the total costs to date, in terms of loss of life and resources expended, have dwarfed the benefits, from the perspectives of Afghanistan, Iraq and the intervening state and institutional actors in each country.

The aforementioned costs of intervention in both Afghanistan and Iraq to date mean the level of perceived threats to the United States at home emanating from weak, fragile and failing states in the future must be pronounced for Washington to even consider intervening, let alone planning and engaging in endeavors comparable to Operation Enduring Freedom or Operation Iraqi Freedom. While such conditions are not certain to preclude any future American-led interventions and subsequent leadership of nation- and state-building operations, they will surely foreclose the possibility of any efforts on the scale of those already played out in Afghanistan and Iraq. The United States has already deceased its commitments to nation- and state-building efforts in each of those countries, given the military withdrawal from Iraq in December 2011 and the ongoing drawdown in Afghanistan, the completion of which will be left to Obama's successor in the White House, President Donald J. Trump.

Chapter Notes

Introduction

1. J. Garry Clifford, Kenneth Hagan, Thomas Paterson, *American Foreign Policy: A History Since 1900* (Lexington: D.C. Heath and Company, 1991), 537; Benjamin Schwarz, "American Counterinsurgency Doctrine and El Salvador: The Frustrations of Reform and the Illusions of Nation Building" (Santa Monica: RAND, 1991), 7.

2. Francis Fukuyama, *State-Building: Governance and World Order in the 21st Century* (Ithaca, NY: Cornell University Press, 2004), 99.

3. James Dobbins et al., *The Beginner's Guide to Nation-Building* (Santa Monica, CA: RAND Corporation, 2007), xvii.

4. FM 100–5, *Operations* (Washington, DC: Department of the Army, 1993), 13–6.

5. *Ibid.*, 13–6.

6. *Ibid.*, 13–6.

7. *Ibid.*, 13–6.

8. United Nations Peacebuilding Support Office, "Peacebuilding and the United Nations," http://www.un.org/en/peacebuild ing/pbso/pbun.shtml.

9. Andy Sumner and Michael Tribe, *International Development Studies: Theories and Methods in Research and Practice* (Los Angeles: Sage, 2008), 10.

10. Robert Chambers, *Ideas for Development* (New York: Routledge, 2005), 185.

11. Ravi Kanbur, "What's Social Policy Got to Do with Economic Growth?" Accessed June 23, 2011. http://www.arts.cornell. edu/poverty/kanbur/SocPolEconGrowth. pdf.

12. Lynnell Simonson and Virginia Bushaw, "Participatory Action Research: Easier Said than Done," *The American Sociologist* 24, no. 1 (Spring 1993): 28.

13. David Tucker, "Facing the Facts: The Failure of Nation Assistance," *Parameters* (Summer 1993): 34.

14. *Decentralization and Democratic Local Governance Programming Handbook* (Washington, DC: Center for Democracy and Governance, 2000), 63.

Chapter 1

1. Fukuyama, *State-Building*, 1.

2. *Ibid.*, 6.

3. There are numerous other terms that reflect various nuances and agendas, such as weak, fragile, collapsing, diminished, and premodern.

4. Steven Lamy et al., *Introduction to Global Politics* (New York: Oxford University Press, 2013), 137.

5. Fukuyama, *State-Building*, 96.

6. *Ibid.*, 7.

7. *Ibid.*, 7.

8. Stewart Patrick, "Weak States and Global Threats: Fact or Fiction?" *The Washington Quarterly* 29, no. 2 (Spring 2006): 30.

9. Liana Sun Wyler, CRS Report for Congress: "Weak and Failing States: Evolving Security Threats and U.S. Policy, 2008," accessed June 6, 2010. http://www.fas.org/sgp/crs/row/RL34253.pdf.

10. The Failed States Index 2009: FAQ & Methodology, accessed June 6, 2009. http://www.foreignpolicy.com/articles/2009/06/22/2009_failed_states_index_faq_metho dology.

11. Thucydides, *The History of the Peloponnesian War*, Book 5, 5.89.

12. Hans Morgenthau, *Politics Among Nations: The Struggle for Power and Peace*, 5th ed., rev. (New York: Alfred A. Knopf, 1978), 4–15.

13. Edward Hallett Carr, *The Twenty Years' Crisis: 1919–1939* (London: Macmillan, 1948), 109–120.

14. Andrew Moravcsik, "Taking Preferences Seriously: A Liberal Theory of International Politics," *International Organizations* 51, no. 4 (Autumn 1997), 516–521.

15. Immanuel Kant and Ted Humphrey, *To Perpetual Peace: A Philosophical Sketch* (Hackett, 2003), 13–14 and 345.

16. Russell Bova, *How the World Works: A Brief Survey of International Relations* (New York: Longman, 2009), 20.

17. David Baldwin, *Neorealism and Neoliberalism: The Contemporary Debate* (New York: Columbia University Press, 1993), 12.

18. Francis Fukuyama, *The End of History and the Last Man* (New York: Harper Perennial, 1992), xx.

19. Michael Doyle, "Liberalism and World Politics," *The American Political Science Review* 80 no. 4 (December 1986), 1151.

20. David Ricardo, *On the Principles of Political Economy and Taxation* (Mineola, NY: Dover, 2004), 81.

21. Thomas Friedman, *The World Is Flat 3.0: A Brief History of the Twenty-first Century* (New York: Farrar, Straus and Giroux, 2007), 587.

22. References to Claude, Herz, and Nye are all form Baldwin, 24.

23. *Ibid.*, 24.

24. James McCormick, *American Foreign Policy & Process* (Boston: Wadsworth Cengage Learning, 2014), 176, 182.

25. John Dietrich and George W. Bush, *The George W. Bush Foreign Policy Reader: Presidential Speeches With Commentary* (Armonk, NY: M.E. Sharpe, 2005), 26.

26. Francis Fukuyama, *America at the Crossroads: Democracy, Power, and the Neoconservative Legacy* (New Haven, CN: Yale University Press, 2007), 3, 48–49.

27. McCormick, 182.

28. Fukuyama, *Crossroads*, 46–47.

29. George W. Bush, "President Bush Discussed Iraq Policy at Whitehall Palace in London," November 19, 2003, http://georgew bush-whitehouse.archives.gov/news/releases/2003/11/20031119-1.html.

30. McCormick, 182.

Chapter 2

1. Richard Williamson, "Nation-Building: The Dangers of Weak, Failing, and Failed States," *The Whitehead Journal of Diplomacy and International Relations* (Winter/Spring 2007), 15.

2. Paul D'Anieri, *International Politics: Power and Purpose in Global Affairs* (Boston: Wadsworth, 2014), 363.

3. Gerald Parshall, "1943: The Pull of Distant Shores," *U.S. News & World Report*, 25 October 1993, 25.

4. Roméo Dallaire, *Shake Hands with the Devil: The Failure of Humanity in Rwanda* (New York: Da Capo Press, 2004), 375.

5. The Responsibility to Protect," http://www.un.org/en/preventgenocide/adviser/responsibility.shtml.

6. Definitions of human security range from focusing on all the broad threats to personal well-being and dignity to specific challenges posed by political violence. For general information on the concept of human security, see Amos Jordan et al., *American National Security* (Baltimore: Johns Hopkins University Press, 2009), 4 and 548–551; Henry Nau, *Perspectives on International Relations* (Washington, DC: CQ Press, 2007), 26; Joshua Goldstein and Jon Pevehouse, *International Relations* (New York: Longman, 2010), 425; Kofi Annan, "Secretary-General Salutes International Workshop on Human Security in Mongolia," Two-Day Session in Ulaanbaatar, May 8–10, 2000, Press Release SG/SM/7382.

7. Jordan, 551.

8. D'Anieri, 363.

9. Scott Burchill et al., *Theories of International Relations* (New York: Palgrave Macmillan, 2005), 58.

10. D'Anieri, 363.

11. Michael Ignatieff, "Power in the Service of Morality Abroad," *U.S. News & World Report*, 18 November 1996, 70.

12. *U.S. National Security Strategy* (Washington, DC : Department of State, 2002), http://2001–2009.state.gov/r/pa/ei/wh/15421.htm.

13. Michael Doyle, "Kant, Liberal Lega-

cies, and Foreign Affairs," *Philosophy and Public Affairs* 12, no. 3 (Summer 1983), 229.

14. *Ibid.*, 230.

15. *Ibid.*, 231.

16. *Ibid.*, 232.

17. Fukuyama, *History*, 4.

18. George W. Bush, "President Bush Discusses Iraq Policy at Whitehall Palace in London," November 19, 2003, available http://georgewbush-whitehouse.archives.gov/news/releases/2003/11/20031119-1.html.

19. D'Anieri, 48.

20. Lamy, 89.

21. Paul Miller, "Why and How to Fix Failed States," *Prism* 3, no. 1 (December 2012): 65.

22. Williamson, 13.

23. Miller, 68.

24. See for example Williamson, 16–17.

25. Fukuyama, *State-building*, 100.

26. *Ibid.*, 100.

27. Tucker, 34.

28. Robert Tomes, "Operation Allied Force and the Legal Basis for Humanitarian Interventions," *Parameters* (Spring 2000): 39–40.

29. Anna Simons and David Tucker, "The Misleading Problem of Failed States: A 'Sociogeography' of Terrorism in the Post-9/11 Era," *Third World Quarterly* 28, no. 2 (2007): 388.

30. *Ibid.*, 400.

31. *Ibid.*, 399. It should be noted that Simons and Tucker are rather short on the details of how this should be done, other than that it involve "means other than military force" (387).

32. Justin Logan and Christopher Preble, *Failed States and Flawed Logic: The Case Against a Standing Nation-Building Office*, Cato Institute Policy Analysis 560 (January 11, 2006), 11. http://www.cato.org/sites/cato.org/files/pubs/pdf/pa560.pdf.

33. James Dobbins, et al., *America's Role in Nation-Building: From Germany to Iraq* (Santa Monica, CA: RAND, 2003), xix, xx.

34. Fukuyama, *State-Building*, 38.

35. *Ibid.*, 39.

36. For a fairly representative criticism of Suri's conclusion, see Robert Kagan's "Nation-Building, Our National Pastime," *New York Times*, October 14, 2011. http://www.nytimes.com/2011/10/16/books/review/libertys-surest-guardian-by-jeremi-suri-book-review.html?_r=0.

37. Dobbins, *Beginner's Guide*, 256–258.

38. Charles Dunlap, Jr., "The Origins of the American Military Coup of 2012," *Parameters* (Winter 1992-1993): 4.

39. *Ibid.*, 11.

40. Tucker, 39.

41. Kenneth Allard, "Lessons Unlearned: Somalia and Joint Doctrine," *Joint Forces Quarterly* (Autumn 1995): 89–90.

42. *Ibid.*, 93.

43. Douglas Blaufarb, *The Counterinsurgency Era: U.S. Doctrine and Performance 1950 to the Present* (New York: Free Press, 1977), 287.

44. Harry Summers, *Strategy: A Critical Analysis of the Vietnam War* (Novato, CA: Presidio, 1982), 78–79.

45. Allard, "Lessons Unlearned," 91.

46. Fukuyama, *State-Building*, 99.

47. S.L. Arnold, "Somalia: An Operation Other Than War," *Military Review* (December 1993), 31.

48. James MacGregor Burns, *The Vineyard of Liberty* (New York: Alfred Knopf, 1982), 457.

49. E. Allen Richardson, "Architects of a Benevolent Empire: The Relationship between the American Missionary Association and the Freedmen's Bureau in Virginia, 1865–1872," in *The Freedmen's Bureau and Reconstruction: Reconsiderations*, ed. Paul Cimbala and Randall Miller (New York: Fordham University Press, 1999), 122–123.

50. Kipling's poem was published originally in *McClure's Magazine* 12 (February 1899).

51. Paul Haalsam, et al., *Introduction to International Development: Approaches, Actors, and Issues* (New York: Oxford University Press, 2009), 54.

52. *Ibid.*, 55.

53. Thomas Paterson, "Bearing the Burden: A Critical Look at JFK's Foreign Policy," *The Virginia Quarterly Review* 54 (Spring 1978): 208.

54. *Ibid.*, 209.

55. Tucker, 37.

56. Lawrence Harrison, *Culture Matters: How Values Shape Human Progress* (New York: Basic Books, 2001), 2.

57. David Landes, *The Wealth and Poverty of Nations: Why Some are So Rich and Some So Poor* (New York: W.W. Norton, 1999), 413.

58. *Ibid.*, xx.

59. Dobbins, *Beginner's Guide*, 3.

60. Benjamin Schwarz, *American Counterinsurgency Doctrine and El Salvador: The Frustrations of Reform and the Illusions of Nation Building* (Santa Monica: RAND, January 1991), viii–ix.

61. Thomas Montgomery, PBS *Frontline* interview, "Ambush in Mogadishu," at http://www.pbs.org/wgbh/pages/frontline/shows/ambush/interviews/montgomery.html.

62. Stanley Karnow, *Vietnam: A History* (New York: Penguin, 1991), 251.

63. Schwarz, 83.

64. Dietrich and Bush, 26–27.

65. See, for example, Michael Isikoff and David Corn's *Hubris: The Inside Story of Spin, Scandal, and the Selling of the Iraq War* (New York: Crown, 2006) as one of the more critical.

66. Fukuyama, *State-building*, 100.

67. *Ibid.*, 37.

68. Edward Mansfield and Jack Snyder, "The Sequencing 'Fallacy,'" *Journal of Democracy* 18, no. 3 (July 2007): 6.

69. Thomas Carothers, "How Democracies Emerge: The 'Sequencing' Fallacy," *Journal of Democracy* 18, no. 1 (January 2007): 22.

70. Rory Stewart and Gerald Knaus, *Can Intervention Work?* (New York: W.W. Norton, 2011), 71.

Chapter 3

1. Kimberly Martin, "Warlordism in Comparative Perspective," *International Security* 31, no. 3 (Winter 2006): 41.

2. Helen Metz, ed., *Somalia: A Country Study* (Washington, DC: Headquarters, Dept. of the Army, 1993), xiv, xxx–xxxiv; Frederick Fleitz, *Peacekeeping Fiascoes of the 1990s: Causes, Solutions, and U.S. Interests* (Westport, CN: Praeger, 2002), 130–131; "UN-mandated Force Seeks to Halt Tragedy: Operation Restore Hope," *UN Chronicle*, March 1993, 14.

3. Caspar Weinberger, "The Uses of Military Power," *Defense* 85 (January 1985): 2.

4. *Ibid.*, 10.

5. Edwin Arnold, "The Use of Military Power in Pursuit of National Interests," in *Parameters* (Spring 94), 5–7. Several alternatives to the Weinberger Doctrine were put forward in the aftermath of the Cold War.

President George Bush's Chairman of the Joint Chiefs of Staff, General Colin Powell, argued that force should be used only as a last resort, there should be a clear-cut military objective, that the military objective must be measurable, and that military force should only be used in an overwhelming fashion. While similar in most ways to the Weinberger Doctrine, Powell's criteria significantly omitted the requirement of vital interest. However, others such as President Bill Clinton's Secretary of Defense Les Aspin did not feel that Powell's criteria went far enough in recognizing the changed world environment. At particular issue was the idea of using the military only as a last resort. Aspin and others argued for a more activist role in what is known as the "limited objective school." The heart of this thinking is that the military can be applied in one place to compel an adversary to change his behavior elsewhere. President Bush was also one of those who viewed the military as one of the means available at any time to achieve national interests, not only the means of last resort. See *Ibid.*, 8–9.

6. Jeffrey Record, "A Note on Interests, Values, and the Use of Force," *Parameters* (Spring 2001): 16.

7. McCormick, 24.

8. *Ibid.*, 24.

9. Record, 10–11.

10. J.F.O McAllister et al., "Taking on the Thugs," *Time*, 12 December 1992, 29.

11. Bruce Nelan, "Today, Somalia…" *Time*, 21 December 1992, 29.

12. Russell Watson, "It's Our Fight Now," *Newsweek*, 14 December 1992, 31.

13. *Ibid.*, 30.

14. Thomas Dye, *The Irony of Democracy: An Uncommon Introduction to American Politics* (Belmont, CA: Wadsworth, 2011), 114.

15. Matthew Harmon, "The Media, Technology and United States Foreign Policy: A Re-examination of the 'CNN Effect,'" *Swords & Ploughshares: A Journal of International Affairs* 8, no. 2 (Spring 1999), 1.

16. Stephen Livingstone, "Clarifying the CNN Effect: An Examination of Media Effects According to Type of Military Intervention," The Joan Shorenstein Center for Press, Politics, and Public Policy (June 1997), 2.

17. Dye, 73 and 111.

18. Bruce Jentleson, *American Foreign Policy: The Dynamics of Choice in the 21st Century* (New York: W.W. Norton, 2003), 55.

19. Livingstone, 6.

20. *Ibid.*, 6.

21. Michael Mandelbaum, "The Reluctance to Intervene," *Foreign Policy* 95 (Summer 1994), 10.

22. Nik Gowing, "Real Time Television Coverage of Armed Conflicts and Diplomatic Crises: Does It Pressure or Distort Foreign Policy Decisions?" The Joan Shorenstein Center for Press, Politics, and Public Policy, 1994, 49.

23. Craig Hines, "Pity, Not U.S. Security, Motivated Use of GIs in Somalia, Bush Says," *Houston Chronicle*, October 24, 1999.

24. *U.S. Army Forces, Somalia, 10th Mountain Division (LI), AAR Summary* (Fort Drum, NY: Headquarters, 10th Mountain Division, 1993), 1.

25. Speech by Anthony Lake to the Trans-Africa Forum, Washington, DC, June 29, 1995, in *U.S. Department of State Dispatch* 6, no. 27 (July 3, 1995): 539.

26. David Pearce, *Wary Partners—Diplomats and the Media* (Washington, DC: Congressional Quarterly, 1995), 18.

27. Donald Snow, *Peacekeeping, Peacemaking and Peace-Enforcement: The U.S. Role in the New International Order* (Carlisle, PA: U.S. Army War College Strategic Studies Institute, 1993), 4.

28. "Confrontation in the Gulf: Transcript of President's Address to Joint Session of Congress," *New York Times*, 12 September 1990, http://www.nytimes.com/1990/09/12/us/confrontation-gulf-transcript-president-s-address-joint-session-congress.html.

29. Robert Bauman and Lawrence Yates, *"My Clan Against the World": U.S. and Coalition Forces in Somalia, 1992–1994* (Fort Leavenworth, KS: Combat Studies Institute, 2004), 24; Robert Oakley, "An Envoy's Perspective," *Joint Forces Quarterly* (Autumn 1993), 45; McAllister, 29.

30. Watson, 31.

31. Snow, 3.

32. S.L. Arnold, 35; *10th Mountain AAR*, 25.

33. Kenneth Allard, *Somalia Operations: Lessons Learned* (Washington, DC: National Defense University Press, 1995), 8–9.

34. Dobbins, *Beginner's Guide*, 3.

35. Dennis Jett, *Why Peacekeeping Fails* (New York: St. Martin's Press, 1999), 133.

36. Walter Clarke and Jeffrey Herbst, "Somalia and the Future of Humanitarian Intervention," *Foreign Affairs* 75, no. 2 (March-April 1996): 74.

37. Norman Cooling, "Operation Restore Hope in Somalia: A Tactical Action Turned Strategic Defeat," *Marine Corps Gazette* (September 2001): 95.

38. Allard, *Somalia Operations*, 13.

39. Thomas Montgomery, PBS *Frontline* interview, "Ambush in Mogadishu," at http://www.pbs.org/wgbh/pages/frontline/shows/ambush/interviews/montgomery.html.

40. S.L. Arnold, 33.

41. William Wunderle, *Through the Lens of Cultural Awareness: A Primer for U.S. Armed Forces Deploying to Arab and Middle Eastern Countries* (Fort Leavenworth, KS: Combat Studies Institute, 2006), 133–134.

42. Dobbins, *America's Role*, 59–60.

43. Clarke and Herbst, 74.

44. Mandelbaum, "Social Work," 16–17.

45. Watson, 31.

46. "Senator calls for Somalia pullout," *Columbus Ledger-Enquirer*, 14 July 1993. In fact, on October 15, 1993, the U.S. Senate adopted an amendment proposed by Byrd to cut off funds for military operations in Somalia after March 31, 1994, unless the president obtained additional spending authority from Congress. See P.L. 103–109, Section 8151.

47. See Allard, "Lessons Unlearned," 109, for a characterization of operations in Somalia as "muddling." See Donald Snow, *When America Fights: The Use of U.S. Military Force* (Washington, DC: CQ Press, 2000), 111, for a criticism of the halfhearted nature of U.S. state-building efforts in Somalia.

48. Oakley says, "My own personal estimate is that there must have been 1,500 to 2,000 Somalis killed and wounded that day." Oakley, *Frontline* interview.

49. Bruce Auster and Louise Lief, "What Went Wrong in Somalia?" *U.S. News & World Report*, 18 October 1993, 37.

50. David Rieff, "A New Age of Imperialism?" *World Policy Journal* 16, no. 2 (Summer 1999): 5.

51. Elaine Sciolino, "New U.S. Peacekeep-

ing Policy Deemphasizes Role of the UN," *New York Times*, May 6, 1994, A1. Quoted in Michael Mandelbaum, "Foreign Policy as Social Work," *Foreign Affairs* 75, no. 1 (Jan.-Feb. 1996), 20.

52. Mandelbaum, "Social Work," 18, 20, 30.

53. McAllister, 29.

54. Watson, 35.

55. Carl Hodge, "Woodrow Wilson in Our Time: NATO's Goals in Kosovo," *Parameters* (Spring 2001): 130.

56. Clarke and Herbst, 82.

57. Gordon Rudd, *Humanitarian Intervention: Assisting the Iraqi Kurds in Operation Provide Comfort, 1991* (Washington, DC: Center of Military History, 2004), 245.

58. Paul Horvitz, "Christopher Calls Plan by Senator 'Offensive' to the U.S. Constitution: White House Acts to Block Dole Move over Haiti," *New York Times*, October 19, 1993, http://www.nytimes.com/1993/10/19/news/19iht-haiti_9.html (accessed May 13, 2011). Douglas Brinkley argues in "Democratic Engagement: The Clinton Doctrine" *Foreign Policy* no. 106 (Spring 1997): 118–119, that ultimately what led President Clinton to intervene in Haiti was "mostly in response to domestic pressures" from the Cuban-American community in Florida and the Congressional Black Caucus.

59. Leslie Gelb and Justine Rosenthal, "The Rise of Ethics in Foreign Policy," *Foreign Affairs* 82, no. 3 (May-June 2003): 7.

60. Hodge., 128.

61. *Ibid.*, 131.

62. Ignatieff, 69.

63. *Ibid.*, 69.

64. Clarke and Herbst, 84.

65. McAllister, 29.

66. Belb and Rosenthal, 5.

67. Strobe Talbott, "Dealing with Anti-Countries," *Time*, 14 December 1992, 35.

68. Clarke and Herbst, 84.

69. James Fearon and David Laitin, "Neotrusteeship and the Problem of Weak States," *International Security* 28, no. 4 (Spring 2004): 7.

70. *Ibid.*, 43.

71. Rieff, 8.

72. Rieff, 9.

73. Stephen Walt, "Two Cheers for Clinton's Foreign Policy," *Foreign Affairs* 79, no. 2: 64.

74. Snow, 1.

75. Clarke and Herbst, 84.

76. *Ibid.*, 76.

77. Fearon and Laitin, 26.

Chapter 4

1. William Reitzel, "Mahan on the Use of the Sea," *Naval War College Review* 25 no. 5 (May-June 1973): 82.

2. Alfred Thayer Mahan, *The Influence of Sea Power upon History, 1660–1783* (Boston: Little, Brown, 1890), 25.

3. Ltr., Mahan to Ashe, March 12, 1880. Quoted in Peter Paret, *Makers of Modern Strategy from Machiavelli to the Nuclear Age* (Princeton, NJ: Princeton University Press, 1986), 463.

4. James Henretta et al., *America: A Concise History*, vol. 2 (Boston: Bedford/St. Martin's, 2002), 621.

5. *Ibid.*, 623.

6. Dana Munro, *Intervention and Dollar Diplomacy in the Caribbean, 1900–1921* (Princeton, NJ: Princeton University Press, 1964), 113.

7. Theodore Roosevelt's Annual Message to Congress for 1904; House Records HR 58A-K2; Records of the U.S. House of Representatives; Record Group 233; Center for Legislative Archives; National Archives.

8. Henretta, 623.

9. Richard Haggerty, ed., *Dominican Republic and Haiti Country Studies* (Washington, DC: Library of Congress, Federal Research Division, 1989), 21.

10. *Ibid.*, 21–22.

11. *Ibid.*, 21–22.

12. *Ibid.*, 22.

13. Theodore Roosevelt: "Fourth Annual Message," December 6, 1904. Online by Gerhard Peters and John T. Woolley, *The American Presidency Project*: http://www.presidency.ucsb.edu/ws/?pid=29545.

14. Haggerty, 23.

15. *Ibid.*, 22–23.

16. Haggerty, 23.

17. Theodore Roosevelt: "Fifth Annual Message," December 5, 1905. Online by Gerhard Peters and John T. Woolley, *The American Presidency Project*: http://www.presidency.ucsb.edu/ws/?pid=29546.

18. Haggerty, 23–24.

19. Haggerty, 24; Munro, 263.

20. Haggerty, 24; Munro, 264–265, 274.
21. Haggerty, 24.
22. Quoted in Munro, 534.
23. Munro, 270.
24. *Ibid.*, 292.
25. Haggerty, 24; Munro, 292–293.
26. Haggerty, 24–25; Munro, 294–295, 305–306.
27. Quoted in Max Boot, *The Savage Wars of Peace: Small Wars and the Rise of American Power* (New York: Basic Books, 2002), 168.
28. Haggerty, 26; Munro, 305–306; Boot, 168–169.
29. Haggerty, 26.
30. Haggerty, 26; Munro, 307–314.
31. Stephen Fuller and Graham Cosmas, *Marines in the Dominican Republic, 1916–1924* (Washington, DC: Headquarters U.S. Marine Corps, 1974), 25.
32. William Pulliam, "The Bare Facts about Santo Domingo," in *Current History: A Monthly Magazine of the New York Times* 13 (October 1920–March 1921), 401.
33. Haggerty, 26; Munro, 314–315, 533.
34. Munro, 315–316; Fuller, 52, 56.
35. Fuller, 54, 56–57.
36. Munro, 317–318; Fuller, 57–58, 60.
37. Haggerty, 26; Munro, 316–317; Fuller; 25, 35.
38. Fuller, 45.
39. Richard Millet, *Searching for Stability: The U.S. Development of Constabulary Forces in Latin America and the Philippines* (Fort Leavenworth, KS: Combat Studies Institute, 2010), 79–80; Haggerty, 26.
40. Fuller, 46–52.
41. Munro, 540.
42. Millett, 77.
43. Fuller, 48–51.
44. McCormick, 25.
45. Haggerty, 27.
46. Haggerty, 27; Fuller, 61–62.
47. Fuller, 66.
48. Haggerty, 27.
49. Fuller, 69.
50. Boot, 180.
51. Haggerty, 27–28.
52. Boot, 181.
53. Roosevelt, "Fifth Annual Message."
54. Munro, 115–116.
55. Munro, 271.
56. *Ibid.*, 131.
57. Fuller, 69.

Chapter 5

1. Dobbins, *Beginner's Guide*, xxxvi.
2. Jeremi Suri, *Liberty's Surest Guardian* (New York: Free Press, 2011), 106.
3. Earl Ziemke, *The U.S. Army in the Occupation of Germany, 1944–1946* (Washington, DC: Government Printing Office, 1975), 320.
4. Suri, 89–93.
5. Graham A. Cosmas, ed. *Correspondence Relating to the War With Spain Including the Insurrection in the Philippine Islands and the China Relief Expedition, April 15, 1898, to July 30, 1902* (Washington, DC: Government Printing Office, 1993), 858–859.
6. Congressional Serial Set, "Affairs in the Philippine Islands," Field Orders 26 (Washington, DC: Government Printing Office, 1902), 986.
7. *Elihu Root Collection Of United States Documents Relating to the Philippine Islands*, vol. 97, "Supplement to the Official Gazette" (Washington, DC: Government Printing Office, 1903), 2.
8. John Gates, *Schoolbooks and Krags: The United States Army in the Philippines, 1898–1902* (New York: Praeger, 1973), 70.
9. *Ibid.*, 82–83.
10. Testimony of Jesse Lee Hall, *Affairs in the Philippine Islands, Hearings before the Committee on the Philippines of the United States Senate*, SD 331, 57th Congress, 1st Session, part 3, 2430.
11. Field Orders No. 26, Headquarters 2nd Division, 8th Army Corps, April 22, 1899, *Affairs in the Philippine Islands, Hearings before the Committee on the Philippines of the United States Senate*, SD 331, 57th Congress, 1st Session, part 2, 893.
12. Gates, 86–87.
13. A reference to the Krag-Jorgensen rifles then fielded by the U.S. Army. A common ditty of the era advocated the Army's role to "civilize 'em with a Krag." See Edward Coffman, *The Regulars: The American Army, 1898–1941* (Cambridge, MA: Belknap Press of Harvard University Press, 2004), 35.
14. "General Otis Says the War is Over," *Leslie's Weekly* 90 (June 16, 1900), 462.
15. *Ibid.*, 462.
16. William Howard Taft to Elihu Root, 14 July 1900, Reel 463, Series 8, William Howard Taft Papers, Microfilm Collection,

Wisconsin Historical Society Library, Madison, WI; Suri, 95.

17. Suri, 100.

18. *Ibid.*, 94 and 96–97.

19. "The Philippine-American War, 1899–1902," Department of State, Office of the Historian. Accessed August 8, 2013. http://history.state.gov/milestones/1899–1913/War.

20. Russell Ramsey, *Savage Wars of Peace: Case Studies of Pacification in the Philippines, 1900–1902* (Fort Leavenworth, KS: Combat Studies Institute, 2008), 24–25.

21. *Ibid.*, 44–50.

22. *Ibid.*, 51.

23. Brian Linn, *The U.S. Army and Counterinsurgency in the Philippine War, 1899–1902* (Chapel Hill: University of North Carolina Press, 1989), 57–58.

24. Root, vol. 6, 325.

25. *Facts about the Filipinos* 1, no. 1 (May 1, 1901): 47.

26. Ramsey, *Savage Wars*, 51.

27. *Facts about the Filipinos*, 50.

28. Ramsey, *Savage Wars*, 55.

29. *Ibid.*, 55.

30. *Correspondence*, 1237.

31. Maurice Matloff, *American Military History* (Washington, DC: Department of the Army, 1973), 358.

32. Gates, 207.

33. Matloff, 358.

34. Ramsey, *Savage Wars*, 57.

35. Linn, *U.S. Army*, 60.

36. Ramsey, *Savage Wars*, 61.

37. Linn, *U.S. Army*, 59.

38. *Facts about the Filipinos*, 118.

39. *Correspondence*, 1287.

40. *Facts about the Filipinos*, 118.

41. Ramsey, *Savage Wars*, 73; Brian Linn, *The Philippine War, 1899–1902* (Lawrence: University of Kansas Press, 2000), 122–123.

42. Ramsey, *Savage Wars*, 79–80.

43. Linn, *U.S. Army*, 126.

44. John Jordan to My dear mother, 29 Oct. 1900, Jordan papers.

45. *Annual Report of Major General Arthur MacArthur, U.S. Volunteers, Commanding, Division of the Philippines* (Manila, Philippine Islands: Division of the Philippines, 1900), 35.

46. Ramsey, *Savage Wars*, 87.

47. Robert Ramsey, *A Masterpiece of Counterguerrilla Warfare: BG J. Franklin Bell in the Philippines, 1901–1902* (Fort Leavenworth, KS: Combat Studies Institute Press, 2007), 39.

48. Ramsey, *Masterpiece*, 35.

49. *Ibid.*, 37.

50. Congressional Serial Set, "Affairs in the Philippine Islands," 1609.

51. Ramsey, *Masterpiece*, 70.

52. U.S. War Department, *Five Years of the War Department Following the War With Spain, 1899–1903* (Washington, DC, 1904), 258.

53. Matloff, 359.

54. Quoted in Suri, 93.

55. Gary Hess, "Roosevelt's Practical Idealism and the Successful Management of the Alliance," in Thomas Paterson and Dennis Merrill, *Major Problems in American Foreign Relations*, vol. 2: *Since 1954* (Lexington, MA: D.C. Heath and Company, 1995), 203.

56. Atlantic Charter," available http://avalon.law.yale.edu/wwii/atlantic.asp.

57. Gorrest Pogue, *George C. Marshall: Organizer of Victory, 1943–1945* (New York: Viking Press, 1973), 466.

58. German Occupation Policy, Oct 44, in ASW, 370.8. Cited in Ziemke, 104.

59. Dobbins, *America's Role*, 4.

60. Ziemke, 320.

61. *Ibid.*, 291.

62. Ziemke, 390–391, 395; Dobbins, *America's Role*, 13.

63. Dobbins, *America's Role*, 14.

64. Ziemke, 336.

65. *Ibid.*, 334–335.

66. *Ibid.*, 336.

67. FM 3–24, *Counterinsurgency* (Washington, DC: Department of the Army, 2006), 1–13.

68. Ziemke, 396.

69. This ratio presents a stark contrast to the Philippines. In northern Luzon, for example, MacArthur commanded 25,000 American soldiers in an area of 30,000 square miles and nearly two million Filipinos. The resulting 12.5 soldiers per 1,000 inhabitants falls well below the FM 3–24 recommended minimum of twenty. See Ramsey, *Savage Wars*, 44.

70. Ziemke, 339.

71. *Ibid.*, 341.

72. Kendall Gott, *Mobility, Vigilance, and Justice: The U.S. Army Constabulary in Germany, 1946–1953* (Fort Leavenworth, KS:

Combat Studies Institute Press, 2005), 30–31.

73. Gott, 29–30.

74. Dobbins, *America's Role*, 21.

Chapter 6

1. *Columbia Daily Phoenix*, September 23, 1865.

2. *Journal of the Convention of the People of South Carolina: Held in Columbia, S.C., September, 1865* (Columbia: J.A. Shelby, 1865), 14–15.

3. *Journal of the Convention*, 103.

4. Richard Zuczek, *State of Rebellion: Reconstruction in South Carolina* (Columbia: University of South Carolina Press, 1996), 15.

5. Dan Carter, *When the War Was Over: The Failure of Self-Reconstruction in the South, 1865–1867* (Baton Rouge: Louisiana State University Press, 1985), 177; Zuczek, *Rebellion*, 16.

6. The first quote is from *New York Tribune*, April 15, 1866. Cited in Zuczek, *Rebellion*, 36–37, from a reprint of the *New York Herald* in *Greenville Southern Enterprise*, January 31, 1867. The second is from *New York Tribune*, April 15, 1866. Cited in Lilian Kibler, *Benjamin F. Perry: South Carolina Unionist* (Durham, NC: Duke University Press, 1946), 446.

7. *New York Tribune*, April 15, 1866. Cited in Zuczek, *Rebellion*, 37.

8. *New York Tribune*, September 22, 1866. Cited in Kibler, 411.

9. Zuczek, *Rebellion*, 39.

10. *Ibid.*, 39–42 and 50.

11. Alfred Williams, *Hampton and his Red Shirts: South Carolina's Deliverance in 1876* (Charleston, SC: Walker, Evans & Cogswell, 1935), 22.

12. Zuczek, *Rebellion*, 57.

13. *Ibid.*, 55.

14. *Ibid.*, 57.

15. W. Lewis Burke, "All we ask is Equal Rights." available http://law.sc.edu/equal_rights/5s-randolph.shtml.

16. William Tolbert, quoted in *Additional Papers in the Case of Hoge vs. Reed*, 41st Cong., 1st sess., H. Doc. 18 (Serial 1403), 34.

17. Zuczek, *Rebellion*, 60.

18. *Ibid.*, 60–61.

19. *Ibid.*, *Rebellion*, 62–63.

20. Rod Andrew, *Wade Hampton: Con-federate Warrior to Southern Redeemer* (Chapel Hill: University of North Carolina Press, 2008), 352.

21. Andrew, 352.

22. Zuczek, *Rebellion*, 72.

23. *Ibid.*, 74.

24. *Ibid.*, 75–76.

25. *Ibid.*, 77.

26. Kelly Greenhill and Solomon Major, "The Perils of Profiling: Civil War Spoilers and the Collapse of Intrastate Accords," *International Security* 31, no. 3 (Winter 2006/2007): 9.

27. *Ibid.*, 9; Wade Hampton to James Connor, April 11, 1869, in Box 5, Hampton Family Papers, SCL. Quoted in Zuczek, *Rebellion*, 77.

28. Herbert Shapiro, "The Ku Klux Klan During Reconstruction: The South Carolina Episode," *The Journal of Negro History* 49, no. 1 (January 1965): 40.

29. *Ibid.*, 40.

30. *Ibid.*, 41.

31. *Ibid.*, 41–42.

32. Richard Zuczek, "The Federal Government's Attack on the Ku Klux Klan: A Reassessment," *The South Carolina Historical Magazine* 97, no. 1 (January 1996), 53.

33. James Richardson, *A Compilation of the Messages and Papers of the Presidents, 1789–1897: 1869–1881*, vol. 7 (Washington, DC: Government Printing Office, 1898), 163–164.

34. Zuczek, "The Federal Government's Attack," 55.

35. *Ibid.*, 55.

36. *Ibid.*, 56.

37. *Ibid.*, 56.

38. *Ibid.*, 56.

39. *Ibid.*, 63.

40. *Ibid.*, 63.

41. Shapiro, 46.

42. Zuczek, "The Federal Government's Attack," 60.

43. Corbin to Williams, House Executive Document No. 268, Serial Set 1515, 42nd Congress, 2nd Session. Emphasis in original. Quoted in Zuczek, "The Federal Government's Attack," 60.

44. Zuczek, "The Federal Government's Attack," 64.

45. Timothy Smith, *James Z. George: Mississippi's Great Commoner* (Jackson: University Press of Mississippi, 2012), 99.

46. Nicholas Lemann, *Redemption: The Last Battle of the Civil War* (New York: Farrar, Straus, and Giroux, 2006), 87–88.

47. Lemann, 74.

48. *Ibid.*, 91–94.

49. *Ibid.*, 95.

50. *Ibid.*, 96.

51. *Ibid.*, 98.

52. *Ibid.*, 99.

53. *Ibid.*, 111–113.

54. *Ibid.*, 113–114.

55. *Ibid.*, 123.

56. *Ibid.*, 125–127.

57. Smith, 102.

58. Lemann, 129–131; Smith, 105–107.

59. Smith, 106.

60. *Ibid.*, 108.

61. *Ibid.*, 109.

62. Philip Dray, *Capitol Men: The Epic Story of Reconstruction through the Lives of the First Black Congressmen* (Boston: Houghton Mifflin Harcourt, 2008), 249.

63. Smith, 111, 113.

64. Zuczek, *Rebellion*, 167.

65. *Ibid.*, 167; Vernon Burton, "Race and Reconstruction: Edgefield County, South Carolina," *Journal of Social History* 12, no. 1 (Autumn 1978), 43.

66. Williams, 65–66.

67. Andrew, 376–377.

68. Burton, 43.

69. H. Leon Prather, "The Red Shirt Movement in North Carolina 1898–1900," *The Journal of Negro History* 62, no. 2 (April 1977), 175.

70. Williams, 105.

71. Prather, 175.

72. Williams, 255–256.

73. Zuczek, *Rebellion*, 169–170.

74. *Ibid.*, 170; Francis Simkins and Robert Woody, *South Carolina During Reconstruction* (Chapel Hill: University of North Carolina Press, 1932), 503.

75. Andrew, 367.

76. Zuczek, *Rebellion*, 171.

77. *Ibid.*, 173.

78. *Ibid.*, 172.

79. Andrew, 386.

80. Melinda Meek Hennessey, "Racial Violence During Reconstruction: The 1876 Riots in Charleston and Cainhoy," *The South Carolina Historical Magazine* 86, no. 2 (April 1985), 104–05; Williams, 121–122.

81. *Ibid.*, 101–102, 105, 112.

82. Theodore Barker, "To the People of Charleston," *Charleston News and Courier*, September 8, 1876.

83. Hennessey, 106.

84. Williams, 123, 125–126.

85. *Ibid.*, 246.

86. Williams, 364.

87. Zuczek, *Rebellion*, 197.

88. Greenhill and Major, 9.

89. Zuczek, *Rebellion*, 197–198.

90. Ulysses S. Grant, in *New York Tribune*, February 18, 1877. Quoted in Zuczek, *Rebellion*, 198.

91. Greenhill and Major, 13.

92. See Francis Simkins, "The Ku Klux Klan in South Carolina, 1868–1871," *The Journal of Negro History* 12, no. 4 (October 1927): 606–647.

93. Alfred Williams, "General Wade Hampton Campaigns in the 'Black Belt,'" in Katharine Jones, *Port Royal Under Six Flags* (Indianapolis: Bobbs-Merrill, 1960), 315 and 316.

94. Laura Towne, *Letters and Diary of Laura M. Towne*, ed. Rupert Sargent Holland (Cambridge, MA: Riverside Press, 1912), 289.

95. Dray, 306 and 309.

96. Stephen Stedman, "Spoiler Problems in Peace Processes," *International Security*, 22, no. 2 (Fall 1997): 5.

97. *Ibid.*, 12.

98. *Ibid.*, 8.

99. *Ibid.*, 8.

100. *Ibid.*, 8.

101. Zuczek, *Rebellion*, 55.

102. *Ibid.*, 55.

103. Stedman, 10.

104. Foner, 425–426.

105. Stedman, 12.

106. *Ibid.*, 12.

107. *Ibid.*, 13.

108. *Ibid.*, 13.

109. *Ibid.*, 7.

110. *Ibid.*, 15.

111. Greenhill and Major, 12.

112. Stedman, 15.

113. *Ibid.*, 15.

114. Zuczek, *Rebellion*, 210.

115. Andrew Birtle, *U.S. Army Counterinsurgency and Counterinsurgency Doctrine, 1860–1941* (Washington, DC: Center of Military History, 1998), 57–58.

Chapter 7

1. Esther Pan, "UNITED NATIONS: Nation-Building." doi: October 2003. accessed February 2014.

2. *Decentralization and Democratic Local Governance Programming Handbook*, 65.

3. Jeffrey Clarke, *The United States Army in Vietnam, Advice and Support: The Final Years, 1965–1973* (Washington, DC: Center of Military History, 1988), 171–172.

4. Lawrence Yates, "A Feather in their CAP? The Marines' Combat Action Program in Vietnam," in *U.S. Marines and Irregular Warfare, 1898–2007: Anthology and Selected Bibliography*, ed. Stephen Evans (Quantico, VA: Marine Corps University Press, 2008), 148.

5. Robert Komer, "Pacification," *Army* 20, no. 5 (June 1970): 23.

6. Maxwell Taylor, *Swords and Plowshares* (New York: W.W. Norton, 1972), 340. For other commentary on the lack of security, see George Herring, *America's Longest War: The United States and Vietnam, 1950–1975* (New York: Newberry Award Records, 1979), 159; Guenter Lewy, *America in Vietnam* (New York: Oxford University Press, 1978), 89; William Willoughby, "Revolutionary Development," *Infantry* (Nov.-Dec. 1968): 6; Thomas Thayer, *War Without Fronts: The American Experience in Vietnam* (Boulder, CO: Westview Press, 1985), 137; John Cleland, "Principle of the Objective and Vietnam," *Military Review* (July 1966): 86; Edwin Chamberlain, "Pacification," *Infantry* (November-December 1968): 32–39; Larry Cable, *Conflict of Myths: The Development of American Counterinsurgency Doctrine and the Vietnam War* (New York: New York University Press, 1986), 257.

7. James William Gibson, *The Perfect War: Technology in Vietnam* (Boston, MA: Atlantic Monthly Press, 1986, 273–274; Lewy, 89.

8. Philip Catton, *Diem's Final Failure: Prelude to America's War in Vietnam* (Lawrence: University of Kansas Press, 2003), 52.

9. Catton, *Diem*, 63–64.

10. Philip Catton, "Counter-insurgency and Nation-building: The Strategic Hamlet Programme in South Vietnam, 1961–1963," *The International History Review* 21, no. 4 (December 1999): 919.

11. *Ibid.*, 919–920.

12. Quoted in Michael Latham, "Redirecting the Revolution? The USA and the Failure of Nation-building in South Vietnam," *Third World Quarterly* 27, 1 (2006): 28.

13. *Ibid.*, 34.

14. *Ibid.*, 34.

15. Catton, *Diem*, 66–67. See also Catton, "Counter-insurgency," 927.

16. Catton, *Diem*, 67.

17. *Ibid.*, 68–69.

18. *Ibid.*, 60–70.

19. Latham, 34.

20. Anthony James Joes, *The War for South Viet Nam, 1954–1975* (New York: Praeger, 2001), 64; Catton, *Diem*, 73, 93–97; Latham, 35.

21. Latham, 35.

22. *Ibid.*, 35–36.

23. Report of visit by Joint Chiefs of Staff Team to South Vietnam, January 1963, National Security Files, Box 197, "Vietnam, General, 1/10–1/30/63," John F. Kennedy Library. Quoted in Latham, 36.

24. *Decentralization and Democratic Local Governance Programming Handbook*, 5.

25. Latham, 36.

26. George Kahin and John Lewis, *The United States in Vietnam* (New York: Dial Press, 1967), 140.

27. Latham, 37.

28. *Ibid.*, 36.

29. Tucker, 38.

30. Lewy, 112; Robert Doughty, *American Military History and the Evolution of Western Warfare* (Lexington, MA: D.C. Heath and Company, 1996), 642–643; Karnow, 272–273.

31. Lewy, 25.

32. *Ibid.*, 112.

33. Dave Palmer, *Summons of the Trumpet: U.S.-Vietnam in Perspective* (San Rafael, CA: Presidio Press, 1978), 221.

34. Latham, 37.

35. Thayer, 137.

36. Lewy, 25.

37. Thomas Scoville, *Reorganizing for Pacification Support* (Washington, DC: Center of Military History, 1982), 24; Clarke, 171.

38. Samuel Smithers, "Combat Units in Revolutionary Development," *Military Review* (Oct. 1967): 38. See Louis Swenson, "The Revolutionary Development Program,"

Infantry (Jan.-Feb. 1968): 28 for a similar definition.

39. Willoughby, 4.

40. Scoville, 12.

41. Clarke, 172.

42. Scoville, 26; Clarke, 172.

43. Robert Komer, *The Organization and Management of the New Model Pacification Program—1966-1969* (Santa Monica, Calif.: RAND Corporation, 1970), 44–45. Interestingly, contrary to most other observers, Lodge argued, "Ambassador Porter does not now absorb substantial responsibilities which distract his attention from revolutionary development." See Scoville, 41. Komer considers Knowlton to have been one of MACV's "brightest young generals." See Komer, 44.

44. Scoville, 26; Clarke, 172.

45. Clarke, 172–173.

46. Willoughby, 9.

47. Herring, 158.

48. Clarke, 172–173; Thayer, 169; Matloff, 640; Lewis Sorley, "The Quiet War: Revolutionary Development," *Military Review* (November 1967): 13–19; Willoughby, 5–11; Swenson, 28–31; Smithers, 37–41.

49. Herring, 158.

50. Swenson, 31.

51. Millet and Maslowski, 556.

52. Cleland, 85–86.

53. Herring, 158.

54. Dale Andrade and James Willbanks, "CORDS/Phoenix: Counterinsurgency Lessons from Vietnam for the Future," *Military Review* (March-April 2006): 90.

55. Yates, 148.

56. *Ibid.*, 148–149; Al Hemingway, *Our War Was Different: Marine Combined Action Platoons in Vietnam* (Annapolis, MD: Naval Institute Press, 1994), 178; Anthony James Joes, *Resisting Rebellion: the History and Politics of Counterinsurgency* (Lexington: University Press of Kentucky, 2006), 115.

57. Yates, 149; Lewy, 116–117; Birtle, 399–400; Swenson, 28; R.E. Williamson, "A Briefing for Combined Action," *Marine Corps Gazette*, March 1968, 41–43.

58. Lewy, 63.

59. William Westmoreland, *A Soldier Reports* (Garden City, NY: Doubleday, 1976), 166.

60. Yates, 148.

61. Lewy, 117.

62. James Olson and Randy Roberts, *Where the Domino Fell: America and Vietnam, 1945 to 1990* (New York: St. Martin's Press, 1991), 144.

63. John Tolson, *Vietnam Studies: Airmobility, 1961-1971* (Washington, DC: Department of the Army, 1989), 181.

64. Lewy, 143.

65. Julian Ewell and Ira Hunt, *Sharpening the Combat Edge: The Use of Analysis to Reinforce Military Judgment* (Washington, DC: Dept. of the Army, 1995), 160.

66. Joint Pub 1-02, *Department of Defense Dictionary of Military and Associated Terms* (Washington, DC: Joint Chiefs of Staff, 2010), 289.

67. Yates, 150, 156.

68. Gibson, 271.

69. *Ibid.*, 273.

70. *Ibid.*, 156.

71. Brigham, 49–50; Gibson, 305–308; Thayer, 138–139.

72. Gibson, 305.

73. Erwin Brigham, "Pacification Measurement," *Military Review* (May 1970): 51–53; Maurice Roush, "The Hamlet Evaluation System," *Military Review* (September 1969): 12–13; Gibson, 305.

74. Lewy, 134.

75. Gibson, 313.

76. *Ibid.*, 312; Gregory Daddis, *No Sure Victory: Measuring U.S. Army Effectiveness and Progress in the Vietnam War* (New York: Oxford University Press, 2011), 149–150.

77. Gibson, 313.

78. *Ibid.*, 313.

79. *Decentralization and Democratic Local Governance Programming Handbook*, 64.

80. Smithers, 41.

81. Chamberlain, 39.

82. Mike Sedra, "Afghanistan: It Is Time for a Change in the Nation-Building Strategy," *Foreign Policy in Focus*, November 15, 2002, https://www.hsdl.org/?view&did=438086.

83. "Revisiting Afghanistan's Reconstruction Teams," National Public Radio, April 7, 2013. Transcript available at http://www.npr.org/2013/04/07/176482780/revisiting-afghanistans-reconstruction-teams.

84. Michael McNerney, "Stabilization and Reconstruction in Afghanistan: Are PRTs a Model or a Muddle?" *Parameters* (Winter 2005-2006): 33.

Chapter 8

1. L. Paul Bremer III, with Malcolm McConnell, *My Year in Iraq: The Struggle to Build a Future of Hope* (New York: Simon & Schuster, 2006): 3.

2. For an in-depth examination of American participation in nation- and state-building projects, please James Dobbins, John G. McGinn, Keith Crane, Seth G. Jones, Rollie Lal, Andrew Rathmell, Rachel Swanger and Anga Timilsina, *America's Role in Nation-Building: From Germany to Iraq* (Santa Monica, CA: RAND, 2003).

3. *The Oxford English Dictionary Online*: http://www.oxforddictionaries.com.

4. *Ibid.*

5. James Dobbins, Seth G. Jones, Keith Crane and Beth Cole DeGrasse, *The Beginner's Guide to Nation-Building* (Santa Monica, CA: RAND, 2007), xvii.

6. Francis Fukuyama, *State-Building: Governance and World Order in the 21st Century* (Ithaca, NY: Cornell University Press, 2004), ix.

7. *Ibid.*, 99.

8. For an in-depth discussion of the characteristics of weak, fragile, failing and failed states, please consult the following sources: "2016 Fragile States Index," *Foreign Policy* (July-August 2016); Daron Acemoglu and James Robinson, *Why States Fail: The Origins of Power, Prosperity and Poverty* (New York: Crown Business, 2013); Ashraf Ghani and Clare Lockhart, *Fixing Failed States: A Framework for Rebuilding a Fractured World* (New York: Oxford University Press, 2009); Susan E. Rice and Stewart Patrick, "Index of State Weakness in the Developing World," Brookings Institution (2008) (http://www.brookings.edu/~/media/Files/rc/reports/2008/02_weak_states_index/02_weak_states_index.pdf); and Robert I. Rotberg, *When States Fail: Causes and Consequences* (Princeton, NJ: Princeton University Press, 2003).

9. Larry Diamond, *Squandered Victory: The American Occupation and the Bungled Effort to Bring Democracy to Iraq* (New York: Times Books, 2005), 21–22.

10. For an in-depth account of the 1991 Persian Gulf War, please see Steve A. Yetiv, *The Persian Gulf Crisis* (New York: Greenwood, 1997).

11. For an in-depth examination of the diplomatic prologue to (and prosecution of) the U.S.-led Operation Iraqi Freedom, please see Tom Lansford and Robert J. Pauly, Jr., *Strategic Preemption: U.S. Foreign Policy and the Second Iraq War* (Aldershot, UK: Ashgate Publishing Limited, 2004).

12. *The Oxford English Dictionary Online*: http://www.oxforddictionaries.com.

13. Samuel P. Huntington, "The Clash of Civilizations?" *Foreign Affairs* 72–3 (Summer 1993): 22–49.

14. Samuel P. Huntington, *The Clash of Civilizations and the Remaking of World Order* (New York: Simon & Schuster, 1996).

15. *Ibid.*, ix.

16. Geert Hofstede Center: http://geert-hofstede.com/national-culture.html.

17. Bernard Lewis, *The Multiple Identities of the Middle East* (New York: Schocken Books, 2001), 6–7.

18. Albert Hourani, *A History of the Arab Peoples* (Cambridge, MA: Harvard University Press, 1991), 4.

19. "Rightly Guided Caliphs," *Oxford Islamic Studies Online*: http://www.oxfordislamicstudies.com/article/opr/t236/e0687.

20. "2015 Corruption Perceptions Index," *Transparency International* (2015): http://www.transparency.org/cpi2015.

21. For detailed retrospectives on the planning and implementation of the de-Baathification process in Iraq, please see Bremer, *My Year in Iraq*, 19, 30, 39–42, 53–59, 83, 115, 155, 320 and 343–44.

22. George W. Bush, *Decision Points* (New York: Crown, 2010), 392.

23. For a thorough assessment of Operation Iraqi Freedom, please see Michael R. Gordon and Gen. Bernard E. Trainor, *COBRA II: The Inside Story of the Invasion and Occupation of Iraq* (New York: Pantheon Books, 2006).

24. *Ibid.*, 411–56.

25. George Packer, *The Assassins' Gate: America in Iraq* (New York: Farrar, Strauss and Giroux, 2006), 101.

26. Francis Fukuyama, *The Origins of Political Order: From Prehuman Times to the French Revolution* (New York: Farrar, Strauss and Giroux, 2011), 13.

27. For an in-depth examination of ISIS, please see Jack Covarrubias, Tom Lansford and Robert J. Pauly, Jr., ed., *The New Islamic*

State: Ideology, Religion and Violent Extremism in the 21st Century (New York: Routledge, 2016).

28. Larry Diamond, "What Went Wrong and Right in Iraq," in Francis Fukuyama, ed., *Nation-Building: Beyond Afghanistan and Iraq* (Baltimore: Johns Hopkins University Press, 2006), 181–82.

29. *Ibid.*

Chapter 9

1. *Decentralization and Democratic Local Governance Programming Handbook*, 2.

2. Dobbins, *Beginner's Guide to Nation-Building*, 200.

3. *Decentralization and Democratic Local Governance Programming Handbook*, 46.

4. Dobbins, *Beginner's Guide to Nation-Building*, 200.

5. Michael Roskin et al., *Political Science* (Boston: Longman, 2012), 121.

6. *Decentralization and Democratic Local Governance Programming Handbook*, 46.

7. Dobbins, *Beginner's Guide*, 200; Roskin, 121.

8. See for example Roskin, 121.

9. Edward Pierce to Salmon Chase, January 19, 1862, item 36, Port Royal Correspondence, National Archives.

10. *The War of the Rebellion: A Compilation of the Official Records of the Union and Confederate Armies*, Series 1, Volume 6, Chapter XV (Washington, DC: Government Printing Office, 1880–1901), 222–223.

11. *Ibid.*, 30.

12. Edward Pierce to the Reverend Mr. Jacob Manning, January 19, 1862, Edward Atkinson MSS, Massachusetts Historical Society.

13. Willie Lee Rose, *Rehearsal for Reconstruction: The Port Royal Experiment* (New York: Bobbs-Merrill, 1964), 35.

14. *First Annual Report of the Boston Educational Commission for Freedmen* (Boston: D. Clapp, 1863), 4; Rose, 35.

15. *The Freedmen's Journal*, vol. 1 (Boston: New England Freedmen's Aid Society, 1865), 13.

16. Kay Ann Taylor, "Mary S. Peake and Charlotte L. Forten: Black Teachers During the Civil War and Reconstruction," *The Journal of Negro Education* 74, no. 2 (Spring, 2005): 125.

17. Rose, 40–41.

18. American Missionary Association, *History of the American Missionary Association: With Illustrative Facts and Anecdotes* (New York: The Association, 1891), 10.

19. 1872 AMA report quoted in John Rachal, "Gideonites and Freedmen: Adult Literacy Education at Port Royal, 1862–1865," *The Journal of Negro Education* 55, no. 4 (Autumn 1986), 59.

20. AMA, 10.

21. *Ibid.*, 11–12.

22. Rose , 26.

23. *Ibid.*, 41.

24. *Ibid.*, 219.

25. E. Allen Richardson, "Architects of a Benevolent Empire: The Relationship between the American Missionary Association and the Freedmen's Bureau in Virginia, 1865–1872," in *The Freedmen's Bureau and Reconstruction: Reconsiderations*, ed. Paul Cimbala and Randall Miller (New York: Fordham University Press, 1999), 123.

26. *Ibid.*, 122.

27. Eric Foner, *Reconstruction: America's Unfinished Revolution, 1863–1877* (New York: Harper & Row, 1988), 52.

28. W.J. Richardson to George Whipple, May 21, 1864, uncatalogued box labeled "1862—A–J," AMA MSS.

29. Richardson, 124.

30. *Ibid.*, 119.

31. Rose, 333–334.

32. Fish Haul Creek Park marker. See also listings in *The Freedmen's Journal*.

33. Rose, 322.

34. Edward Pierce, *The Negroes at Port Royal: Report of E.L. Pierce, Government Agent, to the Hon. Salmon P. Chase, Secretary of the Treasury* (Boston: R.F. Wallcut, 1862), 5–6.

35. Elizabeth Hyde Botume, *First Days Amongst the Contrabands* (Boston: Lee and Shephard Publishers, 1893), 16.

36. Pierce, "Report," 5–6.

37. Towne, 73–75. The description of St. Helenaville is from Guion Griffis Johnson, *A Social History of the Sea Islands* (Chapel Hill: University of North Carolina Press, 1930), 110.

38. Botume, 35.

39. *Ibid.*, 79. The *New Georgia Encyclopedia* concurs with this estimate. See http://www.georgiaencyclopedia.org/nge/Article.jsp?id=h-1084.

40. Rose, 320. See Elizabeth Pearson, *Letters From Port Royal: Written at the Time of the Civil War* (Boston: W.B. Clarke, 1906), 293, and Towne, 148–149, for descriptions of the conditions of the march.

41. Rose, 321.

42. Towne, 149.

43. Botume, 133.

44. Rose, 322.

45. Pierce, "Report," 7.

46. Towne, 57.

47. *Ibid.*, 75.

48. Botume, 16.

49. Rose, 332.

50. *Ibid.*, 50–51.

51. *Ibid.*, 52.

52. *Ibid.*, 51 and 62.

53. *New York Times*, October 8, 1862, 1. Quoted in Michael Trinkley and Debi Hacker, "The Archaeological Manifestations of the 'Port Royal Experiment' at Mitchelville, Hilton Head, South Carolina" (Columbia, SC: Chicora Foundation, Inc, 1987), 4.

54. Joseph Danielson, *War's Desolating Scourge: The Union's Occupation of Northern Alabama* (Lawrence: University Press of Kansas, 2012), 79–81.

55. Trinkley, 4.

56. *New York Times*, "Gen. Mitchell and the Contrabands," October 30, 1862. Accessed July 1, 2013. http://www.nytimes.com/1862/10/30/news/gen-mitchel-and-the-contrabands.html.

57. Robert Carse, *Department of the South: Hilton Head Island in the Civil War* (Columbia, SC: The State Printing Company, 1961), 81.

58. Maj. Gen. Ormsby M. Mitchel to Secretary of the Treasury Salmon P. Chase, 13 October 1862, in "Gen. Mitchel and the Contrabands," *New York Times*, 30 October 1862.

59. William Sherman, *Memoirs* (New York: D. Appleton, 1875), 246.

60. *The New South*, August 22, 1863. Cited in JoAnn Zeise, "'Dawn of Freedom': The Freedmen's Town of Mitchelville on Hilton Head Island, SC." Master's thesis, University of South Carolina, 2012, 42.

61. *The New South*, "Dedication of the Negro Church," October 18, 1862.

62. Trinkley, 4. See also Phineas Camp Headley, *The Patriot Boy: Or, The Life and Career of Major-General Ormsby M. Mitchel* (New York: W.H. Appleton, 1865), 256.

63. Carse, 91.

64. *New York Times*, "Gen. Mitchell and the Contrabands," October 30, 1862.

65. Charles Carleton Coffin, *Four Years of Fighting: A Volume of Personal Observation with the Army and Navy, from the First Battle of Bull Run to the Fall of Richmond* (Boston: Ticknor and Fields, 1866), 231–32.

66. *The Freedmen's Journal*, vol. 1, 13.

67. *Ibid.*, 13.

68. *The New South*, November 18, 1862; *New York Commercial Advertiser*, April 27, 1865; *The National Republican*, January 2, 1877.

69. Whitelaw Reid, *After the War: A Southern Tour: May 1, 1865, to May 1, 1866* (New York: Moore, Wilstach & Baldwin, 1866), 91.

70. Among the numerous definitions and connotations of "development," one common theme is that development encompasses "change" in a variety of aspects of the human condition. See Andy Sumner and Michael Tribe, *International Development Studies: Theories and Methods in Research and Practice* (Los Angeles: Sage, 2008), 10. Robert Chambers notes that the preference is for "good change," but because "any development agenda is value-laden," interpretations of what "good change" is are also problematic. See Robert Chambers, *Ideas for Development* (New York: Routledge, 2005), 185.

71. Rose, 229.

72. Dobbins, *Beginner's Guide*, 200.

73. Rose, 315.

74. Pierce, "Report," 24.

75. Clarence Mohr, "Before Sherman: Georgia Blacks and the Union War Effort, 1861–1864," *The Journal of Southern History* 45, no. 3 (August 1979): 349.

76. Fish Haul Park marker.

77. Mohr, 349.

78. Pierce, *Report*, 10 and 31–32.

79. Edward Pierce, "The Freedmen at Port Royal," *The North American Review* 101, no. 208 (July 1865): 9.

80. *The New South*, "Church Organization at Hilton Head," August 30, 1862. Accessed July 23, 2013. http://digital.tcl.sc.edu/cdm/compoundobject/collection/NSN/id/102/show/100/rec/1.

81. *New York Times*, "A Negro Conventicle—The Rev. Abraham Murchison—Trip to Seabrook—The Drayton Plantation—The

Elliott Plantation—Rose and Her Family—A Negro Bayoneted—The Contrabands at Seabrook—A Human Phenomenon—Cotton Planting—The Bombardment of Fort Pulaski to Commence," April 19, 1862. Accessed July 23, 2013. http://www.nytimes.com/1862/04/19/news/negro-conventicle-rev-abraham-murchison-trip-seabrook-drayton-plantation-elliott.html?pagewanted=1.

82. "Arming the Negroes of the South:; Inauguration of the Policy in South Carolina The First Meeting of the Blacks to Consider the Question Their Enthusiasm for the Government and Willingness to Fight. & c.," *New York Times*, May 1, 1862. Accessed July 24, 2013. http://www.nytimes.com/1862/05/01/news/arming-negroes-south-inauguration-policy-south-carolina-first-meeting-blacks.html.; Mohr, 349.

83. *New York Times*, "A Negro Conventicle," April 19, 1862. Accessed July 23, 2013. http://www.nytimes.com/1862/04/19/news/negro-conventicle-rev-abraham-murchison-trip-seabrook-drayton-plantation-elliott.html?pagewanted=1.

84. Mohr, 349.

85. *The Island Packet*, August 13, 1995.

86. "St. James Baptist Church Marks its Faith," *The Beaufort Gazette*, May 23, 2011. Accessed July 23, 2013. http://www.islandpacket.com/2011/05/23/1664052/st-james-baptist-church-marks.html.

87. "Queen Chapel AME Church: A beacon for freedom, the community," *Beaufort Gazette*, September 11, 2010. Accessed July 23, 2013. http://www.islandpacket.com/2010/09/11/1368736/queen-chapel-ame-church-a-beacon.html?referredfrom=netnewsreports.com. See also Fish Haul Park marker.

88. Pierce, *Freedmen*, 9.

89. Pierce, *Report*, 28.

90. Rose, 229.

91. William Pease, "Three Years Among the Freedmen: William C. Gannett and the Port Royal Experiment," *Journal of Negro History* 42 (1957): 101.

92. Botume, 57.

93. Towne, 27.

94. Rose, 88.

95. *Ibid.*, 203.

96. Oliver Howard, *Report of Brevet Major General O.O. Howard Commissioner Bureau of Refugees, Freedmen, and Abandoned Lands to the Secretary of War, Oct. 20, 1869* (Washington, DC: Government Printing Office, 1869), 11.

97. Zeise, 45.

98. *The Freedmen's Journal*, vol. 1, 118.

99. Richard Butchart, *Schooling the Freed People: Teaching, Learning, and the Struggle for Black Freedom, 1861–1876* (Chapel Hill: University of North Carolina Press, 2010), 117.

100. Jane Briggs Smith to William Fuller Fisk, July 31, 1866. Jane Briggs Smith Fiske Papers, American Antiquarian Society, Worcester, Massachusetts. Accessed July 24, 2013. http://faculty.assumption.edu/aas/Manuscripts/fiske/09-08-1866.html.

101. *The Freedmen's Journal*, vol. 1, 13.

102. *Annual Report of the Missionary Society, Sunday-School Union and Tract Society of the Methodist Episcopal Church*, vols. 44–47 (New York: The Society, 1863–1866), 153; *The Freedmen's Journal*, vol. 1, 14.

103. See, for example, Dobbins, *Beginner's Guide*, xxxvii, and Fukuyama, *State-building*, 100.

104. Fort Howell, National Register of Historic Places Registration Form, 4. Available http://www.nationalregister.sc.gov/beaufort/S10817707070/S10817707070.pdf.

105. Fort Howell, 14–15, citing Brig. Gen. Edward E. Potter, Hilton Head District, to Col. George W. Baird, 32nd United States Colored Infantry, 19 August 1864, National Archives Record Group 393, Records of United States Army Continental Commands, 1821–1920, National Archives and Records Administration, Washington, DC.

106. *OR*, Series 1, vol. 35, part 2, 302; Ezra Warner, *Generals in Blue: Lives of the Union Commanders* (Baton Rouge: Louisiana State University Press, 1964), 240.

107. Fort Howell, 15–16, citing Suter to Potter, 2 September 1864, and Captain Charles R. Suter, *Journal of Engineering Operations*, Department of the South, United States Army, 1863–1864, National Archives RG 77, copy on file at South Carolina SHPO.

108. Fort Howell, 16–17.

109. Establishment of Mitchelville on Hilton Head Island, General Orders No. 3, Bvt. Brig. Gen. M.S. Littlefield, February 16, 1865. See also Trinkley, 4; Reid, 89–91; Martin Abbott, "Freedom's Cry: Negroes and Their Meetings in South Carolina, 1865–

1869," *The Phylon Quarterly* 20, no. 3 (3rd Quarter 1959), 266.

110. Reid, 127–129.

111. Ira Berlin, et al, *Freedom: A Documentary History of Emancipation, 1861–1867.* Series I, vol. III (New York: Cambridge University Press, 1990), 314–316; the Rev. Abram Mercherson to his excellency Maj. Gen. J.G. Foster, 12 Aug. 1864, M-268 1864, Letters Received, ser. 4109, Dept. of the South, RG 393 Pt. 1 [C-1327]; Lt. Col. James F. Hall to Col. M.S. Littlefield, 4 Oct. 1864, Vol. 209/475 DS, p. 62, Letters Sent by the Provost Marshal General, ser 4270, Dept. of the South, RG 393, Pt. 1 [C-1327].

112. Christopher T. Espenshade, "Contraband, Refugee, Freedmen: Archaeological and Historical Investigations on the Western Fringe of Mitchelville, Hilton Head, South Carolina," (Charleston, SC: Brockington and Associates, 1991), 17.

113. Trinkley, 5–6.

114. *Ibid.*, 5.

115. "The Civil War, Hilton Head, and The Evolution of Mitchelville" (Columbia, SC: Chicora Foundation, 1995), 8–10.

116. Sumner and Tribe, 142–144.

Chapter 10

1. For an incisive primer on U.S. and broader Western intervention in Afghanistan, please see Tom Lansford, *A Bitter Harvest: U.S. Foreign Policy and Afghanistan* (Aldershot, UK: Ashgate, 2003).

2. James Dobbins, Seth G. Jones, Keith Crane and Beth Cole DeGrasse, *The Beginner's Guide to Nation-Building* (Santa Monica, CA: RAND, 2007), ix–xx.

3. Richard Haass, *The Reluctant Sheriff: The United States After the Cold War* (New York: Council on Foreign Relations Press, 1997), 6.

4. United States Agency for International Development (USAID), "Mission Statement": https://www.usaid.gov/who-we-are/mission-vision-values.

5. For an in-depth examination of the Marshall Plan and its implications for the European integration process during the Cold War, please see Geir Lundestad, *"Empire" by Integration: The United States and European Integration, 1945–1997* (New York: Oxford University Press, 1998).

6. John Lewis Gaddis, *We Now Know: Rethinking Cold War History* (New York: Oxford University Press, 1997), 38.

7. Quoted in USAID, "USAID History": https://www.usaid.gov/who-we-are/usaid-history.

8. *Ibid.*

9. For a thorough assessment of the British-Russian "Great Game" for control over Central Asia, please see Evgeny Sergeev, *The Great Game, 1856–1907: Russo-British Relations in Central and East Asia* (Baltimore: Johns Hopkins University Press, 2014).

10. For a thorough assessment of the rise of the Taliban in Afghanistan during the 1990s, please see Ahmed Rashid, *Taliban: Militant Islam, Oil and Fundamentalism in Central Asia*, 2nd ed. (New Haven, CT: Yale University Press, 2010).

11. For insiders' accounts of the Navy SEAL operation that eliminated Al Qaeda leader Osama bin Laden, please see Michael Morell, *The Great War of Our Time: The CIA's Fight Against Terrorism—From Al Qaida to ISIS* (New York: Twelve, 2015), 144–76, and Robert M. Gates, *Duty: Memoirs of a Secretary at War* (New York: Alfred A. Knopf, 2014), 538–46.

12. Barack H. Obama, "An Update on Our Mission in Afghanistan," White House Office of the Press Secretary: https://www.whitehouse.gov/blog/2016/07/06/update-our-mission-afghanistan.

13. *Oxford English Dictionary Online*: http://www.oxforddictionaries.com/us/definition/american_english/economic-growth?q=economic+growth.

14. World Bank, "Glossary": http://www.worldbank.org/depweb/english/beyond/global/glossary.html.

15. For an incisive assessment of the roots of the Taliban insurgency in Afghanistan, please see Seth G. Jones, "The Rise of Afghanistan's Insurgency: State Failure and Jihad," *International Security* 32–4 (Spring 2008): 7–40.

16. *Ibid.*, 34.

17. "Afghanistan: Donors Pledge $4.5 billion in Tokyo," United Nations Development Program (22 January 2002): http://reliefweb.int/report/afghanistan/afghanistan-donors-pledge-45-billion-tokyo.

18. Transparency International, "Corruption Perception Indices," 2007–15: http://

www.transparency.org/research/cpi/cpi_2004/0/.

19. Michael O'Hanlon, "Afghanistan Index" (March 2016), Brookings Institution: https://www.brookings.edu/wp-content/uploads/2016/07/index20160330.pdf.

20. "2014 United Nations Human Development Index": http://hdr.undp.org/en/indicators/137906.

21. Francis Fukuyama, *Political Order and Political Decay: From the Industrial Revolution to the Globalization of Democracy* (New York: Farrar, Strauss and Giroux, 2014), 23.

22. Michael O'Hanlon, "Afghanistan Index" (March 2016), Brookings Institution: https://www.brookings.edu/wp-content/uploads/2016/07/index20160330.pdf.

23. United Nations Economic and Social Committee Online Thesaurus: http://vocabularies.unesco.org/browser/thesaurus/en/page/concept6966.

24. International Institute of Social Studies, "Indices of Social Development": http://www.indsocdev.org/defining-social-development.html.

25. "Afghanistan," in Tom Lansford, ed., *Political Handbook of the World* (Washington, DC: Congressional Quarterly Press): 3–15.

26. *Ibid.*

27. John L. Esposito, *The Oxford Dictionary of Islam* (New York: Oxford University Press, 2003), 333.

28. *Ibid.*, 275.

29. O'Hanlon, "Afghanistan Index" (March 2016): https://www.brookings.edu/wp-content/uploads/2016/07/index20160330.pdf.

30. *Ibid.*

31. *Ibid.*

32. *Oxford English Dictionary Online*: http://www.oxforddictionaries.com/us/definition/american_english/intergovernmental?q=inter-governmental.

33. *Oxford English Dictionary Online*: http://www.oxforddictionaries.com/us/definition/american_english/organization.

34. United Nations Rule of Law Website: https://www.un.org/ruleoflaw/what-is-the-rule-of-law/.

35. For details on the work of these organizations please see the following websites: Amnesty International (https://www.amnesty.org/en/), Doctors Without Borders (http://www.doctorswithoutborders.org/), the Global Partnership for Afghanistan (http://www.gpfa.org/), International Red Cross and Red Crescent Movement (http://www.ifrc.org/), International Rescue Committee (https://www.rescue.org/), Human Rights Watch (https://www.hrw.org/), Oxfam (https://www.oxfam.org/) and Transparency International (http://www.transparency.org/).

Chapter 11

1. For in-depth examinations of the history of ethnic and religious division and conflict in Bosnia-Herzegovina, please see Robert Kaplan, *Balkan Ghosts: A Journey Through History* (New York: St. Martin's Press, 1993).

2. For in-depth examinations of U.S., NATO and UN intervention and operations in Bosnia-Herzegovina during the 1990s, please see Wesley K. Clark, *Waging Modern War: Bosnia, Kosovo, and the Future of Combat* (Washington, DC: Public Affairs, 2002), and Richard Holbrooke, *To End a War* (New York: Random House, 1998).

3. *The Oxford English Dictionary Online*: http://www.oxforddictionaries.com/us/definition/american_english/intergovernmental.

4. *The Oxford English Dictionary Online*: http://www.oxforddictionaries.com/us/definition/american_english/organization.

5. The United Nations Rule of Law Website, "Non-Governmental Organizations": http://www.unrol.org/article.aspx?article_id=23.

6. Hans J. Morgenthau, *Politics Among Nations: The Struggle for Power and Peace* (New York: Alfred A. Knopf, 1948).

7. Kenneth N. Waltz, *Theory of International Politics* (Reading, MA: Addison Wesley, 1979).

8. John Mearsheimer, *The Tragedy of Great Power Politics* (New York: W.W. Norton, 2001).

9. John Locke, *Two Treatises of Government*, ed. Peter Laslett (New York: Cambridge University Press, 1988).

10. Robert O. Keohane and Joseph S. Nye, *Power and Interdependence: World Politics in Transition* (Boston: Little, Brown, 1977).

11. Robert O. Keohane, "Institutional Theory and the Realist Challenge After the

Cold War," in David A. Baldwin, ed., *Neorealism and Liberalism* (New York: Columbia University Press, 1993), 273–74.

12. For a detailed account of the history of the European deepening and widening processes, please see "The History of the European Union": http://europa.eu/about-eu/eu-history/index_en.htm.

13. For a detailed account of the history of NATO, please see "Introduction to NATO": http://www.nato.int/cps/en/natohq/68147.htm#intro.

14. John Lewis Gaddis, *We Now Know: Rethinking Cold War History* (New York: Oxford University Press, 1997), 288–89.

15. Huntington, "The Clash of Civilizations?"

16. Huntington, *The Clash of Civilizations.*

17. *Ibid.*

18. Fukuyama, *History.*

19. Robert D. Kaplan, "The Coming Anarchy: How scarcity, crime, overpopulation, tribalism, and disease are rapidly destroying the social fabric of our planet," *The Atlantic* (February 1994).

20. For a thorough assessment of the causes, characteristics and consequences, please see Margaret Macmillan, *Paris 1919: Six Months that Changed the World* (New York: Random House, 2002).

21. Kaplan, *Balkan Ghosts.*

22. Holbrooke, *To End a War.*

23. *Oxford English Dictionary Online*: http://www.oxforddictionaries.com/us/definition/american_english/economic growth.

24. World Bank Glossary: http://www.worldbank.org/depweb/english/beyond/global/glossary.html.

25. "U.S. Foreign Assistance to Bosnia-Herzegovina": http://us-foreign-aid.insidegov.com/l/21/Bosnia-and-Herzegovina.

26. United Nations Development Program, "Progress towards the Realization of Millennium Development Goals in Bosnia and Herzegovina, 2013 Report" (March 2014): file:///C:/Users/MPAULY~1/AppData/Local/Temp/MDG_BiH_2013_ProgressReport-4.pdf.

27. European Union, "Bosnia-Herzegovina Page": http://ec.europa.eu/enlargement/pdf/publication/2015/near_factograph_bih.pdf.

28. World Bank, "Projects and Programs in Bosnia-Herzegovina": http://www.worldbank.org/en/country/bosniaandherzegovina/projects.

29. *Ibid.*

30. Francis Fukuyama, *Political Order and Political Decay: From the Industrial Revolution to the Globalization of Democracy* (New York: Farrar, Strauss and Giroux, 2014), 23.

31. Freedom House, "Freedom in the World Indices for Bosnia-Herzegovina, 1998–2016": https://freedomhouse.org/report/freedom-world.

32. Transparency International. "Corruption Perception Indices, 1995–2015": www.transparency.org/research/cpi/.

33. European Commission, "Bosnia and Herzegovina Page": http://ec.europa.eu/enlargement/countries/detailed-country-information/bosnia-herzegovina/index_en.htm.

34. *Oxford English Dictionary Online:* http://www.oxforddictionaries.com/definition/english/justice.

35. International Center for Transitional Justice, "Definition of Transitional Justice": https://www.ictj.org/about/transitional-justice.

Bibliography

Abbott, Martin. "Freedom's Cry: Negroes and Their Meetings in South Carolina, 1865–1869." *The Phylon Quarterly* 20, no. 3 (3rd Quarter 1959): 263–272.

Acemoglu, Daron, and James Robinson. *Why States Fail: The Origins of Power, Prosperity and Poverty*. New York: Crown Business, 2013.

"Afghanistan: Donors Pledge $4.5 billion in Tokyo." United Nations Development Program (22 January 2002): http://reliefweb.int/report/afghanistan/afghanistan-donors-pledge-45-billion-tokyo.

Allard, Kenneth. "Lessons Unlearned: Somalia and Joint Doctrine." *Joint Forces Quarterly* (Autumn 1995): 105–109.

_____. *Somalia Operations: Lessons Learned*. Washington, DC: National Defense University Press, 1995.

American Missionary Association. *History of the American Missionary Association: With Illustrative Facts and Anecdotes*. New York: The Association, 1891.

Andrade, Dale, and James Willbanks. "CORDS/Phoenix: Counterinsurgency Lessons from Vietnam for the Future." *Military Review* (March-April 2006): 77–91.

Andrew, Rod. *Wade Hampton: Confederate Warrior to Southern Redeemer*. Chapel Hill: University of North Carolina Press, 2008.

Annual Report of Major General Arthur MacArthur, U.S. Volunteers, Commanding, Division of the Philippines. Manila, Philippine Islands: Division of the Philippines, 1900.

Annual Report of the Missionary Society, Sunday-School Union and Tract Society of the Methodist Episcopal Church. 44–47. New York: The Society, 1863–1866.

Arnold, Edwin. "The Use of Military Power in Pursuit of National Interests." *Parameters* (Spring 1994): 4–12.

Arnold, S.L. "Somalia: An Operation Other Than War." *Military Review* (December 1993): 26–35.

Auster, Bruce, and Louise Lief. "What Went Wrong in Somalia?" *U.S. News & World Report*, 18 October 1993, 33–37.

Baldwin, David. *Neorealism and Neoliberalism: The Contemporary Debate*. New York: Columbia University Press, 1993.

Bauman, Robert, and Lawrence Yates. *"My Clan Against the World": US and Coalition Forces in Somalia, 1992–1994*. Fort Leavenworth, KS: Combat Studies Institute Press, 2003.

Belknap, Margaret. "The CNN Effect: Strategic Enabler or Operational Risk?" *Parameters* (Autumn 2002): 100–114.

Berlin, Ira, et al. *Freedom: A Documentary History of Emancipation, 1861–1867*. Series I, vol. 3. New York: Cambridge University Press, 1990.

Birtle, Andrew. *U.S. Army Counterinsurgency and Counterinsurgency Operations Doctrine, 1942–1976*. Washington, DC: Center of Military History, 2006.

Blaufarb, Douglas. *The Counterinsurgency Era: U.S. Doctrine and Performance 1950 to the Present*. New York: The Free Press, 1977.

Bolger, Daniel. *Savage Peace: Americans at War in the 1990s*. Novato, CA: Presidio Press, 1995.

Boot, Max. *The Savage Wars of Peace: Small Wars and the Rise of American Power*. New York: Basic Books, 2002.

Botume, Elizabeth Hyde. *First Days Amongst the Contrabands*. Boston: Lee and Shephard, 1893.

Bova, Russell. *How the World Works: A Brief Survey of International Relations*. New York: Longman, 2010.

Bowden, Mark. *Black Hawk Down: A Story of Modern War*. New York: Grove Press, 2010.

Bremer, L. Paul III, with Malcolm McConnell. *My Year in Iraq: The Struggle to Build a Future of Hope*. New York: Simon & Schuster, 2006.

Brigham, Erwin. "Pacification Measurement." *Military Review* (May 1970): 47–55.

Brinkley, Douglas. "Democratic Enlargement: The Clinton Doctrine." *Foreign Policy*, no. 106 (Spring 1997): 111–127.

Burchill, Scott, et al. *Theories of International Relations*. New York: Palgrave Macmillan, 2005.

Burns, James MacGregor. *The Vineyard of Liberty*. New York: Alfred Knopf, 1982.

Burton, Vernon. "Race and Reconstruction: Edgefield County, South Carolina." *Journal of Social History* 12, no. 1 (Autumn 1978): 31–56.

Bush, George H.W. *All the Best, George Bush: My Life in Letters and Other Writings*. New York: Scribner, 2013.

Bush, George W. *Decision Points*. New York: Crown, 2010.

Butchart, Richard. *Schooling the Freed People: Teaching, Learning, and the Struggle for Black Freedom, 1861–1876*. Chapel Hill: University of North Carolina Press, 2010.

Cable, Larry. *Conflict of Myths: The Development of American Counterinsurgency Doctrine and the Vietnam War*. New York: New York University Press, 1986.

Carothers, Thomas. "How Democracies Emerge: The 'Sequencing' Fallacy." *Journal of Democracy* 18, no. 1 (January 2007): 12–27.

Carr, E.H. *The Twenty Years' Crisis: 1919–1939*. London: Macmillan, 1948.

Carse, Robert. *Department of the South: Hilton Head Island in the Civil War*. Columbia, SC: The State Printing Company, 1961.

Carter, Dan. *When the War Was Over: The Failure of Self-Reconstruction in the South, 1865–1867*. Baton Rouge: Louisiana State University Press, 1985.

Catton, Philip. "Counter-insurgency and Nation-building: The Strategic Hamlet Programme in South Vietnam, 1961–1963." *The International History Review* 21, no. 4 (December 1999): 918–940.

_____. *Diem's Final Failure: Prelude to America's War in Vietnam*. Lawrence: University of Kansas Press, 2003.

Chamberlain, Edwin. "Pacification." *Infantry* (November-December 1968): 32–39.

Chambers, Robert. *Ideas for Development*. New York: Routledge, 2005.

Church, George. "Anatomy of a Disaster." *Time*, 18 October 1993, 40–50.

"The Civil War, Hilton Head, and The Evolution of Mitchelville." Columbia, SC: Chicora Foundation, 1995.

Clark, Wesley K. *Waging Modern War: Bosnia, Kosovo, and the Future of Combat*. Washington, DC: Public Affairs, 2002.

Clarke, Jeffrey. *The United States Army in Vietnam, Advice and Support: The Final Years, 1965–1973*. Washington, DC: Center of Military History, 1988.

Clarke, Walter, and Jeffrey Herbst. "Somalia and the Future of Humanitarian Intervention." *Foreign Affairs* 75, no. 2 (March-April 1996): 70–85.

Clausewitz, Carl von. *On War*. Edited by Michael Howard and Peter Paret. Princeton, NJ: Princeton University Press, 1984.

Cleland, John. "Principle of the Objective and Vietnam." *Military Review* (July 1966): 82–86.

Clinton, William. "Speech to the Nation: Somalia." 7 October 1993.

_____. "Why Bosnia Matters to America." *Newsweek*, 13 November 1995, 55.

Clifford, J. Garry, Kenneth Hagan, and Thomas Paterson. *American Foreign Policy: A History Since 1900*. Lexington, MA: D.C. Heath and Company, 1991.

Coffin, Charles Carleton. *Four Years of Fighting: A Volume of Personal Observation with the Army and Navy, from the First Battle of Bull Run to the Fall of Richmond*. Boston: Ticknor and Fields, 1866.

Coffman, Edward. *The Regulars: The American Army, 1898–1941*. Cambridge, MA: Belknap Press of Harvard University Press, 2004.

"Congress Questions Peace Goal." *Columbus Ledger-Enquirer*, 1 December 1995.

Cooling, Norman. "Operation Restore Hope

in Somalia: A Tactical Action Turned Strategic Defeat." *Marine Corps Gazette* (September 2001): 92–106.

Cosmas, Graham, ed. *Correspondence Relating to the War With Spain Including the Insurrection in the Philippine Islands and the China Relief Expedition, April 15, 1898, to July 30, 1902.* Washington, DC: Government Printing Office, 1993.

Covarrubias, Jack, Tom Lansford, and Robert J. Pauly, Jr., ed. *The New Islamic State: Ideology, Religion and Violent Extremism in the 21st Century.* New York: Routledge, 2016.

Daddis, George. *No Sure Victory: Measuring U.S. Army Effectiveness and Progress in the Vietnam War.* New York: Oxford University Press, 2011.

Dallaire, Roméo. *Shake Hands with the Devil: The Failure of Humanity in Rwanda.* New York: Da Capo Press, 2004.

Dalleck, Robert. *Flawed Giant: Lyndon Johnson and His Times, 1961–1973.* New York: Oxford University Press, 1998.

Danielson, Joseph. *War's Desolating Scourge: The Union's Occupation of North Alabama.* Lawrence: University Press of Kansas, 2012.

D'Anieri, Paul. *International Politics: Power and Purpose in Global Affairs.* Boston: Wadsworth, 2014.

Davenport, David. "The New Diplomacy." *Policy Review* (December 2002 and January 2003): 17–30.

Decentralization and Democratic Local Governance Programming Handbook. Washington, DC: Center for Democracy and Governance, 2000.

Diamond, Larry. *Squandered Victory: The American Occupation and the Bungled Effort to Bring Democracy to Iraq.* New York: Times Books, 2005.

Dietrich, John, and George W. Bush. *The George W. Bush Foreign Policy Reader: Presidential Speeches with Commentary.* Armonk, NY: M.E. Sharpe, 2005.

Dobbins, James, et al. *America's Role in Nation-Building: From Germany to Iraq.* Santa Monica, CA: RAND, 2003.

_____. *The Beginner's Guide to Nation-Building.* Santa Monica, CA: RAND, 2007.

Dougherty, Kevin, and Jason Stewart. *The Timeline of the Vietnam War.* San Diego, CA: Thunder Bay Press, 2008.

Doughty, Robert, et al. *American Military History and the Evolution of Western Warfare.* Lexington, MA: D.C. Heath and Company, 1996.

Doyle, Michael. "Kant, Liberal Legacies, and Foreign Affairs." *Philosophy and Public Affairs* 12, no. 3 (Summer 1983): 205–235.

_____. "Liberalism and World Politics." *The American Political Science Review* 80, no. 4 (December 1986): 1151–1169.

Dray, Philip. *Capitol Men: The Epic Story of Reconstruction through the Lives of the First Black Congressmen.* Boston: Houghton Mifflin Harcourt, 2008.

Dunlap, Charles, Jr. "The Origins of the American Military Coup of 2012." *Parameters* (Winter 1992-1993): 2–20.

Dye, Patrick. *The Irony of Democracy: An Uncommon Introduction to American Politics.* Belmont, CA: Wadsworth, 2011.

Espenshade, Christopher. "Contraband, Refugee, Freedmen: Archaeological and Historical Investigations on the Western Fringe of Mitchelville, Hilton Head, South Carolina." Charleston, SC: Brockington and Associates, 1991.

Esposito, John L. *The Oxford Dictionary of Islam.* New York: Oxford University Press, 2003.

European Commission, "Bosnia and Herzegovina Page": http://ec.europa.eu/enlargement/countries/detailed-country-information/bosnia-herzegovina/ index_en.htm.

European Union, "Bosnia-Herzegovina Page": http://ec.europa.eu/enlargement/pdf/publication/2015/near_factograph_bih.pdf.

Ewell, Julian, and Ira Hunt. *Sharpening the Combat Edge: The Use of Analysis to Reinforce Military Judgment.* Washington, DC: Dept. of the Army, 1995.

The Failed States Index 2009: FAQ & Methodology, http://www.foreignpolicy.com/articles/2009/06/22/2009_failed_states_index_faq_methodology, accessed June 6, 2009.

Fearon, James, and David Laitin. "Neotrusteeship and the Problem of Weak States." *International Security* 28, no. 4 (Spring 2004): 5–43.

First Annual Report of the Boston Educational Commission for Freedmen. Boston: D. Clapp, 1863.

Fleitz, Frederick. *Peacekeeping Fiascoes of the 1990s: Causes, Solutions, and US Interests.* Westport, CN: Praeger, 2002.

FM 3–24. *Counterinsurgency.* Washington, DC: Headquarters, Department of the Army, 2006.

FM 100–5. *Operations.* Washington, DC: Headquarters, Department of the Army, 1993.

Foner, Eric. *Reconstruction: America's Unfinished Revolution, 1863–1877.* New York: Harper & Row, 1988.

Fort Howell, National Register of Historic Places Registration Form, 4. http://www.nationalregister.sc.gov/beaufort/S10817707070/S10817707070.pdf.

The Freedmen's Journal, vol. 1. Boston: New England Freedmen's Aid Society, 1865.

Freedom House. "Freedom in the World Indices for Bosnia-Herzegovina, 1998–2016": https://freedomhouse.org/report/freedom-world.

Friedman, Thomas, ed. *Nation-Building: Beyond Afghanistan and Iraq.* Baltimore: Johns Hopkins University Press, 2006.

______. *The World Is Flat 3.0: A Brief History of the Twenty-first Century.* New York: Farrar, Straus and Giroux, 2007.

Fukuyama, Francis. *America at the Crossroads: Democracy, Power, and the Neoconservative Legacy.* New Haven, CN: Yale University Press, 2007.

______. *The End of History and the Last Man.* New York: Harper Perennial, 1992.

______. *The Origins of Political Order: From Prehuman Times to the French Revolution.* New York: Farrar, Strauss and Giroux, 2011.

______. *State-building: Governance and World Order in the 21st Century.* Ithaca, NY: Cornell University Press, 2004.

Fuller, Stephen, and Graham Cosmas. *Marines in the Dominican Republic, 1916–1924.* Washington, DC: Headquarters, U.S. Marine Corps, 1974.

Gaddis, John Lewis. *We Now Know: Rethinking Cold War History.* New York: Oxford University Press, 1997.

Gates, John. *Schoolbooks and Krags: The United States Army in the Philippines, 1898–1902.* New York: Praeger, 1973.

Gates, Robert M. *Duty: Memoirs of a Secretary at War.* New York: Alfred A. Knopf, 2014.

Geert Hofstede Center: http://geert-hofstede.com/national-culture.html.

Gelb, Leslie, and Justine Rosenthal. "The Rise of Ethics in Foreign Policy." *Foreign Affairs* 82, no. 3 (May-June 2003): 2–7.

Ghani, Ashraf, and Clare Lockhart. *Fixing Failed States: A Framework for Rebuilding a Fractured World.* New York: Oxford University Press, 2009.

Gibson, James William. *The Perfect War: Technology in Vietnam.* Boston: The Atlantic Monthly Press, 1986.

Goldstein, Joshua, and Jon Pevehouse. *International Relations.* New York: Longman, 2010.

Gordon, Michael R., and Gen. Bernard E. Trainor. *COBRA II: The Inside Story of the Invasion and Occupation of Iraq.* New York: Pantheon Books, 2006.

Gott, Kendall. *Mobility, Vigilance, and Justice: The US Army Constabulary in Germany, 1946–1953.* Fort Leavenworth, KS: Combat Studies Institute Press, 2005.

Gowing, Nik. "Real Time Television Coverage of Armed Conflicts and Diplomatic Crises: Does it Pressure or Distort Foreign Policy Decisions?" The Joan Shorenstein Center for Press, Politics, and Public Policy, 1994.

Graybill, Lyn. "CNN Made Me Do (Not Do) It." *Sarai Reader* (2004): 170–183.

Greenhill, Kelly, and Solomon Major. "The Perils of Profiling: Civil War Spoilers and the Collapse of Intrastate Accords." *International Security* 31, no. 3 (Winter 2006-2007): 7–40.

Haalsam, Paul, et al. *Introduction to International Development: Approaches, Actors, and Issues.* New York: Oxford University Press, 2009.

Haass, Richard. *The Reluctant Sheriff: The United States After the Cold War.* New York: Council on Foreign Relations Press, 1997.

Haggerty, Richard, ed. *Dominican Republic and Haiti: Country Studies.* Washington, DC: Federal Research Division, 1991.

Harmon, Matthew. "The Media, Technology and United States Foreign Policy: A Reexamination of the 'CNN Effect.'" *Swords & Ploughshares: A Journal of International Affairs* 8, no 2 (Spring 1999): http://www.american.edu/sis/students/sword/spring99/USFP.PDF.

Harrison, Lawrence. *Culture Matters: How Values Shape Human Progress*. New York: Basic Books, 2001.

Hastedt, Glenn. *American Foreign Policy: Past, Present, Future*. Upper Saddle River, NJ: Prentice Hall, 2000.

Headley, Phineas Camp. *The Patriot Boy: Or, The Life and Career of Major-General Ormsby M. Mitchel*. New York: W.H. Appleton, 1865.

Hemingway, Al. *Our War Was Different: Marine Combined Action Platoons in Vietnam*. Annapolis, MD: Naval Institute Press, 1994.

Hennessey, Melinda Meek. "Racial Violence During Reconstruction: The 1876 Riots in Charleston and Cainhoy." *The South Carolina Historical Magazine* 86, no. 2 (April 1985): 100–112.

Henretta, James, et al. *America: A Concise History*, vol. 2. Boston: Bedford/St. Martin's, 2002.

Herring, George. *LBJ and Vietnam: A Different Kind of War*. Austin: University of Texas Press, 1994.

Hess, Gary. "Roosevelt's Practical Idealism and the Successful Management of the Alliance." In Thomas Paterson and Dennis Merrill, *Major Problems in American Foreign Relations*, vol. 2: *Since 1954*. Lexington, MA: D.C. Heath and Company, 1995.

Hines, Craig. "Pity, not U.S. Security, Motivated Use of GIs in Somalia, Bush Says." *Houston Chronicle*, October 24, 1999, A11.

"The History of the European Union": http://europa.eu/about-eu/eu-history/index_en.htm.

Hodge, Carl. "Woodrow Wilson in Our Time: NATO's Goals in Kosovo." *Parameters* (Spring 2001): 125–135.

Holbrooke, Richard. *To End a War*. New York: Random House, 1998.

Hourani, Albert. *A History of the Arab Peoples*. Cambridge, MA: Harvard University Press, 1991.

Howard, Oliver. *Report of Brevet Major General O.O. Howard, Commissioner Bureau of Refugees, Freedmen, and Abandoned Lands to the Secretary of War, Oct. 20, 1869*. Washington, DC: Government Printing Office, 1869.

Huntington, Samuel P. "The Clash of Civilizations?" *Foreign Affairs* 72–3 (Summer 1993).

_____. *The Clash of Civilizations and the Remaking of World Order*. New York: Simon & Schuster, 1996.

Ignatieff, Michael. "Power in the Service of Morality Abroad." *U.S. News & World Report*, 18 November 1996, 69–70.

International Center for Transitional Justice, "Definition of Transitional Justice": https://www.ictj.org/about/transitional-justice.

International Institute of Social Studies "Indices of Social Development": http://www.indsocdev.org/defining-social-development.html.

"Introduction to NATO": http://www.nato.int/cps/en/natohq/68147.htm#intro.

Isikoff, Michael, and David Corn. *Hubris: The Inside Story of Spin, Scandal, and the Selling of the Iraq War*. New York: Crown, 2006.

Jentleson, Bruce. *American Foreign Policy: The Dynamics of Choice in the 21st Century*. New York: W.W. Norton, 2003.

Jett, Dennis. *Why Peacekeeping Fails*. New York: St. Martin's Press, 1999.

Joes, Anthony James. *Resisting Rebellion: The History and Politics of Counterinsurgency*. Lexington: University Press of Kentucky, 2006.

_____. *The War for South Viet Nam, 1954–1975*. New York: Praeger, 2001.

Johnsen. William. *US Participation in IFOR: A Marathon, Not a Sprint*. Carlisle, PA: Strategic Studies Institute, 1996.

Johnson, Guion Griffis. *A Social History of the Sea Islands*. Chapel Hill: University of North Carolina Press, 1930.

Joint Pub 1-02, *Department of Defense Dictionary of Military and Associated Terms*. Washington, DC: Joint Chiefs of Staff, 2010.

Jones, Seth G. "The Rise of Afghanistan's Insurgency: State Failure and Jihad." *International Security* 32–4 (Spring 2008).

Jordan, Amos, et al. *American National Security*. Baltimore: Johns Hopkins University Press, 2009.

Kagan, Robert. "Nation-Building, Our National Pastime." *New York Times*, 14 October 2011. http://www.nytimes.com/2011/10/16/books/review/libertys-surest-guardian-by-jeremi-suri-book-review.html?_r=0.

Kahin, George, and John Lewis. *The United States in Vietnam*. New York: The Dial Press, 1967.

Kanbur, Ravi. "What's Social Policy Got to Do with Economic Growth?" http://www.arts.cornell.edu/poverty/kanbur/SocPolEconGrowth.pdf, accessed June 23, 2011.

Kant, Immanuel, and Ted Humphrey. *To Perpetual Peace: A Philosophical Sketch.* Hackett, 2003.

Kaplan, Robert D. *Balkan Ghosts: A Journey Through History.* New York: St. Martin's Press, 1993.

_____. "The Coming Anarchy: How scarcity, crime, overpopulation, tribalism, and disease are rapidly destroying the social fabric of our planet." *The Atlantic* (February 1994).

Karnow, Stanley. *Vietnam: A History.* New York: Penguin, 1991.

Keohane, Robert O., and Joseph S. Nye. *Power and Interdependence: World Politics in Transition.* Boston: Little, Brown, 1977.

Kibler, Lilian. *Benjamin F. Perry: South Carolina Unionist.* Durham, NC: Duke University Press, 1946.

Komer, Robert. "Clear, Hold, and Rebuild." *Army* 20, no. 5 (May 1970): 16–24.

_____. *The Organization and Management of the New Model Pacification Program—1966–1969.* Santa Monica, CA: RAND Corporation, 1970.

_____. "Pacification." *Army* 20, no. 5 (June 1970): 20–29.

Krepinevich, Andrew, Jr. *The Army and Vietnam.* Baltimore: Johns Hopkins University Press, 1986.

Lamy, Steven, et al. *Introduction to Global Politics.* New York: Oxford University Press, 2013.

Landes, David. *The Wealth and Poverty of Nations: Why Some are So Rich and Some So Poor.* New York: W.W. Norton, 1999.

Lansford, Tom. *A Bitter Harvest: US Foreign Policy and Afghanistan.* Aldershot, UK: Ashgate, 2003.

_____, ed. *Political Handbook of the World.* Washington, DC: Congressional Quarterly Press, 15.

Lansford, Tom, and Robert J. Pauly, Jr. *Strategic Preemption: US Foreign Policy and the Second Iraq War.* Aldershot, UK: Ashgate, 2004.

Latham, Michael. "Redirecting the Revolution? The USA and the Failure of Nation-building in South Vietnam." *Third World Quarterly* 27, no. 1 (2006): 27–41.

Lawson, Chris. "Peacekeeping Turned Sour 10 Years Ago, Too." *Army Times*, 25 October 1993, 11.

Lemann, Nicholas. *Redemption: The Last Battle of the Civil War.* New York: Farrar, Straus, and Giroux, 2006.

Lewis, Bernard. *The Multiple Identities of the Middle East.* New York: Schocken Books, 2001.

Lewy, Guenther. *America in Vietnam.* New York: Oxford University Press, 1978.

Linn, Brian. *The Philippine War, 1899–1902.* Lawrence: University of Kansas Press, 2000.

_____. *The U.S. Army and Counterinsurgency in the Philippine War, 1899–1902.* Chapel Hill: University of North Carolina Press, 1989.

Livingstone, Stephen. "Clarifying the CNN Effect: An Examination of Media Effects According to Type of Military Intervention." The Joan Shorenstein Center for Press, Politics, and Public Policy, June 1997.

Locke, John. *Two Treatises of Government,* ed. Peter Laslett. New York: Cambridge University Press, 1988.

Logan, Justin, and Christopher Preble. *Failed States and Flawed Logic: The Case Against a Standing Nation-Building Office.* Cato Institute Policy Analysis 560, 2006.

Lundestad, Geir. *"Empire" by Integration: The United States and European Integration, 1945–1997.* New York: Oxford University Press, 1998.

Macmillan, Margaret. *Paris 1919: Six Months that Changed the World.* New York: Random House, 2002.

Mahan, Alfred Thayer. *The Influence of Sea Power upon History, 1660–1783.* Boston: Little, Brown, 1890.

Mandelbaum, Michael. "Foreign Policy as Social Work." *Foreign Affairs* (January/February 1996): 16–32.

_____. "The Reluctance to Intervene." *Foreign Policy* 95 (Summer 1994): 10.

Mansfield, Edward, and Jack Snyder. "The Sequencing 'Fallacy.'" *Journal of Democracy* 18, no. 3 (July 2007): 5–9.

Martin, Kimberly. "Warlordism in Comparative Perspective." *International Security* 31, no. 3 (Winter 2006): 41–73.

Matloff, Maurice. *American Military History.* Washington, DC: Office of the Chief of Military History, 1973.

McAllister, J.F.O., et al. "Taking on the Thugs." *Time*, 12 December 1992, 29.

McCormick, James. *American Foreign Policy & Process*. Boston: Wadsworth, 2014.

McNerney, Michael. "Stabilization and Reconstruction in Afghanistan: Are PRTs a Model or a Muddle?" *Parameters* (Winter 2005-2006): 32–46.

Mearsheimer, John. *The Tragedy of Great Power Politics*. New York: W.W. Norton, 2001.

Mermin, Jonathan. "Television News and American Intervention in Somalia: The Myth of a Media-Driven Foreign Policy." *Political Science Quarterly* 112: 385–403.

Metz, Helen, ed. *Somalia: A Country Study*. Washington, DC: Headquarters, Department of the Army, 1993.

Miller, Paul. "Why and How to Fix Failed States." *Prism* 3, no. 1 (December 2012): 63–74.

Millett, Allan, and Peter Maslowski. *For the Common Defense: A Military History of the United States of America*. New York: The Free Press, 1984.

Millett, Richard. *Searching for Stability: The U.S. Development of Constabulary Forces in Latin America and the Philippines*. Fort Leavenworth, KS: Combat Studies Institute, 2010.

Mohr, Clarence. "Before Sherman: Georgia Blacks and the Union War Effort, 1861–1864." *The Journal of Southern History* 45, no. 3 (August 1979): 331–352.

Montgomery, Thomas. PBS *Frontline* interview, "Ambush in Mogadishu." Available http://www.pbs.org/wgbh/pages/frontline/shows/ambush/interviews/montgomery.html.

Moravcsik, Andrew. "Taking Preferences Seriously: A Liberal Theory of International Politics." *International Organizations* 51, no. 4 (Autumn 1997): 513–553.

Morgenthau, Hans. *Politics Among Nations: The Struggle for Power and Peace*, 5th ed., rev. New York: Alfred A. Knopf, 1978.

Morell, Michael. *The Great War of Our Time: The CIA's Fight Against Terrorism—From Al Qaida to ISIS*. New York: Twelve, 2015.

Munro, Dana. *Intervention and Dollar Diplomacy in the Caribbean, 1900–1921*. Princeton, NJ: Princeton University Press, 1964.

Nau, Henry. *Perspectives on International Relations*. Washington, DC: CQ Press, 2007.

Nelan, Brian. "Today, Somalia..." *Time*, 21 December 1992, 29.

Oakley, Robert. "An Envoy's Perspective." *Joint Forces Quarterly* (Autumn 1993): 44–55.

_____. PBS *Frontline* interview, "Ambush in Mogadishu." Available http://www.pbs.org/wgbh/pages/frontline/shows/ambush/interviews/oakley.html.

Obama, Barack H. "An Update on Our Mission in Afghanistan." White House Office of the Press Secretary: https://www.whitehouse.gov/blog/2016/07/06/update-our-mission-afghanistan.

O'Hanlon, Michael. "Afghanistan Index" (March 2016). Brookings Institution: https://www.brookings.edu/wp-content/uploads/2016/07/index20160330.pdf.

Oxford English Dictionary Online: http://www.oxforddictionaries.com/.

Packer, George. *The Assassins' Gate: America in Iraq*. New York: Farrar, Strauss and Giroux, 2006.

Palmer, Dave. *Summons of the Trumpet: US-Vietnam in Perspective*. San Rafael, CA: Presidio Press, 1978.

Paret, Peter. *Makers of Modern Strategy from Machiavelli to the Nuclear Age*. Princeton, NJ: Princeton University Press, 1986.

Paris, Roland. *At War's End: Building Peace After Civil Conflict*. New York: Cambridge University Press, 2004.

Parshall, Gerald. "1943: The Pull of Distant Shores." *U.S. News & World Report*, 25 October 1993, 20–25.

Paterson, Thomas. "Bearing the Burden: A Critical Look at JFK's Foreign Policy." *The Virginia Quarterly Review* 54 (Spring 1978): 193–212.

Patrick, Stewart. "Weak States and Global Threats: Fact or Fiction?" *The Washington Quarterly* 29, no 2 (Spring 2006): 27–53.

Pearce, David. *Wary Partners—Diplomats and the Media*. Washington, D.C.: Congressional Quarterly, 1995.

Pearson, Elizabeth. *Letters from Port Royal: Written at the Time of the Civil War*. Boston: W.B. Clarke, 1906.

Pease, William. "Three Years Among the Freedmen: William C. Garnett and the Port Royal Experiment." *Journal of Negro History* 42 (1957): 98–117.

Pierce, Edward. "The Freedmen at Port

Royal." *The North American Review* 101, no. 208 (July 1865): 1–28.

______. *The Negroes at Port Royal: Report of E.L. Pierce, Government Agent, to the Hon. Salmon P. Chase, Secretary of the Treasury.* Boston: R.F. Wallcut, 1862.

Pogue, Forrest. *George C. Marshall: Organizer of Victory, 1943–1945.* New York: Viking Press, 1973.

Pulliam, William. "The Bare Facts about Santo Domingo." *Current History: A Monthly Magazine of the New York Times* 13 (October 1920–March 1921): 399–402.

Rachal, John. "Gideonites and Freedmen: Adult Literacy Education at Port Royal, 1862–1865." *The Journal of Negro Education* 55, no. 4 (Autumn 1986): 453–469.

Ramsey, Russell. *A Masterpiece of Counterguerrilla Warfare: BG J. Franklin Bell in the Philippines, 1901–1902.* Fort Leavenworth, KS: Combat Studies Institute, 2007.

______. *Savage Wars of Peace: Case Studies of Pacification in the Philippines, 1900–1902.* Fort Leavenworth, KS: Combat Studies Institute, 2008.

Rashid, Ahmed. *Taliban: Militant Islam, Oil and Fundamentalism in Central Asia,* 2nd ed. New Haven, CT: Yale University Press, 2010.

Record, Jeffrey. "A Note on Interests, Values, and the Use of Force." *Parameters* (Spring 2001): 15–21.

Reid, Whitelaw. *After the War: A Southern Tour: May 1, 1865, to May 1, 1866.* New York: Moore, Wilstach & Baldwin, 1866.

Reitzel, William. "Mahan on the Use of the Sea." *Naval War College Review* 25 no. 5 (May-June 1973): 73–82.

Ricardo, David. *On the Principles of Political Economy and Taxation.* Mineola, NY: Dover, 2004.

Rice, Susan E., and Stewart Patrick. "Index of State Weakness in the Developing World." Brookings Institution, 2008.

Rieff, David. "A New Age of Imperialism?" *World Policy Journal* 16, no. 2 (Summer 1999): 1–10.

Richardson, E. Allen, "Architects of a Benevolent Empire: The Relationship between the American Missionary Association and the Freedmen's Bureau in Virginia, 1865–1872," in *The Freedmen's Bureau and Reconstruction: Reconsiderations,* ed. Paul Cimbala and Randall Miller. New York: Fordham University Press, 1999: 119–139.

Richardson, James. *A Compilation of the Messages and Papers of the Presidents, 1789–1897:* vol. 7, 1869–1881. Washington, DC: Government Printing Office, 1898.

"Rightly Guided Caliphs," *Oxford Islamic Studies Online:* http://www.oxfordislamic studies.com/article/opr/t236/e0687.

Roberts, Steven. "Will the Smiles Fade?" *U.S. News & World Report,* 11 December 1995.

Rose, Willie Lee. *Rehearsal for Reconstruction: The Port Royal Experiment.* New York: Bobbs-Merrill, 1964.

Roskin, Michael, et al. *Political Science.* Boston: Longman, 2012.

Rotberg, Robert I. *When States Fail: Causes and Consequences.* Princeton, NJ: Princeton University Press, 2003.

Roush, Maurice. "The Hamlet Evaluation System." *Military Review* (September 1969): 10–17.

Rudd, Gordon. *Humanitarian Intervention: Assisting the Iraqi Kurds in Operation Provide Comfort, 1991.* Washington, DC: Center of Military History, 2004.

Schwarz, Benjamin. "American Counterinsurgency Doctrine and El Salvador: The Frustrations of Reform and the Illusions of Nation Building." Santa Monica, CA: RAND, 1991.

Sciolino, Elaine. "New U.S. Peacekeeping Policy Deemphasizes Role of the UN." *New York Times,* 6 May 1994, A1.

Scoville, Thomas. *Reorganizing for Pacification Support.* Washington, DC: Center of Military History, 1982.

Sedra, Mike. "Afghanistan: It Is Time for a Change in the Nation-Building Strategy." *Foreign Policy in Focus,* November 15, 2002. Available https://www.hsdl.org/?view& did=438086.

"Senator Calls for Somalia Pullout." *Columbus Ledger-Enquirer,* 14 July 1993, A-2.

Sergeev, Evgeny. *The Great Game, 1856–1907: Russo-British Relations in Central and East Asia.* Baltimore: Johns Hopkins University Press, 2014.

Shapiro, Herbert. "The Ku Klux Klan During Reconstruction: The South Carolina Episode." *The Journal of Negro History* 49, no.1 (January 1965): 34–55.

Sharkey, Jacqueline. "When Pictures Drive

Foreign Policy." *American Journalism Review* 15, no. 10 (December 1993): 14–19.

Sherman, William. *Memoirs.* New York: D. Appleton, 1875.

Simkins, Francis. "The Ku Klux Klan in South Carolina, 1868–1871." *The Journal of Negro History* 12, no. 4 (October 1927): 606–647.

Simkins, Francis, and Robert Woody. *South Carolina During Reconstruction.* Chapel Hill: University of North Carolina Press, 1932.

Simons, Anna, and David Tucker. "The Misleading Problem of Failed States: A 'Sociogeography' of Terrorism in the Post-9/11 Era." *Third World Quarterly* 28, no. 2 (2007): 387–401.

Simonson, Lynnell, and Virginia Bushaw. "Participatory Action Research: Easier Said than Done." *The American Sociologist* 24, no. 1 (Spring 1993): 27–37.

Smith, Timothy. *James Z. George: Mississippi's Great Commoner.* Jackson: University Press of Mississippi, 2012.

Smithers, Samuel. "Combat Units in Revolutionary Development." *Military Review* (October 1967): 37–41.

Snow, Donald. *Peacekeeping, Peacemaking and Peace Enforcement: The US Role in the New International Order.* Carlisle, PA: U.S. Army War College Strategic Studies Institute, 1993.

_____. *When America Fights: The Uses of U.S. Military Force.* Washington, DC: CQ Press, 2000.

Sorley, Lewis. "The Quiet War: Revolutionary Development." *Military Review* (November 1967): 13–19.

Stedman, Stephen. "Spoiler Problems in Peace Processes." *International Security* 22, no. 2 (Fall 1997): 5–53.

Stewart, Rory, and Gerald Knaus, *Can Intervention Work?* New York: W.W. Norton, 2011.

Summers, Harry. *Strategy: A Critical Analysis of the Vietnam War.* Novato, CA: Presidio, 1982.

Sumner, Andy, and Michael Tribe. *International Development Studies: Theories and Methods in Research and Practice.* Los Angeles: Sage, 2008.

Suri, Jeremi. *Liberty's Surest Guardian.* New York: Free Press, 2011.

Swenson, Louis. "The Revolutionary Development Program." *Infantry* (Jan.-Feb. 1968): 28–31.

Talbott, Strobe. "Dealing with Anti-Countries." *Time,* 14 December 1992, 35.

Taylor, Kay Ann. "Mary S. Peake and Charlotte L. Forten: Black Teachers During the Civil War and Reconstruction." *The Journal of Negro Education* 74, no. 2 (Spring 2005): 124–137.

Taylor, Maxwell. *Swords and Plowshares.* New York: W.W. Norton, 1972.

Thayer, Thomas. *War Without Fronts: The American Experience in Vietnam.* Boulder, CO: Westview Press, 1985.

Thucydides. *The History of the Peloponnesian War.* Book 5.

Tolson, John. *Vietnam Studies: Airmobility, 1961–1971.* Washington, DC: Department of the Army, 1989.

Tomes, Robert. "Operation Allied Force and the Legal Basis for Humanitarian Interventions." *Parameters* (Spring 2000): 38–50.

Towne, Laura. *Letters and Diary of Laura M. Towne,* ed. Rupert Sargent Holland. Cambridge, MA: Riverside Press, 1912.

Transparency International, "Corruption Perception Indices," 1995–2015: http://www.transparency.org/research/cpi/cpi_2004/0/.

Trinkley, Michael, and Debi Hacker. "The Archaeological Manifestations of the 'Port Royal Experiment' at Mitchelville, Hilton Head, South Carolina." Columbia, SC: Chicora Foundation, 1987.

Tucker, David. "Facing the Facts: The Failure of Nation Assistance." *Parameters* (Summer 1993): 34–40.

"2015 Corruption Perceptions Index." *Transparency International* (2015): http://www.transparency.org/cpi2015.

"2014 United Nations Human Development Index": http://hdr.undp.org/en/indicators/137906.

"2016 Fragile States Index." *Foreign Policy* (July/August 2016).

United Nations Development Program. "Progress towards the Realization of Millennium Development Goals in Bosnia and Herzegovina, 2013 Report," March 2014: file:///C:/Users/MPAULY~1/AppData/Local/Temp/MDG_BiH_2013_ProgressReport-4.pdf.

United Nations Economic and Social Committee Online Thesaurus: http://vocab ularies.unesco.org/browser/thesaurus/en/ page/concept6966.

United Nations Rule of Law Website: https:// www.un.org/ruleoflaw/what-is-the-rule- of-law/.

United States Agency for International De- velopment (USAID), "Mission Statement": https://www.usaid.gov/who-we-are/ mission-vision-values.

United States Forces, Somalia After Action Report and Historical Overview: The United States Army in Somalia, 1992–1994. Wash- ington, DC: Center for Military History, 2003.

The War of the Rebellion: A Compilation of the Official Records of the Union and Con- federate Armies. 185 volumes. Washington, DC: Government Printing Office, 1880– 1901.

Walt, Stephen. "Two Cheers for Clinton's Foreign Policy." *Foreign Affairs* 79, no. 2: 63–79.

Waltz, Kenneth N. *Theory of International Pol- itics.* Reading, MA: Addison Wesley, 1979.

Warner, Ezra. *Generals in Blue: Lives of the Union Commanders.* Baton Rouge: Louisi- ana State University Press, 1964.

Watson, Russell. "It's Our Fight Now." *News- week,* 14 December 1992.

Weigley, Russell. *History of the United States Army.* New York: Macmillan, 1967.

Weinberger, Caspar. *Fighting for Peace: Seven Critical Years in the Pentagon.* New York: Warner Books, 1990.

_____. "The Uses of Military Power." *Defense* 85 (January 1985): 2–11.

Westmoreland, William. *A Soldier Reports.* Garden City, NY: Doubleday, 1976.

Williams, Alfred. *Hampton and his Red Shirts: South Carolina's Deliverance in 1876.* Charleston, SC: Walker, Evans & Cogs- well, 1935.

Williamson, Richard. "Nation-Building: The Dangers of Weak, Failing, and Failed States." *The Whitehead Journal of Diplo- macy and International Relations* (Win- ter/Spring 2007): 12–15.

Willoughby, William. "Revolutionary Devel- opment." *Infantry* (Nov-Dec 1968): 5–11.

World Bank. "Glossary": http://www.world bank.org/depweb/english/beyond/global/ glossary.html.

_____. "Projects and Programs in Bosnia- Herzegovina": http://www.worldbank.org/ en/country/bosniaandherzegovina/ projects.

Wunderle, William. *Through the Lens of Cul- tural Awareness: A Primer for US Armed Forces Deploying to Arab and Middle East- ern Countries.* Fort Leavenworth, KS: Combat Studies Institute, 2006.

Wyler, Liana Sun. CRS Report for Congress: "Weak and Failing States: Evolving Secu- rity Threats and US Policy," 2008. Accessed June 6, 2010. http://www.fas.org/sgp/crs/ row/RL34253.pdf.

Yates, Lawrence. "A Feather in their CAP? The Marines' Combat Action Program in Vietnam." In *US Marines and Irregular Warfare, 1898–2007: Anthology and Se- lected Bibliography,* ed. Stephen Evans, 147–157. Quantico, VA: Marine Corps University Press, 2008.

Yetiv, Steve A. *The Persian Gulf Crisis.* New York: Greenwood, 1997.

Zeise, JoAnn. "'Dawn of Freedom': The Freed- men's Town of Mitchelville on Hilton Head Island, SC." Master's thesis, Univer- sity of South Carolina, 2012.

Ziemke, Earl. *The U.S. Army in the Occupa- tion of Germany, 1944–1946.* Washington, DC: Government Printing Office, 1975.

Zinni, Anthony. PBS *Frontline* interview, "Ambush in Mogadishu." Accessed Janu- ary 23, 2012. http://www.pbs.org/wgbh/ pages/frontline/shows/ambush/interviews/ zinni.html.

Zuczek, Richard. "The Federal Government's Attack on the Ku Klux Klan: A Reassess- ment." *The South Carolina Historical Mag- azine* 97, no. 1 (January 1996): 47–64.

_____. *State of Rebellion: Reconstruction in South Carolina.* Columbia: University of South Carolina Press, 1996.

9 780786 497966